Jolie Brise

Jolie Brise

A TALL SHIP'S TALE

Robin Bryer

SECKER & WARBURG
LONDON

First published in England 1982 by
Martin Secker & Warburg Limited,
54, Poland Street, London W1V 3DF

British Library Cataloguing in Publication Data

Bryer, Robin
Jolie Brise: a tall ship's tale.
1. Jolie Brise *(Ship)*—History
2. Pilot boats—History
I. Title
623.8'28 VM371

ISBN 0-436-07181-9

Printed in Great Britain by
Richard Clay (The Chaucer Press) Ltd
Bungay, Suffolk

For David and the girl on the Gosport Ferry

Contents

List of Illustrations

Acknowledgements

Time to say thank you, and there are so many to thank.

From America: Captain John L. Bender; Mr Vincent Monte-Sano II, Secretary of the New York Yacht Club; Mr Stanley Mortimer, one-time owner of *Jolie Brise*, and Mr Charles H. Vilas, Editor and Historian of the Cruising Club of America.

From Portugal: Senhor Luis de Guimarães Lobato and his wife and family, who cared so well for *Jolie Brise* for twenty-nine years.

From Australia: Mr and Mrs W. J. Worsdell, who had had such great plans for *Jolie Brise*.

From France: Monsieur Mistral Cumberlege, and Monsieur J. P. Dole Robbe, enthusiastic authority on Le Havre pilot cutters.

From Holland: Mr J. P. van den Heuvel, model-maker extraordinary.

From Canada: Mr Richard Walker.

From Italy: Signor Bruno Veronese.

From England: Diana Lady Avebury; Mrs Dorothy Bailey; Mr Colin Berry; Viscount Boyd of Merton; Mr J. P. F. Broad; Mr Alfred Broom, sometime deck-hand on *Jolie Brise*; Group Captain and

Mrs Peter Bryer; Captain Eric Bush; Mr and Mrs Boyd Campbell; Mr Richard Chapman; Mr David Chase; Captain J. C. Cockburn; Mr Jack Crossley, sometime deck-hand on *Jolie Brise*; Captain Henry Denham; Lady Festing; Mr Jack Gage; Mrs Griselda Gage; Mrs Molly Gibson (née Warneford); Mr Frank Gibson; Mr David Laurent Giles; Rear-Admiral M. C. Morgan Giles; Major David Goddard, Director of Exeter Maritime Museum; Mr E. A. Green, Secretary of the Royal Ocean Racing Club; Mrs Pam Hoare; Mr Cyril Holland-Martin; Admiral of the Fleet Sir Terence Lewin; Mr David McDonald; Rear-Admiral Morrice McMullen; Mrs A. Mole (née Briggs); Mr P. R. Nicholson of Richardson-Vicks Limited; Mrs W. K. O'Mahony; Mr G. E. Outram of William Stannard and Co. Ltd; Mr C. W. Parish, Commodore of Dauntsey's School Sailing Club; Colonel Stug Perry; Mr Douglas Phillips-Birt; Mr and Mrs Roger Pinckney; Mr Ian Procter; Mr Puttifer; Miss Elspeth Riddick, Secretary of the Cruising Association; Mr David Somerset; Mr Terence Sims; Miss Irene Stannard and Mr N. J. Wollen, Commodore of the Royal Torbay Yacht Club.

Thanks go, too, to the *Yachting Monthly* and *The Yachting World* for providing such a rich source of research for the inter-war years, and to the Cruising Association and the Royal Lymington Yacht Club, whose libraries are so well stocked with them, and to the Royal Cruising Club library for the loan of books by E. G. Martin. I am again indebted to the *Yachting Monthly* and *The Yachting World* for publishing letters by me requesting information from their readers, and to *The Cruising Club News* and *The Daily Telegraph* for prompting a similar response from theirs.

I found particularly helpful the articles of Monsieur J. P. Dole Robbe and Monsieur Paul Bedel in that learned French magazine, *Le Modèle réduit du bateau*. If I have been inaccurate in my description of the last years of the Le Havre pilot service, the fault is mine, not theirs.

Another invaluable source of information was *British Ocean Racing* by the late Douglas Phillips-Birt, published privately in 1960 by the Royal Ocean Racing Club, to whom I am also indebted. The little sketches of *Jolie Brise*'s contemporaries which appear in this book owe much to the sail plan diagrams in Mr Phillips-Birt's book, which he derived in turn from drawings collected by Brigadier L. R. E. Fayle for the *Royal Engineers' Journal* – a rich source indeed, for which all yacht historians should be grateful.

While I was writing *Jolie Brise* two books on kindred subjects were published, and these I commend. One is Ian Dear's *Fastnet*, published by Batsford (1981), and the other is by Pierre-Henri Marin. His *Pilotes* is published by Editions Gallimard (1981). Both feature *Jolie Brise* in a very pleasing way.

And there must be so many more besides, far and wide, whom I should thank. Near at home, however, Gill Ferguson has my lasting gratitude for wrestling so valiantly with my numerous scripts; Oliver Holt, who designed my rebus on the title page; Helen Owen for her indefatigable copy-editing; and my dear wife, Jinks, for her patience and encouragement.

But she who deserves the greatest credit of all is the dear old girl herself, beloved *Jolie Brise*.

ROBIN BRYER
Jolie Brise at Weymouth
November, 1981

PART ONE

Prelude

CHAPTER ONE

Dawn of a Legend

"What people really like," said David, "are stories about sailing and the sea."

"I can tell a story which is every bit as romantic as any tale about Hornblower or Bolitho," I said, "and it's true."

We were in his little back-room in Poland Street and we were looking at the dust-jacket of a novel about the rolling main. It featured a picture of a gaff cutter with sails billowing and foam-topped seas crashing over her bulwarks. I explained that the jib at the end of her perilously long bowsprit could not possibly be hoisted in the way that the artist had suggested.

The publisher in David was awakening.

"Do you know about these things?" he asked.

"Well, yes, actually I do," I said, "because, you see, I sail a boat which is every bit as large and every bit as old, and much more beautiful than the boat in that picture. Only the boat I sail really exists."

"It must be exhilarating to sail a boat like that," said David.

"Yes," I said, "it is, it's very exciting. She's a marvellous boat to sail in, but, more than that, she has a tale to tell, and I've explored the world to find it."

"What's her name?" asked David.

"Her name," I said, "is *Jolie Brise*."

The white painted, stucco houses on the front at Southsea look jauntily out across the waters of Spithead, to the distant shore of the

Isle of Wight. It was a bright February morning in 1927. Out into the sunshine came a sixteen-year-old girl, slight and boyish. She turned right along the front, towards old Portsmouth, and the pleasant breeze cut excitingly across the nape of her neck. She had just recently had her long black hair cut and bobbed in the daring new fashion. She was heading towards the Camber, the old docks of Portsmouth, and her favourite Saturday morning adventure of nosing along the quays looking at the trading schooners, the Thames barges and the fishing boats.

But there was one particular quarry which she had today. She went direct to Point and bought a halfpenny ticket on the Gosport Ferry. She went up on the top deck and there leaned, in her blue sailor jersey and her grey flannel skirt, looking over the rail up-stream to the sheds of Camper & Nicholson's yacht-yard. As the ferry pushed out into the strong tide and crabbed its way across to the Gosport shore, she eagerly watched as she approached a trim, black cutter lying moored just off the shore.

She had a Box Brownie camera with her and this she levelled on the hand-rail and as the ferry came close she clicked the shutter, and then she looked back longingly at the boat as the ferry made its way onwards to the landing-stage. But she didn't get off the ferry when she got there. She came back again, looking and looking at that black cutter sitting on the tideway like a seagull. From her high bows, her sheer ran aft to a delicate counter. Her flush deck was hidden behind bulwarks. Seventeen feet of gleaming bowsprit pointed seawards, seventy-two feet of mast and topmast rose above her, and thirty-eight feet of boom, covered discreetly with a sail-cover, extended the full length of her after deck and even projected out astern.

"It really is *Jolie Brise*," the girl said to herself, and in her mind she imagined the romance of the Ocean Race, the race around the Fastnet Rock which the cutter had sailed on that very first occasion the race had been organized two years before. And she had sailed to victory too. The girl relived, in her mind, the transatlantic crossing which *Jolie Brise* had then made to Long Island Sound in America, the race from there to Bermuda and the voyage back home again.

The girl was used to boats. Looking out from the windows of her father's house she could see the graceful "J" Class yachts racing off Ryde and eastward from Cowes. Sailing boats were part of the back-drop of her life.

It had been a regret to her that her father had never been a nautical man. He was an armchair sailor, fond of boats but quite content to spend the greater part of his years looking out from Southsea on the mainland to Seaview on the island shore. Even on his holidays he was happy enough just to rent a house at Seaview and gaze back again at Southsea, where he spent the rest of his year.

But yachts were a part of her life, albeit vicariously. She had been in and out of the yard at Camper & Nicholson's, she knew Ratsey & Lapthorne, the great sail-makers, she knew them all. But the romance of *Jolie Brise* was something more than the romance of the great gleaming yachts she had seen so often, because *Jolie Brise* was not of these shores. *Jolie Brise* was French. *Jolie Brise* had not been built as a yacht. *Jolie Brise* had been a working boat, a boat every bit as hard-working and built for a rugged life as the schooners, Thames barges and fishing boats which still jostled for places along the quaysides of the Camber. And yet the giant cutter looked so neat and small, her clean lines belying her size, moored there off the Gosport shore. She looked delicate, almost too delicate to believe that she had ever been a pilot cutter, built to take pilots out from Le Havre, to sail out into the Channel to meet ships inward bound.

Oh no, there was nothing "yachty" about *Jolie Brise*, and yet she had come to England to become a yacht, and not just a yacht but a legend, a legend then of only two years' standing, for she had beaten the yachts at their own game. She had become a champion of the very first Ocean Race and she had become an adventurer too. Built for the Channel approaches, she had ventured out across the Atlantic and ventured back again, and there she was lying in the view-finder of the girl's own little camera off that familiar shore. The last of France's sailing pilot cutters, she had become the first of England's ocean racers.

The girl stepped off the ferry at Point again and went along the quay, back towards home and lunch and, as she walked past the tattooists under the railway arch and out towards the green along the front at Southsea, she could not reconcile in her mind the fact that only a few years ago she had very proudly walked the decks of HMS *Victory* which, in those days, used to lie in the middle of the harbour. Then a much smaller girl, in a little straw hat and pigtails, she had looked out from the gun ports and all the patriotism of a little English heart had heaved beneath her sailor-suit.

Yet here was she with a new love, a French boat, and the French and French boats were a complete contrast to all her British naval pride.

But somehow a love for *Jolie Brise* and a love for *Victory* seemed to go together. How many large oil-paintings had she seen over sideboards in Portsmouth dining-rooms, showing full-rigged ships with gaff cutters scuttling along astern? A dozen perhaps? They were just such gaff cutters as *Jolie Brise* herself. Although the paintings depicted a period of a hundred years before, *Jolie Brise* seemed really to belong more to the 1820s than the 1920s, and there seemed to be an affinity between her and HMS *Victory*, now in dry-dock so close by, being lovingly restored at last. This affinity bridged both the century between them and their difference in nationality. One thing in particular which bound them together was that they were both built of oak: *Victory* with the oak of Kent, and *Jolie Brise* with the oak of Normandy. And that oak of which *Jolie Brise* was built was already a fairly mature forest in the hinterland of Normandy when *Victory* was fighting at Trafalgar.

Yes, that was it, oak – or at least that was the girl's explanation to herself of her change of allegiance and change of flag, and it was satisfactory enough for a hungry girl who was just turning in to the door at home, a little late for lunch.

She slipped in quietly and sat in her chair and her father turned round, a white-moustached Elgarian figure, from where he was carving the joint on the sideboard, and her mother said, "Well, Joan, where have you been?"

She said, "I have been to see *Jolie Brise*."

"Yes, dear, do have some potatoes, they are so good."

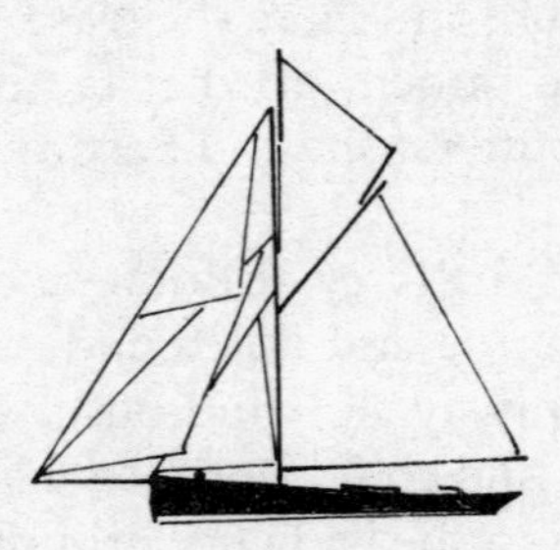

Move now eastwards and northwards by some 900 miles and back in time by 120 years to the year 1806. A vital, hunched figure, his sallow face in silhouette, stood with one knee forward in white breeches and gleaming top-boots, looking out from an upper casement across the waters of the River Warta, where it flows through Posen in distant Poland.

The stocky figure turned back from the window and walked

across to the birchwood table. It served him well enough in place of his campaign desk. It did not feel quite the same, but, for a man with more work to do than just commanding an army, it would do. He pulled the reading lamp towards him and took the next bunch of papers off the pile.

A courier had arrived that morning, his horse more bone than flesh, and it had been strange just thumbing through that pile when it first arrived, looking at the many different subjects of the papers he had been sent by his Ministers back in Paris. He would have to work his way through them now, tired though he was. He could not just turn his back on his Empire. He had got where he was through attention to detail, through knowing more than everybody else about their own special subject.

And something else he could not turn his back on either was that, just the year before, the fleet had been defeated outside Cadiz, off Cape Trafalgar. That had been a blow. He might be succeeding in Eastern Europe, but, if it was the sea and England that he was to contend with, he would have to keep an eye on his coast. By God, those British got everywhere! There was even a colony of Edinburgh merchants here in Posen, as far east as he.

So it was with a determined gesture that he sat down and pulled off the first paper on the pile. He had noticed it before and he did not want it to wait. The heading was: "Imperial Decree for the Regulation of the French Port Pilotage Service." He glanced over the various clauses. There was an indication of how the Channel was to be divided into pilotage areas and the pilot boats were to be based on Le Havre, Brest and Calais, and there were regulations too as to how the pilots should wait for the ships. But what concerned him most, as he thumbed his way through the document, was whether or not the nation would be obliged to foot their bills for them. In Britain it was not the Government who paid the pilotage service – it was the Elders of Trinity House, set up by Henry VIII and confirmed in their autonomy by Elizabeth I.

They were as jealous of their independence as he felt quite sure his adversary, William Pitt, would be unwilling actually to finance their operations. Likewise, if he knew anything about it, there would be no Government finance for his pilotage service. The incoming ships would pay for it and the pilots would have to provide their own boats. Their operations might be controlled by Imperial Decree, but the matter of finance would be for the pilots themselves to sort out.

If that were so, who would be pilots? How many were there to be? How would their skills be passed on? On what would they retire?

He turned the pages to Article Nine, and read:

"A pilot who, as a result of great age or infirmity, becomes unable to fulfil his duty will be obliged to apply to the administrator, who will appoint as his deputy the most experienced assistant pilot in the service to undertake pilotage work in his stead and, at the same time, render to him one third of his salary."

The Emperor nodded with approval, for here he would be avoiding having the water-fronts of his ports littered with retired pilots looking for Government pensions.

He glanced back again over the earlier articles. Article Three laid down the hierarchy of the pilots. There would be a Titular Pilot in charge of any one boat; next in rank an Assistant Pilot, and beneath him a Candidate.

He walked back over to the window. "It could be," he thought, "that all the Titular Pilot would need to do would be to get a medical certificate from his friendly doctor to say that he should no longer go to sea and then retire early, and comfortably, upon a third of the earnings of his hard-working assistant. Well, if he did, all strength to him. He could even run a café if he liked, or a boat-yard, or any number of businesses, just as a Frenchman might have any number of mistresses. All strength to his arm for his initiative!" The main thing was to keep a prosperous, efficient group of pilot boats plying the French shores, going out to meet inbound cargo ships and mail boats, to cut down the appalling number of shipwrecks which they had been suffering along the Breton and Normandy coasts.

Certainly if the minor details of the decree were beneath his concern, the great annual national loss which those shipwrecks constituted was not. If the English and their allies were to be kept out of French ports by the new blockade, it was all the more important that France's ships and the ships of her allies could find their way safely into her harbours.

And what were these independent little pilot boats to be like? He knew well enough those handy gaff cutters which served his navy. He would like these pilots to have cutters just as handy as those fast little messengers of his fleet. That sort of ship had been invaluable in dropping spies off the English shores. They had been handy too at beating those pirate cutters at their own game, as well as the smuggling luggers from the English shore. He smiled as he remembered those similar Moorish marauders that he had known so well from his childhood days in the bays around Corsica.

He shuffled the papers again and looked back to the title page: "Imperial Decree for the Regulation of the French Port Pilotage Service." It would do well enough. He turned to the last page, reached out for his quill, dipped it in the ink and scrawled across it, "Napoléon" – and with that name sent out a ripple which was to effect the building of *Jolie Brise* over a century later, and indeed would dominate the pilot service right up until 1923.

CHAPTER TWO

How It May Have Been

It is some time in the 1860s. The place, Le Havre. It is just a little after five o'clock but on this June morning the sun is already slanting across the *pavé*.

An old woman in a black shawl throws out a bucket of water from the door of a restaurant and a rangey black cat pokes off the lid of a dustbin. But next door a nondescript grey-painted shop is still well shuttered. The name above the door reads *Monet*. The shutters are still closed on the first floor and on the floor above, but the curtains are drawn back in the little *œil-de-boeuf* window high up in the mansard.

The side door opens and a young man slips out. He is wearing a pair of serge trousers and an aggressively new-looking striped sailor's jersey. He heads down the street past the line where the shadow of the houses cuts sharply across from pavement to pavement and the flood of sunlight almost hurts his eyes as he comes round the corner onto the quay.

The braced yards of the trading ships alongside, some even unloading at this early hour hoping to catch the last of the tide, form a network between him and the open sea. The open sea! That is where he is going today, out beyond the breakwater where he has sat for so many hours sketching. But first he must walk a few blocks on to the picture-framer, the man who sells him his drawing paper, Monsieur Boudin. He swings the door open and the bell makes a noise, both as sharp and as sudden, at that early morning hour, as someone laughing in church.

"Ah, Claude, on time – that's good. Have you got everything?"

"I hope so," the youngster replied, holding up his kit-bag.

"Good, good, well, I'll take you down to the Pilot Quay now."

Claude liked Monsieur Boudin. He was not just a shopkeeper, like his father. He was a real painter. As they walked down the quay past the ships, edging their way round the gang-planks, Boudin was saying, "Now remember, Claude, you won't do your best work on a drawing-board in your bedroom at home. Set pieces are fine enough but it's what you see, not what you think you saw, which matters. I think this little trip in *Marie Vendôme* will give you sense enough of that because you've got to know how a ship works before you paint her picture. That doesn't mean to say you've got to put in every line and block but you've got to know *why* she is the shape she is."

Claude nodded. He had heard this before and, of course, Monsieur Boudin was right. Boudin had been the *mousse* or cabin-boy on his father's boat plying between Honfleur, just across the estuary out in the Seine, up-river to Rouen and back.

"Well, here he is, Jacques," Boudin called out. They were further along the quay now, past the big ships, at the pilot station, and there were five or six trim black cutters of the latest style, either alongside the quay or lying just off at moorings, their crews going out in dinghies sculled over the stern. The Jacques whom Monsieur Boudin was talking to was just a red face looking up from the flush deck of a cutter right by them alongside the quay. She looked deceptively tiny from above, no more than forty feet long and it seemed without a cabin, just a hatch a third of the way up the deck and a dinghy stowed by the starboard bulwarks, and another hatch to the forecastle forward of the mast, close by a chimney which was smoking, Claude hoped, with a promise of *petit déjeuner* to come.

"Claude," said Monsieur Boudin, "this is *le patron*, my old friend Jacques Rudeau. He'll look after you, but mind you don't get in the way."

"Come aboard, the two of you," said *le patron*.

Boudin and Claude stepped on the board which held the starboard navigation light in the rigging and flung themselves down onto the capping rail of the bulwark and onto the deck – just as we do on *Jolie Brise* today. Jacques Rudeau pushed back the hatch and they followed him down the ladder into the cabin. It was still dark down there, apart from a patch of sunlight coming through the skylight with specks of dust dancing in its beam.

There were two bunks to one side and two to the other and plain deal benches between them and the cabin sole, with lids you could lift to lockers underneath and, in the middle, a table taking up most of the room. And ahead of that, as his eyes grew accustomed, Claude could just make out a large barrelful – of wine or water, he wondered?

"Jean," called out *le patron*, "*deux calvados*."

A tousled head poked its way around the half-bulkhead.

"*Un moment*."

"Claude, you'd better go and introduce yourself. That's Jean. He's my *mousse*."

Ahead of the bulkhead Claude found the great tree-like base of the mast with a neat, circular series of wedges where it passed through the deck. He had to bend a little here but Jean was on his knees, not because the deckhead was low – in fact he was quite a small boy – but because he was tending the stove.

"I'm Claude, I've come for the cruise."

"Oh!" said Jean. "You'd better be my *moussette*." Being a cabin-boy's cabin-boy momentarily rankled with the young man, but he took it in good part. He was out of his element and he knew it.

"I think it's going now," said Jean and reached up to get two glasses and a couple of splashes of calvados from the wicker carboy for their two elders in the cabin.

"The trouble with my job," he said, "is that at the beginning of a cruise like this everybody is supposed to be on board and ready to go by six o'clock but I have to be here at four or five to get this wretched stove on the go."

"Stop grousing, young 'un," called *le patron* from the cabin. "Charles will soon be taking his pilot's exams, then you can take his place as *lamaneur* and, who knows, we might even press-gang Claude as *mousse* if he's any good."

They all laughed amiably and two bangs on the deck added to the general noise.

A moment later the little square of sunlight in the hatchway was blocked out as first one pair of serge legs and then another rattled down the companionway. With the air of two old hands clocking in for work the new arrivals dumped kit-bags on accustomed bunks. The first took off his beret, said, "*Bonjour, patron*," sat beside Boudin at the table and rolled himself a cigarette.

"Claude, come and meet Charles Bidet. Charles, this is Claude – Monet's son. He's coming for the ride."

"Yes, and box his ears as much as you like," chipped in Boudin with a good-natured laugh. "He's a bit of an artist like me but he's a landlubber too and you'd better knock that out of him."

Charles was only a little older than Claude but he had a residual moustache and beard and eyes wrinkled from looking to windward. A pair of hands like two great hams rested on his knees.

"And that," said *le patron*, indicating to Claude the back of the second man, who was taking books out of his kit-bag and arranging them on a shelf by his bunk, "that," he said, "is Monsieur Magiare, the assistant pilot. He is not to be disturbed."

An introduction as such was not effected. He was clearly a very important man. But somebody more important was to come. A bang on the deck sent *le patron* scuttling up the companionway.

"Well, I must be going," said Boudin, chucking back his calvados and following at his heels. Claude saw his last contact with the shore disappearing and with it all contact with the known world, so he followed too.

There, as he straightened his back, standing before them on the deck, was a very imposing figure indeed in a broadcloth serge suit, bushy side-whiskers and a bowler hat. His valise was being handed down from a pony and trap on the quay above.

"And this," said *le patron*, himself suddenly diminished in stature, "this is Monsieur Dupont, he is the Titular Pilot."

"I am indeed, and it is time we were under way. *L'Etoile* and *L'Agneau Dieu* are already sculling out past the breakwater."

And as he said it the church clock chimed six. Ten days of a pilot cutter's term of duty had begun.

Clearly Dupont was still further ruffled by the fact that he himself was late. The two other boats would be out past the breakwater and heading out on the ebb tide towards the incoming ships and they, not he, would be getting the best pickings since it was first come, first served and the further out to sea, and the sooner away from the port, the more likely that a pilot would be engaged.

"Never mind," said Boudin, "I see my father's ferry under way now."

He took Jacques to one side.

"Show him a line. He'll give you a pluck out."

"Thanks, Louis Eugène, you've got me out of an awkward situation."

"Not at all. If I hadn't brought Claude on board and held you up you'd probably be sculling out there in the harbour now."

The captain of the Le Havre-Honfleur paddle-steamer recognized his son, who by now had leaped ashore and was letting go the lines for them. The starboard paddle splashed close to their port side and Claude got a glimpse of the market people with their pigs and chickens crowded incongruously on the deck beneath the odorous smoke-stack. Charles threw a line to the sailor in the stern, who quickly took a turn. Jean called out, "Quickly, Claude, here," as they pushed the cutter out from the quayside, the quarters threatening to scrape relentlessly along. Her port bow was pulled out sharply with a jerk as the tow-line took up the strain. *Le patron* forced the shuddering tiller over as she slid out into the harbour. The critical moment was over, but Monsieur Dupont with some disdain had already made his way down the companionway.

However, even now there was no time to stand and watch as the breakwaters slid past. *Le patron*, his legs astride the tiller, was now calling out instructions. David Magiare had appeared on deck, his presence diminished, too, by the arrival of Dupont. With his senior in the cabin it was perhaps not the quiet place it had been. Jean took up position with him under the starboard shrouds while Charles called Claude to join him at the pin rail by the port side. The ties were off the mainsail. That at least had been done before Dupont had come aboard. *Le patron*, from his place at the helm, undid the vang which secured the gaff to the boom when stowed.

"Haul away, lads."

Claude, not knowing quite what he was pulling on, did as he was told, his knees sinking to the deck, then his hands reaching up again above his head as he took another pull – as so many newcomers to *Jolie Brise* find themselves doing.

"Now, don't overdo it, Claude," shouted *le patron*.

"The idea is to keep the gaff going up horizontally," Charles explained quietly.

"More on throat," was the next call.

"That's them, not us," whispered Charles again, conspiratorially. "We are on the peak."

Certainly Claude had been pulling with such vigour that the peak of the gaff was pointing skyward before the throat could catch up. The hoops of the sail shuddered up the mast and the mainsail lolloped its way off the boom in lazy folds. When the throat had reached the hounds above them *le patron* called out, "Right, take a turn, David and Jean. Up on peak, Charles and Claude."

And there it was, up. Claude stood back to look at the great white canvas sail, half as big as a tennis court, with the number "12" on it and "H" for Le Havre.

"Come on, come on, come on, what are you waiting for? Brace it up. Brace it up."

Clearly all was not yet done. And not knowing quite why, Claude was made to tail another rope.

"What was all that about?" he asked as they finally belayed it by the rail.

"Well, you see," said Charles, "those two were hoisting the throat on the starboard side and you and I were hoisting the peak on the port side, but to tighten it up properly we pulled on this down-haul which tensioned through the block up there at the hounds and made the whole thing as tight as could be."

Certainly now, looking at the luff of the sail, Claude could see that a man could climb up the hoops and gain the cross-trees without having to make for the ratlines in the shrouds. There was clearly a lot more to it than just artistically draping saggy canvas over a ship as he might in a picture.

They were now out at sea and the roofs and church towers of Le Havre and the yards and masts of her trading ships were as far away from them as Claude had ever been.

When you are on board a gaff cutter it is hard to see quite what is what and to imagine what she looks like from a little distance off. But they were abreast now of their sister-ships, *L'Etoile* and *L'Agneau Dieu*. Their sails were fully set but the only way they were making on this windless morning was from the two seventeen-foot sweeps which they had apiece, braced against the horn timbers of their taff rails, two men on each boat working them with as much nonchalance as they had sculled their dinghies out to where their cutters had lain at their moorings, just an hour before.

"We'll cast off now," said *le patron*. It seemed a little unsporting to scoot past his rivals, particularly as he himself had been so late in starting. Besides, he didn't want too many smuts from the Honfleur ferry's funnel spoiling his fine white mainsail.

Soon they were left in peace as the packet turned up-stream and Rudeau pointed his ship for the open sea with what little way she had left from her tow.

More sails now, first the jib, and Claude watched with some respect as *le mousse* shinned out to the end of the bowsprit to secure its foot so that Charles could set it flying. Then up went the staysail and finally the topsail with its own yard – the whole thing rather like a dipping lug on one of the small inshore fishing boats, only set high up above the mainsail and sheeted into the peak of the gaff.

Le patron himself had picked up one of the sweeps lying on the deck and, emulating his neighbours, was sculling quietly over the stern. Jean, back in again from the end of the bowsprit, was heading down the forecastle hatch and shortly afterwards was calling to Claude as he handed food up from down below.

Hot tin plates of eggs, potatoes and mackerel and a huge pot of coffee. *Petit déjeuner* at sea and *petit déjeuner* on land were clearly two very different affairs. At eight o'clock *le patron* handed the helm over to Charles and he and the two pilots took to their bunks.

The *mousse* and the newly appointed *moussette* washed up the breakfast things in a bucket of water and then set about cleaning the cabin, as quietly as cats so as not to disturb their elders.

It was at about eleven that the whole ship seemed to come alive, each timber quietly taking the strain and the mast at Claude's shoulder feeling like a live thing instead of just a dead tree.

On deck again, he and Jean found Charles smiling as he braced his back to the helm and looked astern at their pursuing rivals. On the starboard bow the top gallants of a full-rigged ship hove across the horizon, while Le Havre was now just a smudge astern. Claude suddenly felt rather vulnerable, even with two foot of bulwark between him and the slightly breaking green-grey sea of the Seine Estuary. Now they were away from the land it was a very different story from the mirror on which they had floated to eat their breakfast.

"Quite a *coup de vent*," he ventured.

"No," laughed Charles. "It's what the English Admiral, Beaufort, would call 'Force 4'. It's what we pilots like best and we don't fiddle about with a scale of fancy numbers – we just call it a *jolie brise*."

After her top gallants, the ship's upper and lower topsails and then her courses emerged out of the horizon ahead of them. Claude gazed at this growing miracle and wondered if those dabs of white against the sky could really be a full-rigged ship made up of rope, wood, canvas and men. Alongside the quay at Le Havre those great sailing ships seemed so complex. There their beauty lay in that complexity. His own drawings had struggled to capture that detail. And yet out here at sea this distant view of sail seemed so effortless, so other-worldly.

"That'll be *L'Esprit*, homeward bound from Australia," Charles' voice cut in on Claude's reverie. From another world indeed! But not quite as he had pictured it.

Claude looked astern at their two fellow cutters, keeping station with them, credit to their equal trim and balance and the skill of their helmsmen that they were so well matched.

"Shouldn't we be cramming on sail to outdistance them?" he asked, sounding as nautical as he could.

"No sense," said Charles. "*L'Esprit* will already have a pilot on board – but stick your head down the hatch and tell Monsieur Dupont if you like."

Claude got even less response from down below.

Nor did there seem to be any sign of increased activity on either of the other cutters.

"There you are, you see," said Charles some minutes later. Claude was not so sure that he did see – but then he noticed a speck had appeared just to windward of the ship, two dashes of white such as Monsieur Boudin's brush might flick onto his canvas. It corresponded in miniature to the silhouette of their own sails.

"That'll be *numéro* 17, or perhaps 20, homeward bound in her wake after putting a pilot aboard. It's the end of their cruise just as it's the beginning of ours. Ten days and back to the wife!"

"They were lucky to pick *L'Esprit*," chipped in Jean, who had joined them on deck, "right at the end of their ten day spell and on the way home!"

Claude took Jean aside.

"How does Charles *know* it's *L'Esprit*?"

"Simple, really. Book of words. We all swot up the *Revue Maritime* for Le Havre. That gives us all the ship movements and what we are likely to get. Then we've got the silhouettes of most of the ships which come this way."

Claude was impressed. Three spots of white on the horizon and a man could make an intelligent guess as to what they were, whence they came, what their cargo and whither bound.

"What's likely to come *our* way, then?"

"Well, I think Monsieur Dupont hopes to meet *Coloniste* first – she's an auxiliary packet, twenty days out of Baltimore. We might meet her off the Casquets, that is if we can shake off those two," Jean gestured at the two cutters just astern.

"Cut the cackle," bellowed Charles from the helm. "Raise *le patron*, and what about our lunch?"

It was a fine day and with the reaching wind from the south everyone came on deck that noon.

The two pilots sat in their braces, wedged against the windward bulwarks, bowlers tilted over their eyes. *Le patron* took over the helm from Charles while Claude helped again to pass the food out from the galley. Onion soup, then fried steak with more onions on top, followed by cheese and jam with *baguettes* bought that morning, but already a little rubbery. Claude was sent down to fetch mugs of wine from the barrel in the centre of the ship – yes, it was for wine, not water after all.

There was something of a festive air as the three pilot cutters sailed towards *L'Esprit* and her pilot cutter homeward bound. They scarcely looked like men doing a job of work on board that day. But one little instance showed that their nonchalance was assumed.

Charles put down his plate, having wiped it clean with some bread and sucked the last drips of gravy and blood through his beard. "All right, *patron*, I'll take her again while you have yours."

"I will, if you like," said Claude. Holding the tiller looked easy enough.

Le patron eyed him with a hostile glance, as if he had proposed going to bed with his wife. "No, that'll be all right, thank you, *moussette*," he said, recollecting his manners. Claude was not to know. The lead over their rivals astern was a precious one and many a race like this was lost at lunch. The awkward moment passed as Charles briefly took the helm again.

Then the climax came. *L'Esprit* passed a little to leeward of them, a clamouring crescendo of sail, every detail in sharp focus with pin-points of colour from the *tricolore*, the pilot flag and the caps of the sailors out on her yards already shortening sail for her homecoming with wool from Australia, perhaps a little gold, all for the citizens of Paris, via barge from Le Havre. Claude was staggered at the succession of masts, the dynamism of the whole incredible structure, which only the rise of a clipper bow and the chiaroscuro of bear yards could hint at when such a ship was at rest beside a quay.

"Yes, and it is *numéro* 17," called out Jean, and sure enough to windward of them the number on the homeward bound pilot's sail could already be discerned.

Soon Dupont got up and made his way back to his bunk. "Let me know when you see Barfleur," he called out. David Magiare soon followed him, and then Charles – so that just *le patron* at the helm, and Claude and Jean were left on deck. The *mousse* and *moussette* duly did the washing up as before.

They were out of sight of land now and only the blue-grey sea told of the great estuary which they were crossing. *Numéro* 17 and *L'Esprit* were now well astern – somehow ships, once passed, seem to slip away to the horizon again far faster than they come. The two other cutters still cut the water, one just astern to port the other just to starboard, as if all three boats were being pulled by the same invisible hand.

"Boats always go better in the afternoon, Claude," commented *le patron*. "When the crew is having a snooze and there aren't people jumping about and slowing them down."

"Surely a great wooden hull like this isn't that sensitive?"

"That's just where you are mistaken."

Even Jean had left them now.

Claude, not yet used to this seemingly lazy habit of retiring to a bunk at the first opportunity, prowled round the boat, gingerly, so as not to upset her after *le patron*'s homily about people "jumping about". He found Jean in the forecastle where the water beat against her bluff bows. He was bent over a manual of seamanship and was not to be disturbed as he moved his finger along the line, or covered a page, closed his eyes and mouthed something silently from memory.

Claude then looked up the mast and wondered if he dare mount the ratlines. Step by swaying step, he distanced himself from the safety of the bulwark capping. Half-way he wished he had not ventured on the climb, but he felt *le patron*'s eyes on him, and shaking in ankles and wrists he ventured on as if it were his last climb on land or sea. But at last he made it to the jaws of the gaff and perched there. He looked up at the curve of the topsail to its yard eclipsing the cap of the topmast, which seemed so much higher again as to make his climb seem paltry indeed – and what a familiar feeling that is to us on board *Jolie Brise* today. His hands, still a little shaky, hugged the top of the mainmast as he scanned the horizon.

"A sail!" he shouted out, raised his right hand to point and then looked down the long curve of the mainsail to where the figure of *le patron* stood at the tiller, tiny beneath him. How he wished he had not! His feet swinging just below him looked so much bigger than that deck far, far below – which looked about as small and useless as some old sailor's ship's model back at home. He closed his eyes and clutched the mast again.

"Yes, I know, I have been watching it," came the still more disconcertingly distant shout from below. So Claude did not even have the satisfaction of having taken his life in his hands to bring fresh news from above.

But as his feet touched the deck again at last, *le patron* did smile encouragingly at him.

"I think it's *Abraham Wannamaker*, four masted schooner with timber out of Boston. Ease off the jib and staysail, will you, and we will try to intercept her."

Claude did, but too much, so Jean had to come up to help him strain them in again, the two boys with their feet braced against the bulwarks. Meanwhile *le patron* eased the main and *Marie Vendôme* gathered speed.

The distance grew between them and their two rivals.

"Ah, yes, but they are staying up-wind of us. We will be throwing away good miles and may even have to tack if the schooner already has a pilot."

"Well, there's no sign of a cutter near her."

"That doesn't mean a thing – it's not often they tag on behind – not like *numéro* 17 and *L'Esprit*."

"What is a four masted schooner?"

No answer. *Le patron* was looking up-wind now at the other cutters.

"Why aren't they making a run for her too?" he was thinking. "Or do they know better?" Someone had gone up the mast aboard one of them and there was a glint of a glass.

"Quick, just by the companionway, get me the telescope."

Claude scuttled back with it.

"Take the helm."

Claude looked surprised.

"Go on, take it."

He did. The feel was so solid and yet so live. She seemed to drop away, and then she pulled like a horse as he strained to get her up to wind again. The luff of the mainsail lifted and the boat yawed like a porpoise as she lost way.

"Hold her still, can't you!" came a curt shout from where *le patron* was wedged by the dead-eyes, trying to steady the side of his glass against the after shroud – and then, "Damn, damn, damn, damn!" He came back to the helm and took it roughly.

"Pull in the sheets – Jean, Claude, jump to it!" They both sweated them in again.

Dupont's head appeared in the companionway – *sans* bowler for once – "What the hell's up, Jacques?"

"I thought that schooner needed a pilot, but I've just seen she's got a pilot flag up."

"More fool you for heading after her," Dupont snapped. "Chances are *numéro* 9 came up with her off Portland. Get this tub to the Casquets and leave me to pick the ships."

Poor *patron*! A flea in his ear from the senior pilot and the lead lost on the other two cutters, *and* he was to leeward of them too.

Oh well, big fleas have little fleas!

"Jean," he called after a suitable pause, "come here, I want to hear your lessons."

It was a matter of routine that *le patron* catechized *le mousse* on what the boy had learnt the day before. On this occasion Jean had just had twenty days ashore, but they had been misspent. He had been sent home with a table of comparative high tides for Cherbourg, Barfleur, Harfleur, Honfleur and Le Havre, all ports of the Seine Estuary, to learn by heart. The spirit was willing, but the flesh was weak. If the truth be known, those few minutes snatched in the forecastle were the only preparation he had made for his test.

Jean looked crestfallen when Claude found him at the helm, *le patron* having just sighted the Barfleur lighthouse, and gone below to log it and tell Dupont.

"What's wrong?"

"I've failed my test – and you know what that means!"

"Search me!"

"I'll have to be on watch from eleven tonight until one."

By supper-time Barfleur was abeam – or at least its long rocky coastline, lighthouse, and squat church tower.

"That place is fit only for scrubbing bottoms," said David dismissively, back on deck again smoking his pipe. A cluster of little lugsail fishing boats setting out for their pots belied the statement, but then those three proud cutters closing with the Cherbourg peninsular were above recognizing such minor water-trade. Not for them holds crammed with fish and crew crammed aft and forward in what little accommodation was left. Indeed, they might claim to be above even the bigger boats. Not for them decks crowded with wind-swept, sea-sick passengers, livestock and all. Not for them crowded gun decks. No, the pilot cutter might be smaller than some, but she was faster and grander than most. Cleanest and proudest of ships afloat, she probably had more space per man than any other type of boat. And she certainly had a more civilized life aboard than you would find even in a yacht, where amateurs sprawled all over the place, getting in the way and calling the tune.

It was with this feeling of effortless superiority that the three cutters glided towards the westering sun. But the wind was dropping, the tide had turned foul and the Barfleur light for long winked that night not far astern. Claude stayed up to help Jean with his punishment watch. The boy was hunched over the binnacle, the little compass lamp being the only light on the ship. They had no navigation lights, since they wanted to slip away from their fellows somehow under cover of dark. But their white lights were ready for hoisting should an inward bound ship fire a white rocket (a "bluebottle") requesting a pilot. If that happened the chances were that all three might reveal themselves at the same time – and then who could claim precedence?

But no bluebottle did go up into the night sky. A gentle off-shore breeze and the turning of the tide wafted *Marie Vendôme* quietly past Cherbourg, and all they could see of their mates was the eclipse of lights ashore as a mainsail passed by.

Just after midnight a figure emerged from the forehatch and stood in the leeward shrouds – time-honoured practice among all male crews, even to this day. It was David Magiare, the assistant pilot. A moment or two later he turned and walked down the deck towards them and spoke in the quiet way one adopts in church, and which is equally a part of night watches – in this instance, not out of respect for God but for the sleep of *le patron* just at the foot of the open companionway in front of them.

Out of consideration, too, for their neighbours; who knows, perhaps just yards away across the water. If not lights – then no sound either if they were to give them the slip.

"Well then, how's it going?"

"Fine thanks, sir."

"Poor old *mousse*, trust you to get the punishment watch."

"Yes, but why should I learn the tide differences on all those harbours; I can always look them up."

"Well, you can't be so sure. You can't always have the book by your side. Besides, Jean, if you want to be a pilot like me, you'd better get used to book-work. This time last year I was sitting my pilot's exams, and you know what that means."

"I know, I know," said Jean.

"What does it mean?" asked Claude.

The young pilot turned to him in the dark and could not tell if he was just making polite conversation, but still, he took his query seriously.

"Well," he said, "first there's an exam on compass correction, logs and soundings. Then there's reading charts and tide tables."

Jean groaned.

"And then after that there's an exam on maritime law. Then there are two exams on the manoeuvring under all types of sail – because, you see, it's not just sailing a cutter like this you've got to be used to."

"And then what?" said Jean.

"Well, then there are exams on steam vessels and anchoring – you know, there's more to dropping an anchor than just plopping it over the side. Then of course comes the main part of the exam – the pilotage of the Channel and the Seine Estuary."

"Well," said Claude, "that should just about button it all up."

"Oh no," said David. "Then they make you translate some of it into German and English; you are not just handling different types of ship but different languages as well."

"Gosh! that must be hard."

"Yes," said David, "but you can pick it up easily enough talking to the sailors on the ships back along the quay-side in Le Havre, you'll see."

"Oh dear," said Jean, "I wonder if I'll ever be a pilot." (So does a boy on board *Jolie Brise* today wonder if he will ever get a yacht master's certificate, or something grander still.)

"You will, you will. Cheer up, you've only got another hour and then you can turn in."

And with that David got up, took a turn round the deck and slipped back down the fore-hatch. By day, the assistant pilot had seemed formidable, though not as formidable as Dupont, no one could be. But there is something about talk on deck in the small hours which makes all of us seem equal.

When Claude finally climbed into the bunk which Jean had showed him, folded his coat and put it as a pillow under his head, he lay, just for a few minutes, looking up through the skylight at the ghost of the mainsail stretching up towards the stars. The unlit brass lamp swung quietly with the ship and the water slid past a few inches away from his ear, with two inches of good solid Normandy oak planking between him and the water. Without the sailor's knack of taking cat-naps during the day, he was by now very tired and soon dead to the world. So dead indeed that when Jean was pulled out of bed at the perilously early hour of four-thirty to stoke the fire at the start of another day, Claude slept through.

When at last he woke, it was to see diffused sunlight reflecting onto the white deckhead and to hear muffled voices from the deck above.

"Well, with those eddies there I reckon we must be half across the Alderney Race. There could be traffic coming through here. Should we sound the fog-horn?"

"No, no. We'll keep quiet. If I'm right, the others, because they were closer inshore, may have been set in to the Race and will either have to go south of Alderney or sail back up into the Channel again. We may *just* be lucky. Judging by the strength of tide I reckon we're still well out in the Channel and it'll be turning west again soon and we'll be just nicely placed off the Casquets." All this sounded a little puzzling to Claude until he pulled on his boots and staggered out on deck to find the cutter in fog as thick as porridge, with dew hanging from the main sheet as it looped and scooped ineffectually in the troubled windless waters.

Time passes quickly in thick fog, all too quickly as you sail across the tiny disc of vision which is yours, never sure if suddenly you might see rocks breaking the water just a bowsprit's length ahead, or the bridge of a steamer bearing down astern. But an age seemed to have passed when, from somewhere to the south-east of them, they heard the long-drawn-out note of a fog-horn.

"The Casquets," said Dupont.

"Thank God for that," said *le patron*, "and it seems we're in just the right place."

"I wouldn't be too sure," said David, so freshly qualified. "Fog can play tricks with hearing; we can't be too sure where they are, or in what direction, or how far away."

"That's as may be," said *le patron*, "but everything tells me we're in the right place. *Mousse*, go and cast the lead, let's take some soundings."

Jean came scurrying up on deck with the lead and, standing between the winch and the starboard bulwarks forward, swung it like the pendulum of a clock with the coil of the cord in his right hand and another coil loosely in his left, and fathom after fathom waiting to run over the side lying on the deck.

The plop sounded precise and loud as the lead hit the water. He had thrown it far ahead. The sea here should be deep and the cutter came up level with the cord long before the shuddering racing lead-line hit the bottom.

"Thirty fathoms," called out Jean, and just as quickly started hauling the cord back in.

"Yes, that puts us about right," said Dupont, looking at David. "We are well into the Channel deep."

"Shall I swing her again?" called Jean.

"No, no, leave it, *mousse*, leave it," and as he said it the fog-horn sounded again and strangely from not far away they heard the plop of another lead and, just as suddenly, the sun broke through, the fog lifted and there, not sucked southward through the Alderney Race as they had hoped but as close as they had ever been before, were their two shadows by day and night, *L'Agneau Dieu* and *L'Etoile*.

"Damn!" said Dupont. But the situation was so ridiculous and the relief from the rising fog so great that laughter broke out in the little fleet.

"You know what this means," said Jean, turning to Claude.

"No. What?"

"We'll have to have a draw. Come on, they'll be wanting the dinghy over; help me with the lashings."

So Jean and Claude were already unlashing the dinghy when the pilot on *L'Agneau Dieu* called out, "Come on over."

"He's the senior pilot here," said Jean.

"What, even above Monsieur Dupont?"

"Oh yes, he's small fry by comparison!"

"That's right. Good boy," said *le patron* as he saw Jean and Claude lifting the dinghy to the gunwale. *L'Etoile*'s dinghy too was going into the water.

"Can you scull?" asked Dupont, turning to Claude.

"Yes, sir," said he, hoping he wouldn't make a mess of it. He had practised enough in the inner harbour at Le Havre on any old dinghy he could set foot in, but to be sculling out here, ten miles from land, even in a flat calm with a fully qualified pilot, would surely seem a little strange.

"Come on then," said Dupont, "take me over to *L'Agneau Dieu*."

The pilot sat amidship wearing his bowler hat. Claude would have liked to have sculled with one hand, looking forward, but he thought prudence was the better part of valour and sculled instead with both hands, facing aft, heading, he hoped, in more or less the right direction. As they moved away from *Marie Vendôme* he was able to appraise his home of the past twenty-four hours.

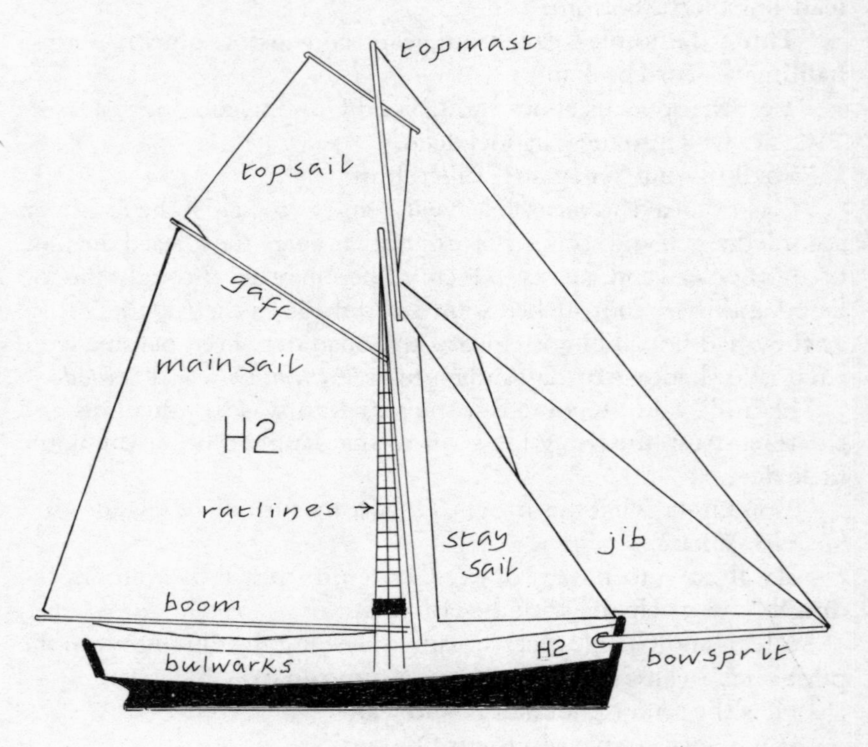

A Havre pilot cutter of 1866

She was an upright little ship. She certainly looked trim enough but was strangely similar to the Dutch trading hoys or a full-bodied fishing smack for, with so few people on board and so little to carry, her lines were buxom. Not for Claude to say, but perhaps with the fullness of time and the eye of a craftsman, those lines could be further refined. He turned, just in time, to find that his exertions had brought them close up to *L'Agneau Dieu*, their own cutter's mirror-image.

Yes indeed, her pilot was venerable compared with Dupont. In place of his bushy side-whiskers was a long white beard.

"Come aboard, Dupont. That was an amusing little race we had of it, but I think no one had the better. Ah, there you are, Blanche."

The dinghy from the other cutter had just appeared beneath his stern. The two pilots and their two boys swung over the bulwarks and the cutter's company hurried on deck with mugs of wine and a large bottle-basket. "More wine?" thought Claude, but no – one of the men handed three numbered balls to the older pilot and he showed them ceremoniously to his fellow pilots. They were numbered one, two and three. He put them in the bottle-basket and handed them to Dupont to put his hand in and draw out a ball.

He drew number one. Blanche picked number three and old White Beard number two.

"Right. That's it, gentlemen. Well done, Dupont. The first ship that comes is yours. I'll take the second and Blanche, you the third. We'll stick to that order of action for the next twelve hours and, if we're all still here, and pray God we won't be, we'll draw again."

The business done, time for conviviality – but not before Dupont had given the thumbs-up to the crew left on board *Marie Vendôme*.

The mugs of wine were handed round and with them a plate of *hors d'oeuvre*. They chatted about this and that, and in particular the pros and cons of the recently imposed westward limit, because they were here, on the line between the Casquets and Portland Bill, at the furthest extremity that they were allowed to go in search of inbound vessels. Before, they had been able to sail as far westward as the line from Ushant to the Isles of Scilly

"Well," said White Beard, "there were problems. Many's the time when a pilot would sail past an incoming ship without a pilot, wanting to get as far west as soon as possible, and too many ships ended up in Le Havre roads before they got assistance."

"That was as may be," said Dupont, "but this new limit's only been in operation for a few years and already we are losing ships on the Casquets. When you think about it, the danger isn't so much getting people into the Seine Estuary but making sure that they don't run into the Channel Isles and the Cherbourg peninsular before they get there!"

"Yes," agreed Blanche, "some of these skippers don't seem to know where the hell they are without a pilot."

"Well," said White Beard, "I doubt if any of us would be too sure if we were twenty-eight days out from Sandy Hook. Come on," he said, "be fair, which of us was too sure where he was this morning? *Mousse*," he called, "fill 'em up again!"

And so the conversation changed; the mugs were filled and the party spirit developed just as it might among as many yachts at the end of an ocean race in years to come.

Back on board their own cutter again, the ship's company, a little muzzy, resigned themselves to a wait and a plate-load of mackerel which Charles had caught as they had been drifting along. But *déjeuner* was interrupted by a cry and a pointed finger towards a smudge of smoke growing quickly bigger from the horizon.

"I'll eat my hat if that's not *Coloniste*," said Dupont.

As she came closer they saw she was indeed a three masted auxiliary, that is to say, a steamship with auxiliary sail power, one of the newer variety without paddles, but with a propeller – the sort they called "up funnel down screw" because the funnel could be lowered, for it would otherwise foul the sails, and the propeller equally could be withdrawn, for it would otherwise have impeded the sailing qualities of the vessel. Soon they saw that she was painted in the livery of the *Compagnie Générale Transatlantique*, and Dupont, as if anyone would have doubted him, finally pronounced:

"Yes, *Coloniste*. David, she's only 600 tons, so you're qualified to take her. I've got bigger ideas for myself."

As the steamer drew closer still they broke out the pilot flag, disproportionately large for the size of the vessel. From the top of the topmast it hung at a slightly drunken angle and limp in the windless air, but it was enough to tell *Coloniste* that theirs was the cutter from which they would collect the pilot. As she drew near she cut her engine and turned across the cutter's bows some hundred yards ahead to take off way. She seemed to be listing ominously towards them, and then Claude realized why. Pink dots of faces were crowding the rail.

Frenchmen homeward bound from America, Americans seeking trade in France, Americans bound for the European tour, twenty-eight days out in a crowded ship, that strange antiquated cutter was certainly the friendliest thing they had seen since they passed the lighthouse on Sandy Hook, an ocean away in time and space. The dark-suited David in his bowler hat sat majestically in the centre of the dinghy as he was sculled across to the waiting gangway. He climbed aboard and was met at the brow by the captain; they saw him mount the bridge and in no time at all it seemed they heard the telegraph ring out across the water and saw a belch of smoke issue from the funnel. A push of water, a jet of spray from under her ornate counter and the steamer was under way again, quickly circling the cutters, soon to be a smudge on the eastern horizon where seemed to float the Cherbourg peninsular and the Isle of Alderney, like two volcanic islands in a southern sea.

"Well, that's him gone," said Dupont, almost amiably. "Bit of luck drawing first and a bit of luck drawing her, because in this flat calm I think it will be some time before any more trade comes this way, unless it's another steamship, and there are none due until tomorrow. But our contract from the draw is fulfilled, so, *patron*, let's get moving!"

Le patron and Charles quietly moved northward, edging stroke by stroke with the sweeps away from the hove-to cutters. By three o'clock they had a wind from the west and on a northward course another fine reach, stronger as the evening wore on.

Marie Vendôme sailed like a thoroughbred as every now and then she dipped her boom end in the water and her bow rose and fell like a swimmer taking breath.

During the afternoon Claude had been exploring in the fore-peak when he found a set of black boards just over a foot square with numbers painted on them in white. What could they be?

"Ah! those," said Jean," are what we use if we all arrive in the same place at the same time, like we did this morning, but when it is too rough for fooling round in dinghies. Then, if Monsieur Dupont is the senior pilot present, he has those propped up along the boom, face-in to the mainsail, and the other pilots have to call out which board they have chosen – he calls last of course because he knows what the numbers are. Then we turn the boards round and all is revealed."

"It's certainly simpler than having to row over to the senior boat."

"Well, I suppose it is – but it doesn't make for much of a party."

Claude had got into the swing of ship life now. He was as quick as the rest of them to turn in as time permitted, and he was up at four-thirty that morning, helping Jean with the stove.

The ship was strangely quiet, hove to. Claude went on deck.

"England," said *le patron*, nodding towards the gentle white cliffs of Dorset, bathed in early sunlight.

"It seems strange to come to England to pilot a ship all the way to Le Havre," thought Claude.

But, as if reading his thoughts, Dupont said, "Yes, with this wind she will have hugged the English coast all the way up from the Lizard and won't want to tangle with the Casquets and from here she'll get a nice angle for the Seine."

"Yes, but who is she?" asked Claude.

"*Firecracker*," said Dupont, "and if she is up to time, and these new clippers go fast, she should be with us by *petit déjeuner*. Two thousand tons, and one of the fastest times last month for the transatlantic crossing to Liverpool, and a valuable cargo of Sheffield metal coming to us in Le Havre."

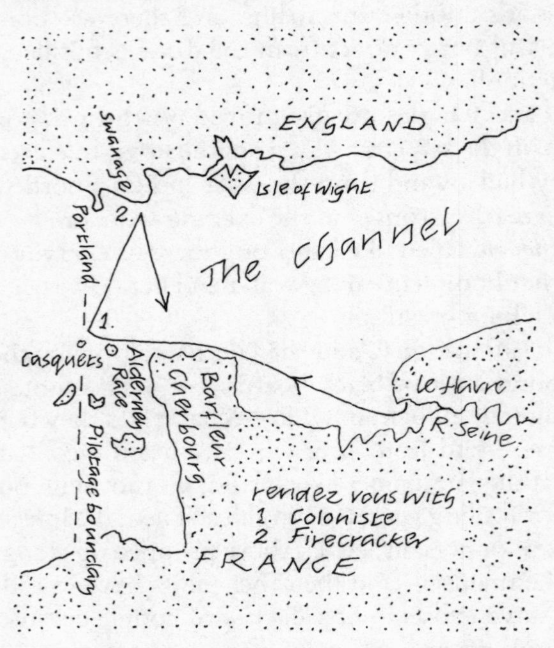

It was at ten o'clock they saw her, growing larger and larger, those dabs of white on the blue horizon, a variation on the symphony of two days before when *L'Esprit* had sailed past them. But today they were not just to be spectators.

This time they broke out the *tricolore* rather than the pilot flag, because they were in English waters. In any event, the number on their sail and the large "H" stated clearly their business and the harbour they were from.

What Claude watched next, standing well back, for this was a matter for the experts, was not so much a symphony but more of a carefully thought out choreography. Half a mile to windward, the great clipper turned suddenly southward and showed her broadside. Three masts instead of one presented themselves now, some of the yards braced one way and some the other, to take way off the ship. At the same time *le patron* had freed the staysail and hoisted the topsail and got his cutter close-hauled to windward, to pass with a cheering wave beneath her bowsprit.

It was like walking round some exquisite sculpture to see *Firecracker* first on her starboard side and then to look back at her port side, as *le patron* did, not himself to admire the beauty of her lines but to judge just where to jibe. And jibe he did, with Charles and Jean quickly handling the backstays and Dupont himself rapidly letting out the mainsheet as the cutter came round and gathered speed to pass beneath the clipper's counter.

As they did so, *Firecracker*, whose captain had still maintained sufficient way to manoeuvre, brought her round to windward and almost simultaneously *le patron* fetched round *Marie Vendôme* too in the lee of the great ship she was about to serve. Quickly they launched the dinghy; Dupont jumped in and Charles with him and they pushed off rapidly towards the waiting gangway.

Now, but for Claude, there were just *le patron* and his *mousse* on board. This was the most difficult time in a pilot cutter's life, a time when she is least manned and possibly has most to do. She hung in the wind for as short a time as possible; *le patron* pulled the helm up again, Jean backed the headsail, and deftly brought it round to leeward as the cutter pulled away, so as not to be blanketed by the great ship. Well clear, they hove to and watched the activity as Dupont stepped on the gangway. *Firecracker*'s squaresails were quickly braced as the clipper's skipper in turn made haste to ensure that his ship was not held in irons. A difficult moment here, and it could well be that the helmsman with his huge wheel high on the poop would be spinning it in the reverse direction, because maybe *Firecracker* was already making sternway. But all was well, she gathered way, first to the south-west almost from whence she came and then, in a final dancing movement, she was borne round towards the Swanage shore.

However, by now *le patron*'s eyes were no longer on her but on his own dinghy with Charles alone in it, drifting back down-wind to the spot in the sea where they had first launched her. Jean again deftly handled the headsail, the cutter gathered way and, as soon as he dared, *le patron* jibed her round and headed back on his previous course.

They passed, luckily, just up-wind of the dinghy, placing it in the cutter's lee, just as the cutter had previously been in the lee of the clipper. The dinghy came alongside, Charles scrambled over the bulwarks and quickly lifted the bow of the boat as Jean and *le patron* leapt forward and pulled it on deck.

By the time the sheets were tightened again and the dinghy lashed down the cutter was on her way from the English shore. The clipper they had served was just three white feathers towards the horizon.

"Where to now, Charles?" said *le patron*.

"Cherbourg, *mon brave*. Put her just east of south and I would say we were just about on course. And, as Monsieur Dupont says, 'once we get there'" (and here he and Jean continued in unison) "'we're not to sit about on our arses because there's a thousand and one jobs on the boat to do'. But we don't want to stay there long, because David could well be back from Le Havre on the train and we might just be able to sail him out to meet a ship at the Casquets, before Monsieur Dupont arrives back on board."

Claude listened to the exchange, apparently forgotten by the cutter's regular crew. It all looked so haphazard and yet was so carefully planned, this meeting of ships at sea and retrieval of pilots from different places ashore.

And did that cutter *Marie Vendôme* really exist? And did David, Jacques, Charles and Jean really make up her crew? Her name and theirs elude the official records of the Le Havre pilot station of that time, such as remain to us, but that is not to say that such as they did not sail together, for indeed they did. They and forty or fifty cutters like them in every generation.

Theirs was not always to be the happy and uneventful fulfilment of duties in summer seas. Sometimes they might return without successfully placing their pilots aboard the incoming ships, or retrieving them from ships outward bound. Then there would be no pilot dues to be shared in proportion among everyone, the boat included, save *le mousse*, who alone had regular, if minuscule, pay.

But economic disaster was far from their only concern. There was the occasion on Friday 7th December in 1888 when, at five o'clock in the morning, the Norwegian steamer *Avon*, ten miles north-east of the Casquets, ran down the pilot cutter *Gustave Victor*. On that fateful morning *le mousse* saw two of his family lost at sea, and with them the cutter named after himself and his brother, and with that much of his family's livelihood and savings.

Another happier story is that told of *L'Hirondelle* (H 28), which set out from Le Havre on 29th January 1902. She had put the pilot Monsieur Dureçu on board the steamer *Cordoba* at eight o'clock the next morning just off the Casquets and had then sailed northward looking for the English shore. The wind had been freshening all the time and she was down to her gaff trysail and a tiny storm jib. Then she hove to in inordinately large seas, even for that time of the year, and on Sunday 2nd February at about seven-thirty she was struck down by a freak wave. Precisely what happened is not clear, but her stove became unshipped and those below had to extinguish a fire on her deckhead, so it would seem that she had almost been capsized. On deck her starboard bulwarks were totally swept away and her stanchions broken level with the decks. Her skylight was a tangled wreck and her dinghy had been completely crushed.

For the rest, it is a tale of endurance as the crew cut away the debris and pumped ship without respite. It was not until Thursday morning at eleven o'clock that they limped into Cherbourg. Having in the storm been swept as far west as Ushant, with jury rig and pumping all the time they had cleaved their way eastward again. It is a tale which foreshadows an adventure in *Jolie Brise* many years later.

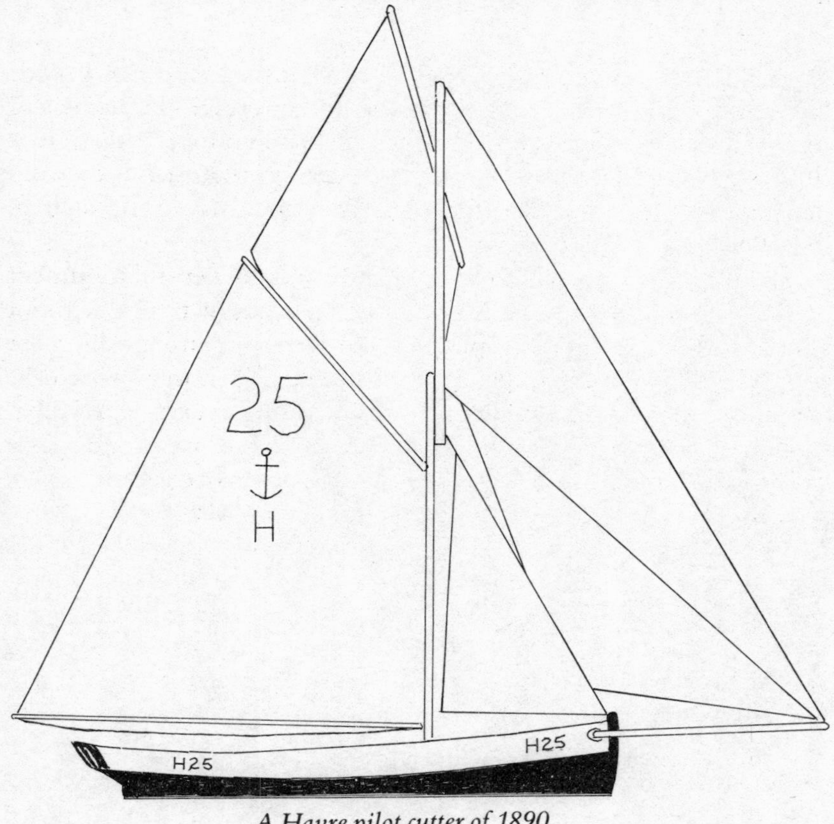

A Havre pilot cutter of 1890

Three hazards, then: one economic; another being run down at sea; and the third being devastated by what the elements themselves had to offer. But of that third tale, I myself feel part of the story. Because *L'Hirondelle*, its battered heroine, had been built in 1894 by one Monsieur Paumelle, a boat-builder of Le Havre, and it is his name on a brass plate on the rudder post of *Jolie Brise* that we still polish up today when we go sailing.

Paumelle was an old man when he built *Jolie Brise*, nineteen years after he had built *L'Hirondelle*: nineteen years of experience, experiences such as hers on those stormy nights in the English Channel, all carefully absorbed in his construction of this, his last-but-one and certainly largest and finest pilot boat creation.

CHAPTER THREE

Conception of a Perfect Ship

The Church and the aristocracy make certain of a well-documented place in posterity. Records of their life and works and relationships are carefully guarded, century after century. If I were writing of bishops or dukes and earls, my way would be as clear as in a well-buoyed channel, however many centuries back I chose to go. But with the captains, pilots and boat-builders of the Seine Estuary, eye-witness records of a century ago are scarcer to come by than are those of the knights and squires of William of Normandy's entourage, nigh on a thousand years before.

But there are exceptions, and the boat-builder Paumelle is one of them. Another is the list of pilot boats at the turn of the century together with their builders and owners and, in another sphere, there are the paintings by those painters who lived and worked around Le Havre. Whether Claude Monet ever did sail in a pilot cutter may not be known, but certainly his paintings of them have an understanding which gives the impression that he did not just appreciate what they looked like, but also knew how they worked and why they were shaped the way they were.

It was in 1874 that he exhibited an oil sketch of the harbour at Le Havre at sunrise which he called an "impression", and from which stemmed the Impressionist movement. No one took those Impressionists too seriously. Any sailor with an eye for a boat and some skill with a brush could paint one of those flat, detailed boat-portraits with every line in place, and claim in the bars around the port that he was a better painter than Monsieur Monet. But if you walk through any major gallery in the world today, as I did recently in Lisbon

(I came suddenly upon a painting of Monet's of a dried-out estuary on the Normandy coast, and of a gaff cutter on the mud), then you will realize that in the paintings of Monet and of his *confrères*, the pilot fleet of Le Havre sails on.

One such *confrère* was Camille Pissarro, who in 1903, the last year of his life, took a room in a hotel overlooking the pilots' jetty at Le Havre and painted there with his laborious *pointilliste* technique the very ordinary scenes of pilots coming and going, even down to the iron light gantry and the public convenience which adorned the quay.

One of the series now hangs in the Tate Gallery in London, eloquent testimony of the funny old painter sitting, silent, hour after hour at his open hotel window. And he would have looked down from there onto the heads of some very real characters in our story. One of the cutters in that cluster of masts must be *L'Hirondelle*, one of the figures on the quay could surely be her builder, Paumelle, another, perhaps, Monsieur Chatel, on whose eye-witness account of her near loss at sea we depend.

It is easy, too, to imagine Monsieur Paumelle turning into the bar beneath where Pissarro was silently painting and calling for a glass of red wine from *le patron* behind the bar – himself possibly, just a few years before, *le patron* of a cutter at sea. Or maybe he was an *ancien pilote*, still with an interest in a cutter at sea, and drawing a third of the salary of the deputy plying his trade on his behalf while he polished the glasses at home.

Whoever he may be, imagine Monsieur Paumelle having his glass of wine and imagine him, too, with another man we know existed, his partner and fellow master-builder, Monsieur Paris. The two specialized not just in the building of pilot cutters, but of yachts as well, and they had some of the new six-metres to their name.

They built their boats in a corner of Monsieur Normand's yard on the Rue de la Mailleraye. Paumelle had started building for Monsieur le Marchand on the other side of the street but when he had died, he had joined forces, as his own master, with Monsieur Paris.

What sort of men were they, these two? They were men with an eye trained for the run of the grain in carefully chosen timber from the oak woods of Normandy, and their skill lay in a knowledge as well of the demands of the run of the waves in the Channel, where their ships would have to serve.

Paumelle may himself have served in pilot cutters. Perhaps his partner had too, for certainly the name of Paris appears in the crew lists as much as fifty years before.

Let us eavesdrop upon their conversation.

"Well, the shape of the cutters has certainly changed over the years."

"It has indeed, Paumelle, it must be ten years now since we built a cutter with a lute stern."

"Yes, and do you remember the outcry when boats like *L'Hirondelle* were first launched with their nearly straight stems, low free-board aft and raked counters?"

"You're right there, and to think that the rudders used to be vertical!"

"Yes, you know, those old cutters were built almost as if they were fishing boats or cargo carriers. They were the same shape fore and aft, and a big box in the middle."

"And pigs to windward," interjected Paris.

"Well, I suppose we've got these racing yachts to thank for the change, but if my cutters ever get as narrow in the beam as some of those six-metres I've been asked to build, then my name's not Paumelle."

"No," said Paris, "I can't see you building a 'plank on edge' cutter like those great racing boats they have over in England on the Solent."

Paris spat on the floor to show appropriate disdain, as he probably had done many times before because "plank on edge" was a boat that seemed as narrow as a plank, being ten times as long as her beam, whereas with their pilot cutters the beam was sometimes as much as a quarter of the overall length.

"Yes, those 'plank on edges' are fine enough for scooting around in the bay on regatta day, but they'd be no good out in the Channel on a December night. And you know," said Paumelle, "I don't really believe they're any faster. They're showy all right, when they've got their scuppers under water and they're heeled right over, but I reckon heeling *stops* them, rather than makes them go."

"And there's another thing," said Paris, "it's some time since we built a hull with much overhang forward."

"Certainly," agreed Paumelle, "these yachting chaps like to have their bows and sterns overhanging far at either end. It makes sense, I suppose, with their boats, because as they heel they increase the waterline length, but if anything, I'd like my stem posts to be *more* vertical than they are now. If I'm making her beamy to keep her upright, there's no particular call for overhang in the bow. But what one of my cutters *does* need is the ability to heave to and a good straight stem, decent free-board in the bow and a long straight keel can help her do that."

"That's right," said Paris. "Where you need the sweet lines is in the counter, 'cod's head and mackerel tail', that's the shape, a bluff entry and sweet lines aft."

"You've got it, Paris. And then when she does heel, we can get her increase in waterline length from the stern and she can shrug off the following seas like waves on the underside of a seagull's tail."

"But why do you have to hang your rudders at an angle of forty-five degrees?" asked an old sailor from across the bar. "Give me the old vertical rudders any day, there was nothing much wrong with the lute stern."

"Well, just think," said Paumelle. "There's a sea coming up behind you and your bow's dipped and the stern comes up and that's the time when you want your rudder to be most effective, and I reckon the slant can help you there."

So, one feels sure, in bars in and around the harbour, the merits of the slowly evolving cutter hulls were discussed by the men who had to sail them and the men who had to build them. There is a myth that, in all boats built before the Great War, building depended simply on the judgement and skill of the builder's eye and his choice of timber. But to think of them as brilliant but unlettered men would be totally wrong. The lines of *Jolie Brise* as we have them today were taken off her hull in the 1920s by one of our most famous yacht designers, Jack Laurent Giles. But that was not the first time that they had appeared on paper. Far from it: the first tentative pencilled design for this final evolution of the ideal cutter had appeared even before the beginning of the century, even before Pissarro was sitting in his upstairs room painting the view of the pilots' jetty, or this imaginary conversation between Monsieur Paumelle and his partner, Monsieur Paris. For you must imagine now a drawing office with high stools and tilted drawing-boards, and a sash window giving a tantalizing view of distant ships' masts, and in the more immediate prospect the straight stem of a cutter on the stocks. There is the sound of the adze outside, fashioning wood for the boat under construction, but inside, sitting on his high stool, is a young man sharpening his pencil. He is wearing a high stiff collar and a cravat, for he is no boat-builder but a member of an important profession. This is young Paris, the son of Paumelle's partner, and he is articled to Emile Galodée, whose main drawing office was on the Rue Frédérick le Maistre.

Paris had found a set of designs for earlier pilot cutters hidden away and forgotten in a drawing chest drawer, and he has them now on the drawing-board, and he is tracing off their lines. To him the lines on the paper tell a story as vividly as the lines of a ship afloat would speak to a sailor, or a ship on the stocks to a master builder. In his mind run phrases which his father or Paumelle himself might not necessarily use. Phrases like "curves of displacement", "centre of buoyancy", "centre of sail area", and others besides.

Paris had studied the works of Colin Archer, that remarkable English boat designer who had gone to Norway and designed the prototype for the new Norwegian lifeboat fleet. Colin Archer favoured beam and had adapted his skill in design to the traditional Viking double-ended hulls with which the Norwegian sailors were familiar. The young Paris had read up Colin Archer's methods and tried to apply them to the traditional shapes of the Le Havre cutters, making corrections to both waterlines and buttocklines. At first this was just an exercise, because no specific commission was in mind, and if it were, you would not expect a newly articled apprentice marine architect to do the work.

Into that drawing office, in the late 1890s, imagine now Monsieur Galodée himself bursting in. He strides up behind Paris and looks over his shoulder, and with fury seizes from the board both the young man's drawings and the drawings which he has copied. A torrent of abuse descends on the boy, such as I cannot imagine in English, let alone in French, and he storms out and down the stairs to his own office. How dare he fiddle on with ideal designs for perfect cutters in his master's time! But as we have it from Paris, in a letter written in 1961, shortly before he died, his boat-building father was able to calm down the ruffled marine architect and explain to him, true or not, that Paris had worked on these drawings at home and in his own time.

Then the real reason for Galodée's fury emerged, and that was that the drawings seemed so extraordinarily good. And so it was suggested by Paumelle's diplomatic partner that the son be allowed to continue on his work at home and submit it to his master, purely as an exercise in designing the hypothetically ideal cutter. Galodée could show him where he was going right and where he was going wrong. And so the seed was sown. Young Paris sat down and worked at full speed designing not one but two boats, before being conscripted for military service in the Sudan.

In 1904 he returned again and the translation from his own letter of 1961 is more eloquent than any dialogue that we could imagine between these more and more vivid characters, as my tale unfolds. Paris writes:

> "I had only one idea, to start again, and I returned the drawing-board to its place. Permanently and boldly I started to draw a pilot cutter, a little larger than the last ones, with an increased draught and with a more rounded forefoot. I gave her a longer counter and a slight rake to the stem. As I had given some hollow to the lower parts of the sections, I increased the beam by 15cm. The stability curves indicated a reliable hull with a good speed to windward."

He took the design to a pilot friend of his, who suggested shortening the counter and straightening the stem. He had hoped to have the larger proportion of ballast on the outside of the hull, but for an all-weather working craft with a strong rig and the necessity of withstanding jerky motion, internal ballast, closer to the centre of gravity, remained essential.

Back to the drawing-board again. The ideal became closer to the realizable, and he handed his finished work to Emile Galodée, his old master. And there the story might have ended. In 1906, Paris went to Rouen. In 1908 he was in Dunkirk, where he designed a *corvette*, or pilot schooner, for the Dunkirk pilot station. It was not until 1912 that the master, who had stormed into the apprentice's office some fifteen years before, wrote to him and asked him to design a fifty-six foot pilot cutter, this time for real. What had been a pipe-dream since before he was old enough to smoke a pipe was at last within a slipway's length of entering the water.

He chose for her a hull of fifty-five feet eight inches overall, on a waterline of forty-eight feet six inches, and a beam of fifteen feet four inches – dimensions which were to change marginally in the building. He gave a forty-five degree rake to her stern-post. She was to be built of grown timbers, four inches by four inches, interspersed with steamed timbers of eight inches by one inch. She was to be nothing if not massively constructed.

"From my earlier designs," he writes, "I knew well where I was going, and I made the design very quickly." The boat's name, even before she left the drawing-board, was *Jolie Brise*. She was to be Paumelle's swan song and also the swan song of Galodée, his designer, who died very shortly after delegating the work to his former apprentice.

Paris never actually saw *Jolie Brise* launched. He passed through Le Havre briefly in 1913 and heard that the owner, Monsieur Dagier, was satisfied, but then he had to go to the war – a war which not only decimated the young men of Europe but which was to change irrevocably the nature of a Le Havre pilot's work.

As so often in the final flowering and final evolution of a thoroughbred species, the large, new, shiny pilot cutter lying off the Pilot Quay was not to be allowed to show her paces – or at least not just yet, and certainly not in the way that her builders and designers had intended.

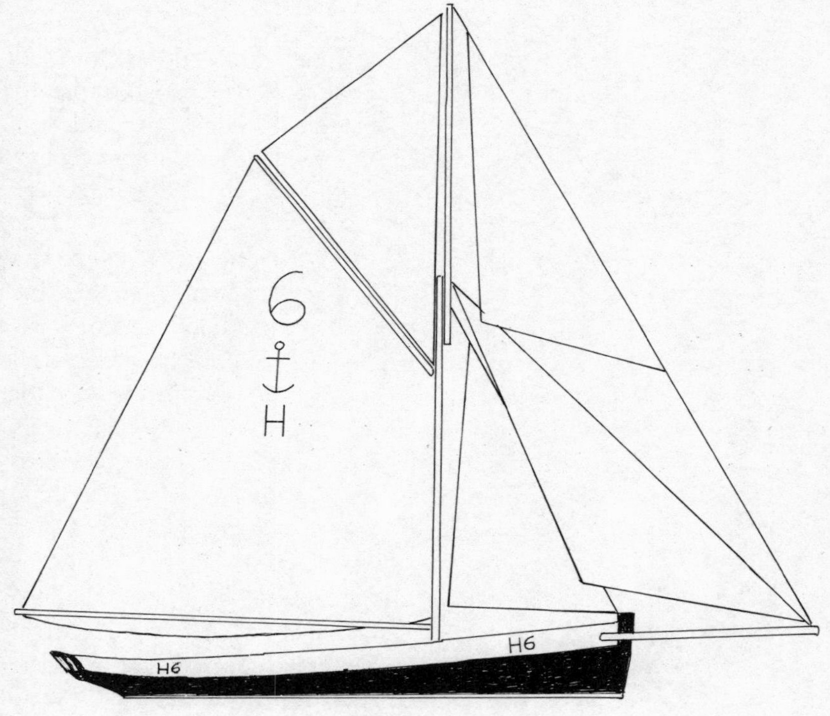

Jolie Brise, *1913*

PART TWO

1913–1923

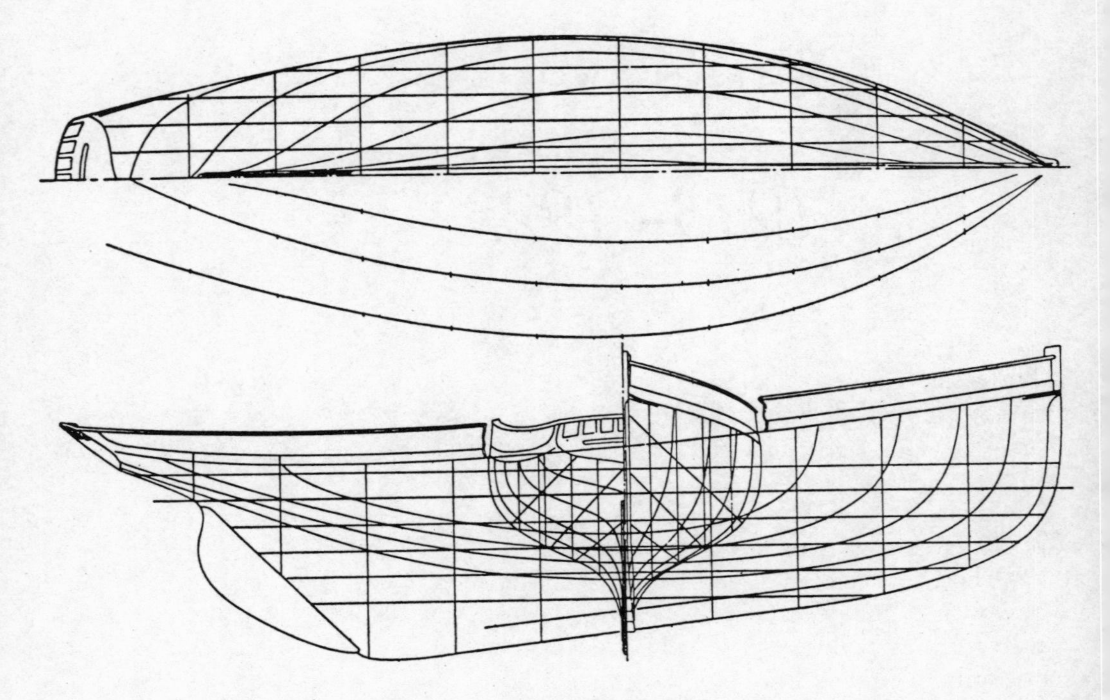

The lines of Jolie Brise

Length overall: 56 feet
Length on the waterline: 48 feet
Beam: 15 feet 9 inches
Draught: 10 feet 2 inches

CHAPTER FOUR

Pilots at War

The assassination of the Archduke Franz Ferdinand at Sarajevo was to have its effect on the newly launched *Jolie Brise*, as indeed it was on every able-bodied man in Europe, and every ship that could put to sea.

The irony was that while in an earlier war her superior size and potential speed in comparison with her fellow pilot cutters might have had her running daring errands up and down the Channel, this new war was on a different scale and required different tools of warfare. Just as the First World War was to see the last of the horse, not only in combat but behind the lines, so too was it to see the last of sail.

None the less, both horse and sail, symbols of a passing age, were pressed in those last few years into desperate use, before both were to lay down tools and become instead vehicles of pleasure and sport for gentlemen.

All this sounds heady stuff. Certainly the First World War was a watershed – nothing after it was ever quite the same again; but even if nations had not entered into combat with one another, another war – a commercial war – a war of evolution – would have brought boats such as *Jolie Brise* permanently ashore. It can be expressed at its simplest as the war between steam and sail.

In that imagined cruise of *Marie Vendôme*, back in the 1860s, the steamship *Coloniste* and her like were small and insignificant beside the square rigged ships, the clippers and schooners, which the pilots served. On one run in particular, that from Australia to European waters, the trade winds ensured the supremacy of the newly evolved clippers transporting large cargoes round the world with both speed and efficiency. The competitions between them, and their apparent supremacy over others of the merchant fleet, must have lulled builders like Paumelle into thinking that sail would always hold its own. However, not only was the steamship developing apace but so too was the ability to build bigger vessels. When Brunel built *Great Britain* in 1843 she was the largest iron ship in the world, but she was a mere 3,270 tons, a little larger than the average cross-Channel British Rail ferry of today. But as the new century grew older the proportion of steamships to sail entering Le Havre was growing more and more challenging, as indeed was the proportion of steamships being built in Le Havre itself.

Such work was not for the yards of men like Paumelle, who worked not in iron and steel but in timber, and on a small and individual scale. But still the illusion of ever-increasing rather than diminishing trade for the sailing pilot cutter seemed borne out by the statistics. In 1898 there had been 3,816,340 tons of shipping entering Le Havre. By 1907, when Alexandre Paris already had his dream pilot cutter firmly on the drawing-board, that figure had increased to 5,671,975 tons of shipping. However, had those pilots been statisticians, they would have noticed that in the same period the number of vessels entering the harbour increased only from 3,832 to 4,018; in other words the tonnage was increasing but so was the size of the vessels, and before long the number of vessels which they were serving annually would actually be diminishing.

Certainly large vessels needed pilots. Certainly too, steamships required pilotage, as did ships under sail, but the steamship could point direct to where she was going regardless of the wind and her navigation was, therefore, that much simpler and more predictable than that of a sailing vessel. The steamer could keep more easily in well buoyed and lighted waters and she could predict her speed and estimate her distance covered with greater surety. Shipwrecks were a favourite subject of photographers at the turn of the century, but it is the sailing vessel which appears in these old sepia photographs far more often than the steamship. One's instinct is to assume that this was because the steamship was still rare upon our waters, but this is not the case. The point had to be faced that she was safer. The slaughter of ships cast up upon the rocks along the French and English Channel coasts, which had been the concern of Napoleon when he signed his pilotage decree, was now decreasing annually, and no longer just through the excellence of the pilot service he had instigated, but through a change in the vessels which they served and in the way in which these could be navigated.

There was a revolution too in communication. Ships no longer had to see one another in order to communicate. Less and less were signal flags and semaphore of importance. In 1910 Crippen was arrested on the liner *Montrose* through the medium of wireless. More and more it was becoming ridiculous that the sailing pilot cutters, with no more than flags for communication, should serve these larger and more complex ships.

The pilots themselves may have known this but in a service which of its nature was built on tradition, father to son, what were they to do? Any form of propulsion, paraffin or steam, would cost as much to install in their boats as the boats themselves, and in any event such power could only be auxiliary, since the ability to heave to under sail while waiting for ships was so much an essential part of a cutter's function.

There had been, in those early years of the century, two reactions. One was to make the cutters more efficient, which led to finer shapes, greater size and greater speed, all achieved by some of the finest exponents of the art of work under sail. The other had been to make an advance before an ultimate withdrawal. In 1856, as we have learnt, the westward limit of the pilotage area had been brought back eastwards from the Ushant-Wolf Rock line to a line from the Casquets to Portland. That had led to loss of ships on the Casquets themselves. It may have been for reasons of safety, but more likely because of the pilots' need for a wider catchment area that in 1896 the Ushant-Wolf Rock western boundary to their area was again granted.

So it was, in those early years of the twentieth century, that they were able to range again over as wide an area as they had first been permitted by Napoleon in the early years of the century before. This in itself must have contributed to the incentive to build bigger and bigger cutters, for over the long passage from Le Havre to the western approaches a bigger boat was clearly at an advantage.

So it seemed that *Jolie Brise*, the biggest and best when she was launched that day in 1913, would have every opportunity to show her paces, to range far and wide in the length and breadth of the Channel. But hardly had she entered the water than the Le Havre pilotage area was reduced again, not this time back to the Casquets-Portland line but to *les petites limites*, the inner limits, a line from

Cherbourg to Trouville, restricting them in effect to the Seine Estuary itself.

This must have been a blow to the owners, builders and designers of those last few craft which the pilots invested in. There were those along the quay-fronts at Le Havre who swore that *Jolie Brise* never in fact served as a pilot at all, but this is not true. She *did* serve throughout the major part of the First World War. Her size was of little use in terms of speed and distance covered, but it did have a function in increasing the comfort of her master and crew, who spent many boring days aboard her. They were boring because there was very little to do. It is doubtful if she ever sailed far even within *les petites limites* because it had not even been thought necessary to supply her with a full mainsail. Instead she would manoeuvre simply under the large, loose-footed gaff trysail which all the pilots used in heavy weather.

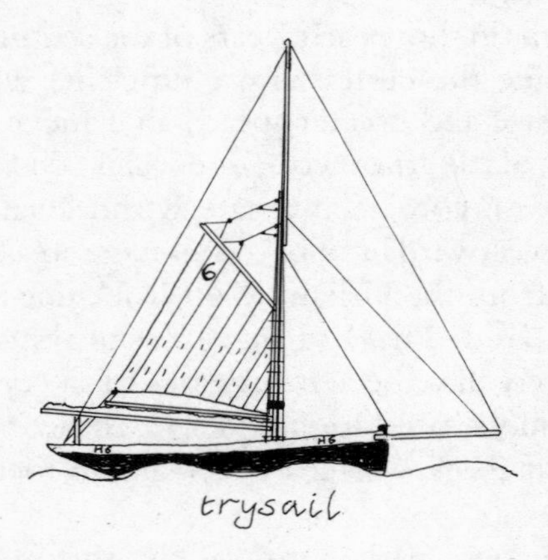

trysail

Her rendezvous with ships would be by prior arrangement and not in competition with other cutters. Indeed, throughout her three years' career, it was probably the ships which came to her rather than vice versa, because she would often be stationed a mere five miles out of Le Havre, close to the Whistle Buoy.

Traditions die hard, and her term of duty would still be the ten days which the Imperial Decree had laid down for a cutter's cruise at sea. But all that ten days might often be spent either anchored in calm or otherwise hove to within sound of that mournful whistle.

And the crew, what of their skills? How could they develop? What romance was there left in a cutter heaving up and down, always on the same patch of water within tantalizing view of the roofs of home? There came the point when pilots, rather than coming out with her at the beginning of her ten day term of duty, would simply leave home after breakfast in their nicely pressed suits and bowler hats, step aboard a new steam pinnace at the Pilot Quay and come out to *Jolie Brise*, almost as any mundane clerk might come to his office.

Even as they left the harbour in the pinnace, they would have a shrewd idea by telegraph which of the larger ships they would be serving. Sometimes indeed it might not even be worthwhile boarding that brand-new cutter lolloping up and down by the Whistle Buoy, because the ship they were bound for was already in sight and it was simpler to step direct from pinnace to gang-plank.

But for *Jolie Brise*, if it was a boring life at least it was an easy life, and one can imagine the pilots out from Le Havre sitting round on her deck for an hour or two, waiting for their ships or turning in down below for a brief sleep while waiting for a night arrival.

Doubtless as the war became more demanding, her crew was probably fewer in number and made up of either the very old or the very young. There must have been time to indulge in the most extravagant feats of cuisine, with the pilots bringing on board fresh fruit every day and the fishing boats being accosted for *fruits de mer* as they bustled backwards and forwards to the ports close by.

There would have been those too whom the crew of *Jolie Brise* would have envied. In those war years there was a final flourishing of sail. Everything which floated had its purpose. Fuel was in short supply, bringing the sailing ship briefly back into its own. The French Government even paid a sailing ship owner a premium for every sea mile sailed, a premium which proved so important to them that a French ship homeward bound from the other side of the world would always, as a matter of course, put into Hobart, Tasmania, simply because it was the furthest practical possible harbour from their homecoming. Those ships, as they sailed into the roads at Le Havre, must have made Monsieur Dagier on his *Jolie Brise* wish that the tiller of his own ship could be alive under his arm, with a mainsail and topsail set above him. With those last of the great traders under sail, doubtless an echo of the time-honoured ballet of sailing under the lee of the waiting ship, dropping the pilot, sailing away and jibing back again to pick up the returning dinghy must have given *Jolie Brise* a shade of adventure in her life, and her crew an inkling of the handiness which Paumelle had built into her, and Paris had anticipated when he set her lines on the drawing-board.

That envy, though, of ships still making long voyages under sail must have been tempered by the realization that some schooners, barques and brigantines scheduled to arrive, never did. For the successor, in this war, of the cutter as a fast and elusive miniature ship was the German submarine which had suddenly been devised to harry the merchant seamen, a hazard from which no navigator and no pilot could save them. There is nothing more evocative of the last days of sail than a film which one of those U-boat captains took, and which still exists to this day, of one of his victims, a three masted topsail schooner, all sails set, sailing effortlessly to death beneath the waves. Had *Jolie Brise* been permitted to meet the incoming ships further out to sea that could have been a fate which she might have shared with them, but whereas a U-boat captain might have coveted her as a yacht, I doubt if he would have wasted a torpedo on her cargo-less hull.

However, if those who were still sailing roused some envy among *Jolie Brise*'s crew doing its ten days of stationary duty off the Whistle Buoy, the sight of their trim new cutter must in turn have raised envy in others. There was in those desperate days a steady flow of steamers making the short passage from Southampton to Le Havre, carrying soldiers to the front in Flanders, and young nurses to field stations or hospitals at Rouen behind the line. As many as ten million men must have passed that cutter as their troop ships neared the end of that short crossing – almost as frequent, but hardly as merry, a water-traffic as the passenger ferries which take the holidaymakers today.

Some of those lads heading for the front may never have been at sea before. Many of the troop ships would, of course, have had their own pilots on board, so they would not have required *Jolie Brise*'s services, but, to the uninitiated, the sight of men in bowler hats waiting in that black cutter with her white bulwarks may have given something momentarily to laugh at, as a feeling of sea-sickness gave way to a sickness of anticipation of what they were to find on land.

And to the others, those who knew the lines of a sailing boat, the sight of her must have been a tantalizing symbol of what they had left behind. I can imagine some young subaltern from Hampshire thinking back to a summer spent in a cutter not dissimilar, racing at Cowes in the Solent, perhaps only a year before. The figure emerging from the fore-hatch might suddenly make him think of a deck-hand, a family friend, whom he may have grown up with over years of summer sailing on the family boat. Where, he might wonder, as he pulled on the last of a packet of Sullivan Powell cigarettes, where might that deck-hand be now? Perhaps already dead somewhere in the trenches towards which he himself was heading.

There would be another type of newly recruited soldier in kilt and tin hat, a Jock from the Clyde, who would break away from the forced boisterousness of banter with his mates as he leant over the stern rail to look at the cutter bobbing in the troop ship's wake. An apprentice boat-builder perhaps, he, so through his mind would run the thought that Milne could have designed that boat to be built up at Fairlie Slip. Surely she was too good to be built in some Frenchie's yard? A boat like that had all the quality of the Clyde about her – and he would not be so far wrong. Just as Milne was a wizard with his six-metre yachts, so too was Paumelle, and breeding will show.

So what of the idle crew looking up at the row upon row of faces gazing down from the passing steamers? A thought perhaps that during those years of war there were many, many fewer of those faces that passed them by outward bound, than they had seen heading towards Le Havre and battle ashore.

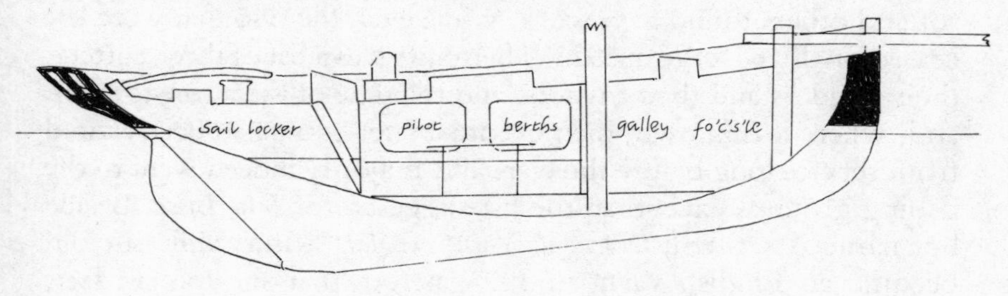

CHAPTER FIVE

In Pursuit of the Tunny

In August 1916 the Le Havre pilots bought their first steamship, *L'Horia*, and she was supported by just two cutters, numbers 27 and 29, but not "*nouveau numéro 6*" as *Jolie Brise* was known, having taken her number six from an earlier cutter. She and all the rest of her breed were paid off.

So what became of her in 1916? Initially she would have been seconded to the French Navy, but was hardly likely to have seen action. It was just a convenient move. The older cutters were left to rot and others found new work, while even the two that were left ceased finally to serve in 1922. There survives a list of those cutters, their builders and their owners, and the date of their construction and, where it is known, their eventual fate. Some had been retired from service long before the war. The majority indeed went to the fishing grounds except, so the list suggests, for *Jolie Brise*. Beside her name is written, "*Devenu Yacht Anglais*". But while she did become an English yacht in 1923, before that she too, in fact, pursued the fish.

It must have been a sad day for Monsieur Dagier and Monsieur Paumelle when they saw *Jolie Brise* set sail for Concarneau one day in 1917. Her new *patron* was one Alain Hervette, a Concarneau man, with a knowledge of tunny fishing, but her owner was still a Le Havre man – what his name was, we still do not know. But we do know that he had a large black beard.

However, for the untried black cutter there were compensations. At last she was clear of *les petites limites*, turning westwards down the Channel in waters of peace again. So we can imagine *Jolie Brise* rounding "the corner" into the Bay of Biscay, and sailing up the long rocky approach to Breton Concarneau, its little walled town straddling the rocks between the old harbour and the new, a contrast indeed in size and character to Le Havre's great commercial port and its sandy and largely rockless shores.

Jolie Brise found herself in strange company, stranger even than the difference between Normandy and Brittany might suggest. While she had been large for a pilot cutter, here in Concarneau she was small for a tunny fishing boat. But she was not dissimilar. Tunny boats too have high stems and long sloping counters, if anything longer and certainly wider than hers. Many were ketches but some were cutters like herself, designed to set the same sort of gaff topsail as she would have carried had she ever been fully rigged. But Hervette sailed her, as it happens, with a jib-headed topsail, such as we use today, rather than one on a jackyard, and a mainsail of enormous proportions. She had been designed to have a boom of thirty-eight feet but he rigged her with one of forty-three. Her gaff should have been some twenty-six feet, but Hervette again went for one of thirty-one. Her mainsail was cut very square in the head, but, as with pilot cutters, it was loose footed so that the tack could be quickly triced up as a rapid form of reducing sail. And why this excessive size of mainsail? Because, sad though Paumelle might be that his cherished pilot cutter was, as it were, losing face by becoming a fishing boat, she was in fact turning into one of a very select fraternity, for the tunny fisherman is no slow old tub. No, she has to sail far into the Atlantic to find her quarry and, once found, the faster she sails, the more easily enticed are the fish to take her bait.

The tunny-men, then, form the *élite* of the fishing fleets, and for a reason other than their speed, too. Not only do they venture far out to sea, and not only do they have to be fast, but also they fish by *line* rather than by net. So it was that the strangest additions to *Jolie Brise* in those weeks of refitting at Concarneau for her new life were those of two thirty-six-feet-long *tangons*, great whisker-like fishing rods stowed in harbour almost vertically up either side of her mast, but, when fishing, lowered at forty-five degrees to the sea, with two lines streaming from each one to either side of her. In addition, further lines would be streamed from each quarter and, on extreme occasions, her dinghy would be towed astern, itself streaming two lines. The tunny is caught by hooks glancing and dancing almost along the surface of the water with some form of yellow coloured lure flashing in the sunlight.

As with the boats, so with the fish. They are monarchs in their own right, with the weight of a single fish being between twenty and fifty pounds.

So in her new guise one can imagine *Jolie Brise* as she moves out past the old town of Concarneau from the inner harbour, up the long rocky entrance against the prevailing westerly winds, in line ahead with other tunny fishermen, behind the fishery steamer, to be cast off out in the waters of the Bay of Biscay. It is said that Alain Hervette, *le patron*, sometimes sailed as many as four hundred miles westwards into the Atlantic in search of the elusive fish. Some tunny-men sailed as far north as the Irish shore in search of their quarry, and it may be that *Jolie Brise* sailed there too, into the waters round the Fastnet which, in her next life, she was to make very much her own.

A tunny-man's crew was similar to a pilot's crew, for she would sail with perhaps three *matelots* and a *mousse*, in addition to *le patron*. The exigencies of her trade were similar too, because if anything the tunny were more elusive than were inward-bound ships in need of a pilot. In ten days at sea *Jolie Brise* might catch a hundred and fifty fish, or she might catch as many in a single day, or perhaps return to port having found no tunny at all. With the fluctuating value of the fish, again, speed was of the essence. Of the essence too because tunny can deteriorate rapidly. For this reason no great hole was cut in the deck of *Jolie Brise*, no fish-hold was made, because the tunny fisherman was possibly unique in storing his fish on deck, where the air could get at them. So on *Jolie Brise*'s deck were erected *chevettes*, or wooden horses, from which the fish were hung.

So we can think of her spanking along on a steady, frisky summer day, with a beam wind to achieve perhaps eight or nine knots, though *le patron* would prefer, say, five or six, speeds at which the hooks would not tear the fishes' mouths. And then, when catches were made on first one, and then another hook, the lines from the *tangons* would be drawn in by side-lines from the deck. Each line would be pulled in individually to unhook the catch, which would be hung, glistening, beneath the *chevettes*. On hot days a sail would be dropped over the fish and the *mousse* would keep this regularly watered with deluges from a bucket.

Alain Hervette, along with many other tunny-men, would claim that sail would always rule in the tunny trade because an engine and propellers frightened the fish away. But there must have been times when *Jolie Brise* idled in a sweltering calm, ten or twenty miles from home. Then it would look as if the catch might be lost before it could be got safely ashore and through the market and out to the canners. Then Hervette could but have wished that he had had an engine at his disposal. But it was the prejudice such as his against engines that kept boats like *Jolie Brise* sailing a little longer in their working lives.

However, this prejudice against engines was not based so much on preference, or theory as to whether or not a fish would come to an engined boat, but on the bare fact of economics. You could get 650 fr. as an average price for a dozen of tunny, and on a total ten day catch of one hundred and fifty fish, that did not amount to much to share between owner, captain, crew and boat. In the early 'twenties, if you had gone to a boat-builder in Concarneau and asked him to build a tunny fishing boat, the price would have been 30,000 to 50,000 fr. for the hull alone. 60,000 to 90,000 fr. if it were ready for the sea, "*barre en main*" or "tiller in hand" but, and here is the rub, had it an engine as well, that engine would cost quite as much as the hull itself.

Did *Jolie Brise* arrive in Concarneau, engineless maybe, but a cheap alternative to a new boat purpose-built for the fish trade? What an indignity! But no, there is another more acceptable explanation. Concarneau had had a boat-yard with a fine reputation for building tunny boats, but that reputation had been lost when a large company had taken over the yard from a personal manager. What a foretaste of things to come! In such circumstances a fine former pilot cutter more than earned her welcome. However, for whatever reason *Jolie Brise* had come to take up her new life, it none the less had much in common with the life she had been designed to lead, while in other respects, as we have seen, it took her to waters which she was later to sail under yet another guise. But there was another factor too which foreshadowed her life to come.

Tunny-men, like the yachts of those days, only sail in the summer months, though for them not because of the sun and the fair weather, but because that is the season when the tunny run.

Jolie Brise only hunted the tunny for three seasons. Why she left the trade is not clear. It could have been because of the precariousness of the economics connected with that elusive fish, or it could have been that the black-bearded owner, at home in Le Havre, felt too much out of touch and wanted his investment for another purpose. It may have been simply because a certain Englishman had been asking questions. However, it was certainly not because she was in any way unsuitable for the fishing trade. Indeed, she was just as good as the rest of them, and Alain Hervette is in fact quoted as saying as much. In terms of seaworthiness she outshone them all. In one of those early post-war fishing seasons a major gale struck the tunny fishing fleet far out in the Atlantic; five of them foundered, but *Jolie Brise* ran before it and returned to Concarneau with herself and her crew safe and unharmed.

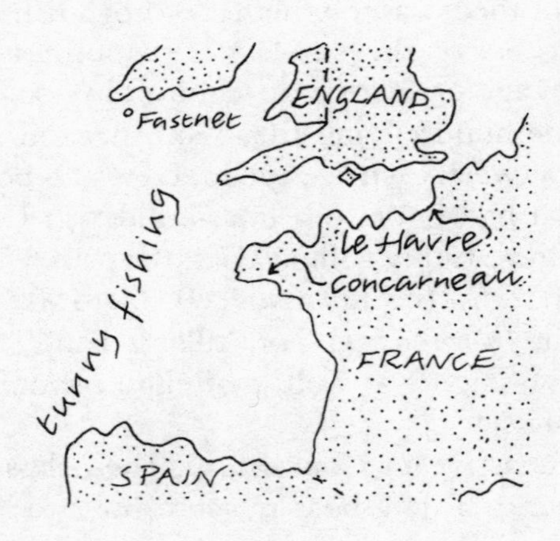

PART THREE

1923–1926

CHAPTER SIX

Enter an Englishman

It is early in the summer of 1923. A 27,000 ton steamer from Plymouth is approaching the Whistle Buoy, five miles off Le Havre. Three English are standing on the after deck, looking down with more than amateur interest at *numéro* 27, on station just off the Whistle Buoy. The woman is wearing a grey flannel skirt and jersey, and one of the men, clearly naval, in fact a Captain J. S. Stewart, turns from his wife to their companion, a man who would be noticeable in any crowd. He stands six feet seven and a half inches, his rugged face surmounted by close-cropped blond hair, which would tend to the curly, were it allowed to do so. His eyes are a piercing bright blue.

"*Marie Fernande* is something like that, only older and a little smaller," said Stewart, turning from his wife and indicating the cutter. His tall blond companion nods, and those blue eyes devour every detail of the cutter lying hove to there beneath them.

This giant is Evelyn George Martin, Old Etonian, Commander RNR and an Officer of the Order of the British Empire for his services on monitor ships and for his command of rescue tugs at Dover during the course of the war. He has come with his friends the Stewarts to help them fetch home a pilot cutter, built not by Paumelle but by Le Marchande in 1891, converted to fishing in 1917, and now about to embark on the more leisurely life of an English cruising yacht.

Marie Fernande, they had been promised, would be ready to sail away in a matter of two days. Such had been the optimism of Captain Stewart's shipping agent in Le Havre. But, as always, there is great disparity between an agent's confidence and what his client actually finds, whether the agent be in Liverpool, Rio or Le Havre. The trio found that there was much work to be done, and the Stewart couple and their bachelor friend had to slave away, first for a week, and then for a fortnight, before the cutter was anywhere near ready for the voyage home.

Martin was not a man who took kindly to ladies afloat and however seamanlike the sporting Mrs Stewart might be, he would escape from time to time along the quayside, looking at the sailing ships, laid up four or five deep, and the old cutters crudely converted or rotting in mud berths. Martin (somehow one seldom called him Evelyn or George, and he never favoured Christian names in return) was a man of forty-three, and one of a breed not known today. A bachelor of independent but modest means, he had undemanding connections with a family bank, and the solitary way of life which, while spartan, always permitted either a housekeeper to look after his affairs ashore or a deck-hand to help him in his sailing adventures. There were perhaps three spheres of his life which he treasured most. The first stemmed from his time at Oxford. He had got his cricket Blue, but it was to sailing that he turned when his doctor ordered a complete rest before he took his medical exams – a rest so complete that he never became a doctor at all. Oxford and sailing had led to various literary associations, for he had in his time sailed with both Kenneth Grahame and Quiller-Couch. Some might hazard that Martin had been a model for Grahame's Ratty in *The Wind in the Willows* and, at a time when "messing about in boats" had not become too hackneyed a phrase, doubtless Martin would have been flattered by such a suggestion. However, it is more likely that Martin modelled himself on Ratty rather than vice versa.

The second sphere which Martin treasured was his connection with the Navy. The First World War had given a new zest to his life and an opportunity for his skill in boats to be put to good purpose. Let it be faced, with the war over he was now slightly high and dry again, and looking for fresh adventures and challenges on water.

The third sphere in Martin's life, and perhaps the dearest to him, was his passion for the traditions of working boats under sail. His father was a colonel in India, so that George and his brother John and sister Dorothy had been left for long periods, often with a friend, Miss Annie Hogg, who lived at Berry Head House in Brixham. So it was that it became his delight at an early age to take passage on a Brixham trawler and go out with the fishing fleet. And his proudest boast to his dying day was that the Brixham skippers had eventually conceded that he was almost as good as one of them.

Knowledge of, and skill with working boats gave Martin two things: first, the sense of aloof superiority over his sailing friends, who confined their sailing to the products of yacht-yards and the chat of yacht clubs, and second, the sense of comradeship with the working man afloat, who treated him with the respect generally afforded to the gentleman tramp, mingled with a certain amount of pride that he should take an interest in their boats and their dying art. Martin, in his turn, probably felt more at ease in such company, less demanding as it was on the social graces to which he, as a shy bachelor, never took naturally.

Be that as it may, on one of those days in Le Havre, the tall Viking-like figure certainly strode with confidence enough into the pilotage office and fell into a half-English, half-French conversation with one of the pilots, who then introduced *le patron* of the cutter which would be sailing out to take up position off the Whistle Buoy the next day.

Martin asked if he might sail with them and got a less than enthusiastic grunt in reply, as *le patron* eyed the shore-going clothes of the gigantic man. But he agreed, on condition that he was on board by six o'clock sharp and would pay for his own food.

As Martin jumped down onto the deck of *Marie Fernande*, he could be excused the slight superiority in his voice when he told the Stewarts of the trip in prospect. Maybe they had bought a pilot cutter, but he was actually going to sail in one which was still in service.

He was to write in detail himself of that day, of how he presented himself promptly at the pilot station, this time wearing sailing clothes – undoubtedly the Breton smock tied with a toggle at the neck which he always affected when sailing, at a time when white shirts and ties were still the more normal wear among gentlemen afloat.

Le patron viewed him with a rather better grace in this rig and, with his arrival, the crew warped the cutter out and made sail off the breakwater.

In deference to their paying passenger, they offered him the helm, and he immediately appreciated the lively, responsive nature of the cutter. When they reached the Whistle Buoy the wind fell calm and they dropped anchor. Martin, always fond of his stomach, with the self-indulgence of a true bachelor, reported with care on what they ate that day – coffee, bread and butter and a sort of *foie gras* was their *petit déjeuner*, and this they had completed when at about ten o'clock the four pilots came aboard from their steam launch, within the hour to board incoming ships.

At noon they had *hors d'oeuvre*, soup, fried steak and onions, salad, cheese, jam, cider and coffee. Then they sat and smoked until one of them spied a small fishing boat. They launched the dinghy and, with two bottles of cider and half a bottle of rum, made over to her to bargain for eleven crabs and five flatfish.

"Now," said *le patron*, back on board, "we will make a collation," and so Martin was feasted on boiled crab and salad with much bread and butter.

All that day Martin's respect for the pilot cutter grew, seen through that happy haze of good food and drink. *Le patron* had shown him his fine vessel from stem to stern, and lifted every locker.

Martin himself in his own boats was not a particularly tidy man. He kept a skipper to look after the spick-and-span aspects of life afloat, but he recognized in this pilot cutter the cleanest ship he had ever seen and praised it to the skies, albeit recognizing that such cleanliness and attention was the product of boredom from the inactivity of spending so many days stationary just five miles off shore.

By the time he left that evening, in the steam launch which had come out with the pilots to board the ships on the evening tide, he was a firm convert to the French pilot-cutter type, firmer than the chores of making *Marie Fernande* ready for sea had made him so far in his stay at Le Havre.

He tried to pay *le patron* for his day on board and, after courteous exchanges, he left a sum with him for distribution among the crew, and as soon as he was ashore he attempted to buy the boat on which he had spent his day.

Yes, she was for sale, but it would be six months before she would be finally withdrawn from service and steam would take over totally the pilot duties in Le Havre roads.

One can imagine the puzzled face atop the shoulders of that giant man, looking like a child deprived of an urgently needed toy. They had another boat for sale, they said, but she was fitted with an enormous engine and that would have been too damaging both to her sailing qualities and Martin's vanity as a sailing man.

He cannot have been too good company aboard *Marie Fernande*, now at last ready for sea, with this sudden ambition to buy a newer and better cutter than his friends' so thwarted. Martin may even have been a little reluctant to sail home with them at all. But just as they were ready to cast off, the Customs' formalities completed, and the English ensign flying for the first time from *Marie Fernande*'s taff rail, there was a call from the quay above, and Martin's pilot friend came clambering down the ladder with a very badly packed paper parcel.

Spilling out of it was the half-model of a cutter. Excitedly, Martin unwrapped it on the cabin table and ran his eyes and his hands over her lines. It was a half-model which had been made by Monsieur Paumelle for his client Monsieur Dagier, who could not, or would not, understand a drawing. It was of course *Jolie Brise* and Martin says that he fell in love with her lines at first sight.

The Stewarts had already made sail and, as Martin's pilot friend cast off their lines, Martin called out that he was serious. If *Jolie Brise* could be located and was really available he would be back by the next boat to make her his own.

And so *Marie Fernande* set out for her new life in England, with those keen blue eyes of Martin's looking back astern to Le Havre, day-dreaming about his next dream ship. The Stewarts and their newly acquired boat now sail out of this tale, or nearly so. They renamed her *Marguerite* and a later owner in turn called her *Leonora*. A few weeks ago I was on board *Jolie Brise* when I was hailed by *Leonora*'s present owner, who keeps her in Salcombe, just two rivers away from where *Jolie Brise* winters now. *Leonora*, then, is a fellow survivor from a once-large fleet, and were it not for the Stewarts' purchase of her all those years ago, there could well be no tale to tell such as I tell today, and no *Jolie Brise* for us to sail.

CHAPTER SEVEN

The Hunt Is Up

And so another chapter opens with a tall blond Englishman leaning on the rail of a steamer entering Le Havre roads. But this time he is alone and he waves, with an air of one who belongs, to the pilot cutter and hopes that he is recognized. Once ashore, events develop at the speed of a French farce – which, after all, it is. He goes straight to see Monsieur Paumelle, who explains with some emotion that, while *Jolie Brise* was not the last cutter he had built, she was the child of his old age and the dearest to his heart. *Jean Madeleine* had been the very last to slide down his slipway but, fast though she was to windward, he had to admit that her sections were too hollow and her stern post too sharply raked for safety in a following sea. No, *Jolie Brise* was the final flowering, the peak of his career. The old man even shook his head and said, "They do say that the forests of Normandy will never be the same again after I had plundered them to get the best timber for her."

As Alexandre Paris had been accumulating plans over the years for this ultimate cutter, so too had Paumelle been gathering his timber.

This talk of finale was in fact just the overture to a pursuit round the streets of Le Havre after a black-bearded man. Contrary to the letter which Martin had received from his pilot contact, negotiations were not really very far advanced at all. The name of the owner was not even known, and is not recorded to this day.

They looked for him at his house, they looked for him at his office and then approached, one after another, gentlemen with black beards. Suddenly Martin's friend spun from the pavement and said, "*Le voilà!*" The beard which he was in pursuit of belonged to a gentleman who had his back to them as he scrutinized a bookshop window, but it was a beard of undeniable blackness and such exaggerated proportions that even from behind it extended, clearly visible, on either side. But it was the wrong man, and Martin's friend had suddenly to adopt an all-absorbing interest in the next-door shop-window which advertised "*cent mille chemises*".

The two recovered from this set-back at a café over a glass of *cassis*, and it was not till that evening that they found the right beard and with it the right man. He and Martin set out for Concarneau the next day, and the journey by train took them twenty hours, since they had to go via Paris.

It was in the late evening that Martin finally set eyes on the object of his love, and the first view was one of profound disappointment. Sitting untended in a mud berth for nine months of the year, *Jolie Brise* had become very dirty and very neglected. Her spars were ramshackle, her rigging suspect in the extreme and her forty-three-foot-long boom was in two pieces, scarfed together at its centre by three heavy iron rings. The halyards were rotten and inadequate, and the sails were extremely heavy; indeed it was a mystery how the one could hold the other. Apart from the mainsheet and the jib halyard, there seemed to be no rope which was of one piece. Everything was cobbled up and spliced together, and the splices refused to run through the blocks.

It must have been a slightly uneasy night that Martin had, wondering what he had agreed to purchase, but the next morning, the man with the black beard by then perhaps safely on the train back to Le Havre, Martin had *Jolie Brise* put on the hard and found her lines just as the half-model had foretold. He found too that her bottom was in quite perfect condition. She did not entirely dry out that day, so the bottom of the keel was not visible, but he could see the garboard strake for the whole of its length, and it showed no signs of ever having been touched since she was launched.

It is strange that Martin had this elaborate concern for the soundness of the vessel, built so massively of oak only ten years before, but probably from that morning of his buying her through to the present day, a span of sixty years, *Jolie Brise* has always been considered as old. Looking back, it seems faintly ridiculous that Martin should have had such fears, but a working boat's life is a hard one and he could not be sure what damage there was under the dirt.

"I shipped on board two Bretons, and we set to work with soft soap and hot water," Martin recalls, using the word "Bretons" much as his cousins in the colonies might refer to "natives". Imagine today a bachelor of modest means buying a fifty-five-ton cutter of ten years of age in the first place, let alone casually engaging labour to scrub her stem to stern. But then, those two men's wages for two days today would probably represent no less than the complete figure which Martin had to lay out on buying the boat – perhaps £300.

The cleaning was rewarding and Martin was relieved to find that, under the dirt, damage was just superficial. *Jolie Brise* has now, and even more then, detachable linings, so that he was able to inspect almost every part of her except the keel. When she was built, cement was laid flush with the frames fore and aft. He would have had trouble shifting the cement to make an inspection and so he took that part of the hull on trust, as we still do to this day, because that cement remains for the most part undisturbed.

The French farce gathered momentum again when Martin discovered that he could not sail his ramshackle ship under the British flag. She would have to return to Le Havre in the late owner's name, still under her fishing licence, before permission for export could be given. Even this arrangement required endless formality and several ceremonious visits with the officials to the wine shop by the harbour office.

At last, three weeks later, *Jolie Brise* was set to sail north again with a *patron* (Alain Hervette himself), a *matelot* and a *mousse*, and the extraordinary English bachelor as "*passager*".

The closest contact Martin ever had with a woman was probably when victualling ship. He gave some money to his skipper's wife and told her to keep what was left over after providing enough to keep himself and her menfolk well fed for a week. Naturally Martin looked after the liquor side of affairs, and repaired to wine cellars to buy the special red wine which French sailors were allowed by law. It was Algerian and he bought forty-seven litres of it for the equivalent of seventeen shillings and sixpence. It was rough, but not acid, and agreeably alcoholic, and they were to drink it at all hours of the day.

At last, all set to go, the weather turned foul and they had to kick their heels for a whole weekend. But on the Monday, after smoking many cigarettes and drinking much red wine in amiable conversation with the captain of the fishery steamship, they at last persuaded him to tow them six miles to windward away from Concarneau's narrow rocky entrance.

It was as well for Martin that he was a passenger on this first voyage in his new ship, both in terms of navigation off a strange coast and of working a strange vessel.

The scene on *Jolie Brise*'s foredeck was chaotic in the extreme as they tried to sort out her anchors and cable, which had been foul of other moorings when they had raised them. As the fishery vessel steamed relentlessly on, the crew separated the rusty chain from the evil-smelling mud and the two enormous and very bent "Trotman" anchors. Martin looked amazed while all this load of junk was stowed right aft, but *le patron* insisted that with the weight forward the boat would not sail well. With it aft? Quite another matter! "*Elle marche comme un poisson*." It is equally strange for us to comprehend this today since we have been at pains to keep the weight away from her counter. However, her disproportionately large mainsail of tunny fishing days may well have had something to do with this strange arrangement.

They got the dinghy on board on that Monday afternoon back in 1923. It was extremely heavy and Concarneau-built. It rowed well, it would have sailed well and it was a good weight-carrier. But though only ten feet long it drew one foot six of water and was the devil to get on board, and was top on Martin's list for jettisoning as he groomed *Jolie Brise* for the life of a yacht. The *tangons* and the *chevettes* had already been sent ashore, of course. The dinghy would be next to go.

Finally they slipped their tow and set their jib to a breeze from the south-west. The cutter gathered way on the port tack. It was an exciting moment for Martin to find just how good were the sailing qualities of his new boat, which he had taken on trust, purely from the look of her half-model, seen just a few weeks before. All was well, she seemed to rejoice in working to windward, or at least, so he claimed. Strange to us today, for *Jolie Brise*, in comparison with the modern Bermudan-rigged cutter, has a decidedly depressing windward performance. No, Martin was well pleased, strain though he had to at the tiller with the enormous weather helm generated by her oversized mainsail. At six o'clock they were past the lighthouse on *Les Iles de Glénans*. They then drifted northwards through a calm and moonlit night.

Breakfast the next day was boiled *langoustines*, hot with bread and butter and swilled down with the red wine drunk from large mugs.

Lunch was *bouillabaisse* and coffee from a half-gallon pot, while for dinner they had veal, gently stewed for many hours with quantities of vegetables.

It fell calm again at sunset that second day. Charles Tangey, the *matelot*, who was himself the skipper of a tunny boat, predicted that the wind would "*chercher la lune*" and so it did, the breeze ruffling the water and the line of the moon's reflection on the sea. They exchanged tales of the war and Martin seemed to be in his element, not just because he was at sea in his new boat, but because he was with seamen and sufficiently far from the drawing-room life.

It had taken an age to make up to the Ar Men lighthouse with a foul tide and light winds, but it was the next day that Martin had the first experience of his ship in a blow of wind. They took the balloon jib and the topsail off her and triced up the main tack, a trick that I would like us to be able to do today, but which we are unable to because *Jolie Brise* now has a fully laced foot to her mainsail. On this occasion she roared along with the water swishing through her scuppers and Martin feared that the boom, bent like a bow, would break at any moment.

It was a hectic, dark-skied hour and a half of rapid sailing, during which time they regaled themselves with three fried eggs and a pint of red wine apiece.

That evening they saw the Eddystone Light and picked up a breeze from the north-north-east. It was a whole day later that they first sighted the Casquets, then Alderney, and then Le Havre.

Jolie Brise was now approaching again the waters for which she had been specifically designed. She reached along the Cherbourg peninsula at a steady seven knots in smooth water.

As day had succeeded day, shipboard routine was a pleasant one and the men exchanged tales in partly comprehensible Breton, as Martin amused himself painting little water-colour sketches, for which he had an agreeable talent. Trawlers putting out from Caen particularly pleased his eye. Then from time to time he would go below and plot *Jolie Brise*'s progress on the chart. Although he was a passenger in his own boat and his skipper was an experienced tunny-man, Martin was the only one on board who understood the mysteries of navigation.

But this first carefree voyage of 343 miles was soon to end. At two thirty the next morning, with a foul tide, they dropped anchor in fourteen fathoms in Le Havre roads. Martin stayed on deck watching his ship and the lights of her birth-place ashore, and the next afternoon they worked her into the harbour on the tide. At this homecoming she did not go to the Pilot Quay, nor to the fishing basin, nor to the slip where she was built, but secured in the corner near the Place Gambetta in the Basin des Yachts. A new phase of her life had begun.

I like to think of old Monsieur Paumelle clucking round her deck and advising Martin on what should be put back where and how. She spent some three weeks there, fitting out further for the voyage home. Martin kept the Bretons for a day or two and then packed them off back to Concarneau on the train. Two friends and a hand from Brixham came over to help him home with his new acquisition, the strange dark horse destined to startle the English yachting scene.

Coincidentally, her first port of call in her new country was Portland. I say that it was coincidental because Portland, as I have written, was the most north-westerly extreme of the Le Havre pilotage area, as defined in 1856, and because from 1978 until 1980, so many, many years later, Portland was to be *Jolie Brise*'s home-port, courtesy of Her Majesty's Navy.

But, on that first occasion that the black cutter sailed between the Portland breakwaters, it was simply to clear Customs and pay modest duty on the cheap wine that she had brought home with her. Her final destination was to be round the Bill and far across the Bay.

A sketch of Jolie Brise *in 1923 by E. G. Martin*

CHAPTER EIGHT

Modest Transformation

At first sight Teignmouth is a strange place to keep a large deep cutter, having as it does a ferocious tide and a difficult bar at the river entrance. But the attraction of Teignmouth was not so much the harbour and the little town, nor indeed the highly reputable boat-yard of Morgan Giles, but one Sidney Briggs, archetype of a breed of men as nearly extinct as the pilots and tunny-men who had handled *Jolie Brise* in her early life. Sidney Briggs was a professional yacht skipper. A cockney by birth, not a Devon man, Briggs had been a sailor-man on a Thames barge. He had put into Teignmouth with a cargo one day and found a pretty girl ashore, married her and never moved away.

After Thames barges, *Jolie Brise* held no mysteries for Briggs. Her new home was a little dock where she could dry out securely alongside but float on every tide, so essential, for if her fine oak was to be kept in good order, it should never be allowed to be completely dry.

Briggs' cottage was in a terrace a hundred yards away, over-looking the boat which was his new charge, and he and Martin busied themselves with her transformation.

New spars were made to the dimensions which Paumelle indicated that they should have been. However, down below there was little change. Always opinionated, Martin would hold forth to his friends about there being no necessity for fancy panelling in the saloon of a sea-going yacht. There were certainly no fancy trimmings in his ship. So you came down the companionway to a saloon lit only by a skylight with two bunks to port and two to starboard. On either side were hand-rails and a pillar up the middle. Ducking to starboard you would come across Martin's own bunk in earshot of the helm, while far aft stretched the sail stowage area, served also by a circular hatch almost at the furthest point to the stern.

That much, then, was little changed from her earliest days (see drawing on p. 51) but a proud innovation was located just to the port of the companionway – a teak chart table. Another innovation, the chief memory of a lady who has just written to me about *Jolie Brise* as she knew her in the early 1930s, was a table-top surmounting a massive zinc water-tank, for Martin had long voyages in prospect.

Forward of the saloon one came to Briggs' personal domain, first the galley with some form of paraffin cooker served by a chimney and ventilator (Martin was particularly concerned with ventilation), and then beyond that the forecastle with pipe cots for skipper Briggs and his assistant cook-cum-steward. Still further forward was the bosun's store.

During the 'twenties there were always long debates about where a yacht's galley should be. They tended usually to be forward of the mast, though that was seldom the most comfortable position. Martin toyed with the idea of a galley further aft, handier for cooking at night when you were serving the watch on deck, but inevitably the forward position for a galley always prevailed because it was the professional skipper or cook who tended to do the cooking, and it was right to have it in their end of the ship.

The position of another important facility was equally one for debate. Flushing lavatories for yachts were a relatively new feature, and certainly *Jolie Brise* in her working days would have been innocent of such a contraption. Martin's new purchase was placed in its own little cubicle on the starboard side, abreast of the galley and just forward of the mast.

And so the newly formed team of Briggs and Martin worked on their vessel's transformation. And sometimes they would lay down their tools and a dinghy would put out from the yard of Morgan Giles across the river, bringing the yard owner and his children to tea. Briggs would appear from the galley with an enormous chocolate cake, for which Martin had a particular weakness. Mr Morgan Giles' sons and daughters would be gathered from the ratlines in the shrouds, which they had been climbing with competitive daring, and be bidden to tuck in. One of those boys, now Admiral Morgan Giles, one-time MP, then aged ten, recalls that their huge jovial host would listen carefully until one of them gave a sigh of repletion, prompting him to roar greatly and declare that the party had been a success.

While Martin was respected among yachtsmen and almost worshipped by children allowed aboard for tea, Briggs too had his following. Sadly he died very recently, living to the end in Teignmouth, where his daughter still lives. His son became foreman at the Morgan Giles yard, but there was another man, of whom we shall hear more, Mr Albert Broom, a thirteenth child, later to be a hand aboard *Jolie Brise*, to whom Briggs was almost a father and always an example. It is he, still hale and hearty today, who sums up that special team of master and man when he says that Martin and Briggs were "both gentlemen in their own spheres".

By the season of 1924 *Jolie Brise* could well and truly be declared a yacht. She often sailed in company with *Vanda*, the family boat of the Warneford family. From a small boy's view of Martin and his boat we now come to a young girl's. Molly Warneford was nineteen, bright, cheerful and precocious, ready to be amused by the shy bachelor and his skipper Briggs. However, she was less pleased when "Martey" sent her ashore on errands in a somewhat perfunctory manner. Molly entered all this in a lively log, peppered with such little comments as, "It is amazing to watch Mr Martin coming down the companion ladder. It seems an age before all 6′7½″ of him are down."

These were the days of novelty in the shape of outboard motors – "the Johnson outboard is a little wonder, it can even tow *Jolie Brise*." A little later Martin pontificates about yachts being at the mercy of the elements and in calm weather helpless and unable to move at all, and the young Molly pokes quiet fun, writing, "the good man had evidently never heard of an engine."

Silent though he so often is, the bachelor more and more turns to the Warnefords for family life as he has no family of his own, other than his Mama, who follows one pace behind, staying in seaside hotels. However, he seems oblivious of any amusement he may cause in the eyes of a bright young girl, or even those of his contemporaries, for Molly's father also finds him all too tempting as a butt for japes in the old tradition. Martin once wrote that an engine was useful in a boat "if you were in a flat calm and there were ladies on board", as if in fear of being compromised by amorous attentions, immobile on the painted sea. This terror of women could not be let slip, so one day during Cowes Week Molly's father takes the steamer to Southampton and returns, having negotiated the purchase of a lifelike female tailor's dummy, clothed only in a substantial corset. Under cover of dark this is propped up just forward of the mast aboard *Jolie Brise*. The eyes of all the yachts in the anchorage peer through half-closed hatches as the next morning the doughty Briggs first emerges through the forehatch and then slowly circumnavigates the dummy. He scuttles down below again. A minute later the head of Martin himself appears in the main hatch, twisting to look forward and then retracting fast. Minutes pass and then Briggs appears again, ties various impediments to the dummy and consigns her to the not-so-deep. Nothing is ever said, until Molly, now a neighbour of mine in Dorset, recalls the tale.

However, there is always a fondness and a respect both for the boat and the man. A typical remark in Molly's log reads, "We saw *Jolie Brise* a good six miles ahead, going well. There was no chance of catching her up. There's no doubt about it, she can move, and it would take more than half a gale of wind to put her rail under."

And it was a respect which an increasing number of yachtsmen were to share as *Jolie Brise* and her owner became a more and more familiar sight, showing their paces against purpose-built yachts in regattas up and down the coast.

CHAPTER NINE

Dawn of a New Sport

Something was afoot in the world of yacht clubs and that of writers concerned with yachting and the sea.

One Weston Martyr comes now onto the scene. He was a regular writer for *The Yachting World* and a delight to the armchair sailor, for he contributed books for the yachtsman's shelf as engagingly entertaining as the stories of W. W. Jacobs and, in a more serious vein, those of Joseph Conrad and H. M. Tomlinson.

I was brought up on those books of Weston Martyr, and one tale in particular, second only perhaps to Erskine Childers' *The Riddle of the Sands*, must have inspired many would-be yacthsmen to get out of their armchairs and put to sea. The tale is called *The Two Hundred Pound Millionaire*, and it is a story of how just such a bachelor as E. G. Martin, with a neat little bottle-green sloop, is able to follow the sun along the coasts and waterways of Europe, totally self-sufficient and contented on a budget of just two hundred pounds a year.

Weston Martyr had knocked about the world a bit himself, rather like Davies the poet and super-tramp. He had experienced the precariousness of a journalist's life in a depressed New York, from which he had escaped with a friend to pool all their resources in the building of a small schooner in Nova Scotia. Hers was a tale to be connected with rum-running in Prohibition days. The experience had ended in financial disaster for Martyr and, in new hands, the schooner had been impounded and finally set on fire. But he had caught one disease which he brought home with him to England and with which he proceeded to infect his friend Martin, and that was the disease of ocean racing.

The yachtsmen of New York, with their handy little schooners, had for some time been racing annually from New London to Bermuda. It was a very different sort of race, appealing to a different sort of boat and a different sort of person, than the racing of the giant "J" Class boats in the elegant waters of the Solent or Long Island Sound.

Martyr himself was no great sailor, albeit that he had served in square-rigged ships. However, he saw in Martin the sort of able and respected man who would rise to the challenge of promoting an ocean race in British waters. So it was to Martin he turned to make a dream into a reality.

The idea of virtually inventing a new British sport must have appealed to Martin's vanity. Both he and Martyr set to to promote ocean racing in the press. Memories of Martin's Oxford days, his connections with Kenneth Grahame and Quiller-Couch, came perhaps to the surface again, and practical but elegantly written articles gave Martin that new purpose in life that possibly he had missed since the active days of the war. But more than blowing on glowing literary embers, there was the matter too of generating support for the idea of an ocean race among the many yacht clubs of which Martin was a member – for like many bachelors he seemed to collect clubs just for the sake of it. In his time he had been a member of the Cruising Association, the Royal Western Yacht Club of England, the Royal Saint George, the Royal Thames, the Yacht Racing Association and, in later life, the Royal Yacht Squadron.

However, there was one other club of which he relinquished membership through this very question of racing at sea. This was the Royal Cruising Club, of which he had been a prominent member but from which he departed when the equally prominent Claude Worth, one of the greatest exponents of cruising under sail, announced that it was foolhardy to promote an ocean race. Cruising in deep water was safe enough, because the individual would shorten sail when prudent and make for ports of refuge if changes in weather threatened his passage. But if he were engaged in the competitive sport of racing, Worth argued, the yachtsman might persuade himself to carry more sail than was seamanlike and stay at sea longer than was prudent, rather than make for ports of refuge.

If cruising men were sceptical so too were racing men, and two brothers, Brooke and Malden Heckstall-Smith, both well known in the pukka world of inshore racing, were later to be at loggerheads on the subject, with Brooke for long canvassing the dangers of ocean-racing – racing in the dark particularly concerned him – while Malden was a staunch supporter.

It is hard to appreciate those ruffled feathers from this distance in time, but Martin and Martyr thrived upon it, and so too did the columns of *The Yachting World*.

In the March number of 1925 it was announced that the Ocean Race would start from Ryde in the Solent on 15th August; that competitors would have to sail from there east-about round the island to the Fastnet Rock off the shores of southern Ireland and thence back to Plymouth. The cards were on the table and endless articles were to appear over the months, preparing readers and would-be competitors for this previously unheard-of novelty of deep-sea racing in European waters.

So it is that in the July issue we find Martin writing in *The Yachting World* about having been nine months ashore and yet still busy preparing *Jolie Brise* for the great race. He speaks of the pleasures of fitting out a pilot boat, whose rugged construction can but respond to loving treatment, whereas a yacht can never look smarter than the day she is launched.

Martin was aware that he must approach his preparations in a different frame of mind from that which he might adopt were he simply embarking on a long cruise. He owns that he would set out upon a passage to Gibraltar or some such distant place with far less consideration than he would upon a 600 mile race. He goes on, "there is perhaps something heroic in the frame of mind that makes a plan and attempts to carry it out whatever the circumstances may be."

He anticipates having a crew on *Jolie Brise* of six or seven amateurs and two paid hands. Normally, he says, there are three, and never more than four on board, all told.

In August we find *Jolie Brise* sailing from Cowes heading for the Plymouth Regatta and trying out a new mainsail just made for her by Ratseys. However, they set sail with only the trysail set for there is rain and they do not want to get the new sail wet, and besides it is blowing hard and Martin is equally loath to reef, for we must remember that those were the days of cotton sails which had to be stretched, carefully broken in, never reefed until already well used, and if made wet, meticulously dried.

They beat westwards down the Solent and out through the

Needles Channel when a sudden loss of wind puts them in some danger of being swept onto the Shingles Bank. In time-honoured pilot fashion the two seventeen-foot sweeps are used to scull her over the stern.

At last they set the new sail and as they reach along the Purbeck shore Martin is well pleased with it. Superseding his first mainsail, which had been laced to the boom, this new sail is loose footed and takes up a perfect curve from luff to leech, standing well despite being unstretched.

Limbering up for the Ocean Race, *Jolie Brise* had some splendid sailing in the Plymouth Regatta, and Martin watched appreciatively the King's great cutter *Britannia* racing to a fine finish.

Then he worked further west and was caught napping sailing into Falmouth on a foul tide and with sudden fog at night. Soon one feels the tension mounting as he will be setting his bowsprit eastwards again for the start of the Ocean Race.

Not just Martin and Martyr were to offer advice to *The Yachting World*'s readers, however. Someone who styled herself simply as "A Woman" also contributed. "The Ocean Race," she writes, "is a very sporting proposition and should cause a great stir in the yachting world, but I feel it should not be undertaken too lightly and without due preparation."

Her chief concern is with what should be worn. "A navy blue sailor hat with stiff brim looks nicer and is nicer than anything." You should take, too, "at least two chiffon motor-veils in blue preferably, not brown, never brown on a boat. These should go right over the hat and face but secure the ends and don't let them wave abroad in the eyes of your neighbours.

"Take also," she advises, "three or four pairs of thick white fabric gloves, long enough to prevent the wrists getting tanned.

"For shoes," she relents, "brown may be permitted," and she recommends "good strong Russian leather".

Practical details settled at last, she lyricizes on the race itself. "Oh, the beauty of sailing at night! Is there anything in the world to compare with it, so '*intrigant*', so enthralling, so refreshing, and, added to that, to put the last touch of gilt on the gingerbread, to feel you are actually racing!"

If the woman-fearing Commander RNR had ever contemplated sailing with ladies on board, sentiments so expressed would certainly have made him think again.

On 8th August the list of entries for the Ocean Race closed and the Skippers Column in *The Yachting World*, written by Weston Martyr, finally assessed the importance of this new departure. "The size of the competing yachts," he reports, "has been limited to those having a waterline length of between thirty and fifty feet, and this in effect has restricted the entries to yachts which normally carry small professional crews."

He talks too about the handicapping: "the effect of the method of hull measurement employed is to penalize yachts designed for speed alone – low freeboard, long overhangs, unduly light displacement and absence of bulwarks, all features undesirable in sea-going craft, are penalized. Whether it is an event which will become popular with British yachtsmen remains to be proved" – or so it did in 1925. We have proof enough today.

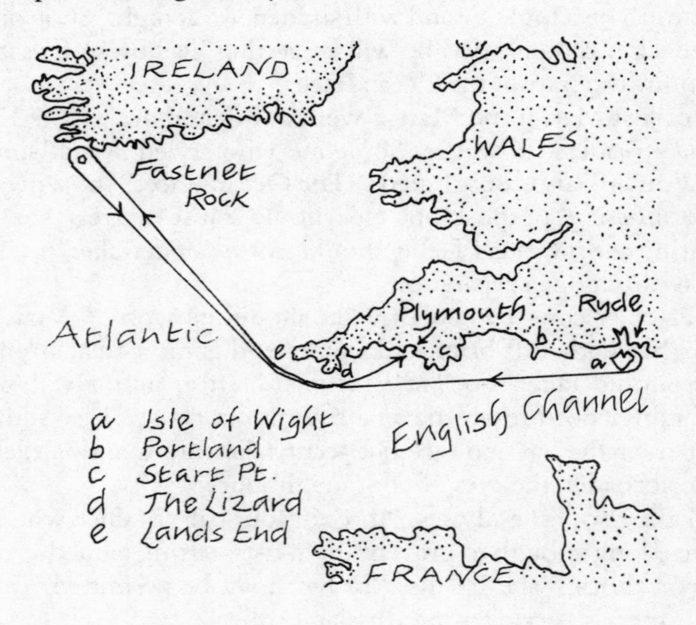

Jolie Brise *and some of her fellow Fastnet competitors, 1925–1931*

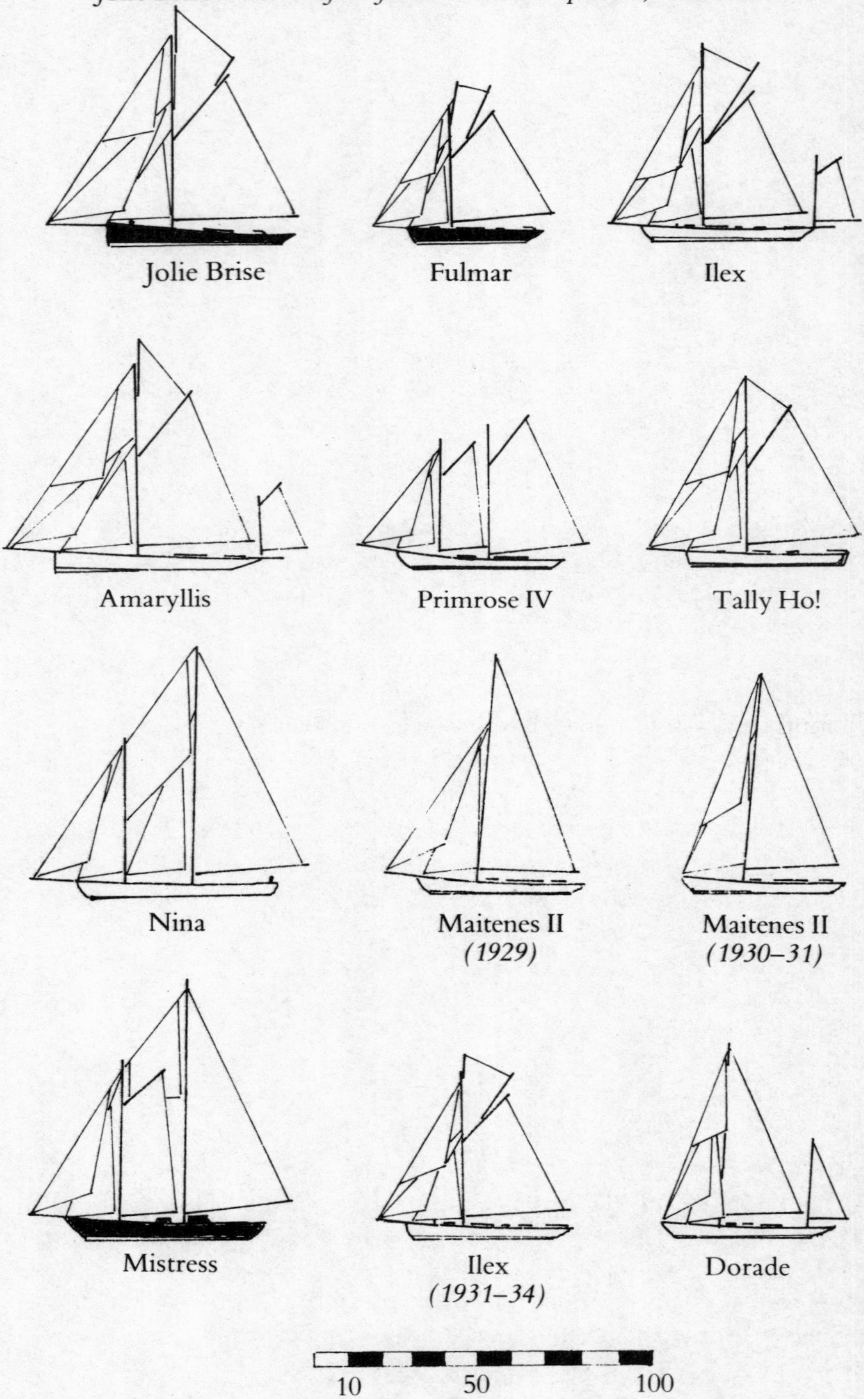

Jolie Brise

Fulmar

Ilex

Amaryllis

Primrose IV

Tally Ho!

Nina

Maitenes II
(1929)

Maitenes II
(1930–31)

Mistress

Ilex
(1931–34)

Dorade

10 50 100
feet

CHAPTER TEN

The First Ocean Race

The Fastnet Race and the Grand National have much in common, the one being the supreme test of racing at sea while the other is the pinnacle of racing on land, but whereas horse-racing is a spectator sport, ocean racing is not. The commentary is fast-moving on the Grand National, but to provide a commentary for its watery counterpart would be well-nigh impossible. But let us just suppose that there was some omniscient commentator on that first race round the Fastnet. His commentary might have run something like this.

"And here we are at the start of the very first Ocean Race, and there are just seven runners from the fourteen entries. Unfortunately the American yawl that was to race is among those that have fallen by the wayside.

Most fancied is *Jolie Brise*, owned and skippered by Commander E. G. Martin, a 1913 French pilot cutter, this. She has no established form, but I think very good prospects.

Martin will be watching *Fulmar*, another rakish black cutter, and she too has been a pilot boat, this time in the Bristol Channel. She's entered by the Royal Engineers Yacht Club, with a crew of enthusiastic lads.

Then the boat for my money is the Irish *Gull*. She has come all the way here from Dublin, owned and skippered by Mr H. P. F. Donegan. He'll be racing back almost as far as the Irish shore and back here to Plymouth. So they are showing great spirit, these Irish contestants. *Gull* herself is the only thoroughbred in the race. She is old, built in 1896, but she does come from the yard of Camper & Nicholson's at Gosport, and I fancy her very much indeed.

And then we've *Saladin*, another traditional straight-stemmed gaff cutter, owned and sailed by Mr Ingo Simon.

Bamba IV is a bit of an outsider, owned and sailed by Mr H. R. Barrett. She's a stout, tubby double-ender gaff ketch with little pretentions to speed, but she should be comfortable enough in a blow.

Mr Hussy's *Jessie L* is the only boat in the fleet with a Bermudan mainsail, and there's been some doubt about the propriety of entering her, particularly as she has a rather controversial roller-reefing gear.

And then finally we have *North Star*, another double-ender built on Norwegian lifeboat lines, a gaff ketch this, owned and sailed by Mr M. Tennant – probably as much an outsider as *Bamba*.

Now it's been blowing from the north-east during the night and none of the competitors have been too comfortable in the exposed conditions off Ryde, but it's beautifully fine now with a light breeze from the east-north-east, which will give them a flog to windward to clear the Isle of Wight with the prospect of a nice run down-Channel.

They are under starter's orders . . . and they're off! *Jolie Brise* is a little late at the start and she's off on the starboard tack, going towards Stokes Bay. *Gull* has started strongly at the Ryde Pier end of the starting line and she has nipped into first position just a few seconds after the starting gun.

Bamba, *Jessie L* and *North Star* are following *Jolie Brise*, but the race is with *Gull*, now followed by *Fulmar*, probably the only boat that can hold her to windward.

But there's a sneaky one over there, *Saladin*'s tacked towards the Ryde sands, taken a quick hitch to windward and she's just behind *Gull* at the Bembridge Buoy. Then it's *Fulmar*, ahead of *Jolie Brise*, and, well behind her, *Bamba* and *Jessie L* bringing up the tail. And the favourite's looking a little more hopeful now.

Jolie Brise has set her enormous spinnaker and yes, she's overhauling *Saladin* and *Fulmar*.

Coming up from St Catherine's, *Gull* is still in the lead, challenged only by *Jolie Brise*, and both of them are pulling away from the rest of the field.

1 Paumelle's pride: the brass capped rudder head is more redolent of a yacht than a working boat. It reads, "*Jolie Brise Havre 1913 Paumelle Constr.*". (Photo Bryer)

2 Pissarro painted this picture of Le Havre pilots' jetty from the first-floor window of a café in 1903. (The Tate Gallery, London)

3 Claude Monet painted this Le Havre pilot cutter entering Honfleur in 1870. (Private Collection)

4 A pilot cutter sails into Le Havre. Note various features evident in Pissarro's picture opposite. (Collection J. P. Dole Robbe)

5 Two pilot cutters being sculled out to sea, while the ferry steams past. The cutter on the left has the sail number 6, but is *Jolie Brise*'s predecessor. *Jolie Brise* was always referred to as "*nouveau numéro six*". (Collection J. P. Dole Robbe)

6 *Jolie Brise* before the wind on a Solent summer's day in the late 1920s. Martin favoured white sails, while Warren Ferrier and Brownlow Smith had a penchant for smart yachting caps. The two combined make the old pilot cutter look every inch a yacht. Notice her sail number is 6, recalling her pilot days . . . although 1 would have been more appropriate for England's first ocean racer. (Beken, Cowes)

7 *Opposite:* Possibly the most famous picture of all. *Jolie Brise* thrashing her way to windward in the Solent in Somerset's day. (Beken, Cowes)

JOLIE BRISE

8 Saved from the scrap-yard and bowling southward in the Lisbon–Algarve race of 1947.

9 Reaching to the northerly Trades in the River Tagus, 1958.

10 Overhauling *Royalist* in the 1980 Tall Ships Race.

11 Ancient and Modern: ocean racing 'twenties and 'eighties style. *Jolie Brise* and a young competitor in the 1981 Round the Island Race. (Beken, Cowes)

12 Secret of success: great depth and sweet lines guide *Jolie Brise* on her effortless way. (Raubenheimer, Cherbourg, 1981)

And the wind has died away now and they're all strung out across Bournemouth Bay. *Gull* is doing slightly better than *Jolie Brise* and *Fulmar* in a drifting match off Portland Bill. And it's a very slow race indeed now but the leaders are off Start Point and *Jolie Brise* has picked up a fresh breeze and she's dropping *Gull* and *Saladin* behind. *Jolie Brise* is at the Manacles and she's hotly pursued by *Gull*, who persists in holding her topsail and her spinnaker in this brisk wind.

Way back in the field *Bamba* looks happier. She's picked up the strong wind off Prawle Point, but no, she's becalmed now off Black Head. *Fulmar*'s in the middle of the field and just off Land's End is *Jolie Brise*, hotly pursued by *Gull*, *Fulmar* some way behind, *Bamba* nowhere in the race at all. And it's *Jessie L* and *North Star* becalmed now just off the Lizard.

The leaders are making good progress, glad to be away from the strong following wind, on course with a reach for the Fastnet. But no, they're becalmed too and within one square mile we've got a drifting match between *Gull* and *Jolie Brise*, and now *Fulmar*'s crept up astern. The three of them look very pretty there but they're not getting very far, although they have got a fifty mile lead on the rest of the field.

The skippers are waving at one another and shouting and, oh dear, yes, *Gull*'s jackyard topsail has suddenly fallen to the deck. Bit of a surprise that, in a dead calm. *Fulmar* and *Saladin* have picked up a little breeze from the eastward and they've come up with the leaders too, but yes, they've stopped as well. So that's *Fulmar*, *Saladin*, *Jolie Brise* and *Gull*, all becalmed together, but it could be anybody's race as it's still a long way to go yet to the Fastnet.

Gull still hasn't managed to get her jackyard topsail up again and she has replaced it with a jibheader. It may very well cost her the race, but there's still all to race for with the four leaders still stationary together on the same piece of water.

But no, *Jolie Brise* is pulling away. She's actually moving. She's picked up a little draught from the north-by-east and yes, things are getting better and better for her. She's now got a westerly Force 1 coming round to west-north-west Force 2, and yes, right up to Force 4 – beautiful sailing breeze with smooth water. And she's making a landfall just between Toe Head and Baltimore Bay. She's certainly given them the slip, but now she's got to tack along the coast before she gets the Fastnet a point under the lee bow. And now she's put her helm up to round the mark – historic moment, this.

And what about the others? There's *Gull* and *Fulmar*, the breeze didn't get to them until an hour and a half after *Jolie Brise* picked it up and they're certainly not getting that extra wind that *Jolie Brise* found. It's *Saladin* and *Gull* having a close match with *Fulmar*. But now *Gull* has jibed to starboard in response to a slight south-west breeze and she's pulling away from *Fulmar*, who's now half a mile in her wake. But they're all becalmed again, and now they've picked up a light south-westerly along the Irish coast and it's *Gull* leading *Fulmar* and *Saladin* at the Rock.

Meanwhile, back down the field, *Bamba* has just avoided the rocks off Land's End and she too is becalmed, though at least she is pointing in the right direction for the Fastnet. She is just laying a course for the Rock on the port tack and the wind is strengthening now. That's fine for *Jolie Brise*, who's creaming her way home with her balloon jib. And the glass is falling fast and it's *Jolie Brise* well ahead, having a splendidly fast passage from Land's End to the Lizard. *Gull* and *Fulmar* are having a closely contested battle coming up to Land's End. Oh, and *Bamba* is having a bad time now – just off the Irish coast, looks as though she is trying to put into Baltimore. But no, she's thought better of it and she's rounding the Rock with a fair wind for home. This is her weather now, at last, and she's setting her large squaresail.

But she's been pipped at the Rock by *North Star*, who, if anything, has been slower, but she hasn't wasted time round Baltimore. *Jessie L* seems to have dropped out of the race. I'm not sure, perhaps trouble there with that roller-reefing gear.

Bamba's just had to dodge there round a steamer approaching the Seven Stones Lightship, and that's dropped her a little too far down to the westward to clear it. She's had to drop her squaresail and she's making up towards the coast. Yes, she's round Land's End and she's got her squaresail up again. Too late to be in the race, but she's making a grand spurt on the homeward leg. Oh dear, and she's becalmed off Looe Island.

But the race is finished now – *Jolie Brise* is home in Plymouth and here's a surprise. *Fulmar* has stayed a little further out than *Gull* and she's beating her into second place. And there's *Saladin* coming in not far astern. *Bamba* and *North Star*, the two heavy double-enders, have still got their own race going. It looks as though *Bamba*'s last – she's becalmed off Looe, some fifteen miles behind *North Star*, who's just coming up to the finishing line – but no, *she*'s becalmed on a foul tide and her skipper's put the engine on. Obviously keen to get in in time for supper, so he's out of the race. And here's *Bamba* drifting up to the finish, not quite sure where she is in the dark. So it's all over bar the shouting. First, *Jolie Brise*; second, *Fulmar*; third, *Gull*; fourth, *Saladin*; fifth, *Jessie L* (how did she get there?), and *Bamba* last but not least because of course *North Star* put her engine on and retired just 200 yards from the finish."

And that is how the commentary might have been had that first Ocean Race lasted ten minutes, whereas in fact the slowest boat took seven and a half days to complete that 600-mile course, and *Jolie Brise*, the winner, took six days, two hours and forty-five minutes.

It was undeniably a motley bunch of eccentric boats which competed in that first race. I think it was Malden Heckstall-Smith who said that they would have made dull company indeed had you met them in a coastal regatta.

Certainly had the King and his "J" Class cronies decided that an Ocean Race would be fun and provided their thoroughbred yachts with modest off-shore rigs, then no doubt *Jolie Brise* and her friends would have been nowhere in the race. But that is not the point. The Ocean Race throughout was conceived as something for the *cruising* man. It was the Cruising Club of America which had taken ocean racing in the United States under its wing and although in Britain the Royal Cruising Club had disdained the idea of racing off shore, all articles connected with the Ocean Race, both before and after, came under the heading "Cruising" in the columns of *The Yachting World*.

Martin had had his share of thoroughbred racing with a six-metre designed by Milne, of which he had been co-owner before the war. He had had his share too of fast, thoroughbred cruising yachts with his ownership of *Amaryllis*, built by Camper & Nicholson's and quite a bit bigger than *Jolie Brise*. But his driving passion was for traditional working boats. That had been behind his ownership of a *boier* before the war, his sailing of *Jolie Brise* and his later infatuation with Thames barges.

So the entrants to the first Ocean Race round the Fastnet Rock, while they were nothing special from the racing man's point of view, in any event drew their inspiration less from the smart competitions round the buoys in sheltered waters and more from the traditional friendly races between fishing boats, bound home to market, or pilot boats bound outward, racing to serve ships.

At a time when many of those traditions were being lost, Martin and his friends were in effect preserving the essence of them in this friendly deep-water match. Ocean racing might be a brand-new sport which racing yachtsmen scoffed at, but it was founded firmly on the skills of fishermen, pilots and lifeboatmen, far predating any yachtsmen's tests of speed.

However unremarkable the company, the *course* they had chosen was certainly very outstanding indeed. Wind changes, tidal peculiarities, differences between the waters of the English Channel and the open waters of the Atlantic Ocean, all contribute to making it a remarkable test of any boat to this day. Further, the time taken to cover its 600-mile course in itself is likely to supply various changes of weather, with inevitably still greater chances of success for the larger and faster, even allowing for handicap, for they can be romping home with a strengthening breeze behind them while the smaller fry are still beating out westward from Land's End.

This was a factor illustrated in this very first race when, after a variety of changes of fortune, the gap between *Jolie Brise*, the leader, and *Bamba IV*, the rearguard, could only grow wider and wider as conditions favoured the homeward bound and thwarted still further those who had yet to round the mark.

Those boats that thrash round the Fastnet today are very different indeed from that little company of 1925, but, relatively speaking, the fun and the challenge is just the same, as too are the implications of some chance mishap such as the breaking of *Gull*'s jackyard topsail halyard, which probably cost her the race, and with it perhaps the revered niche in history which fell instead to *Jolie Brise*.

Such an historic first race deserves mulling over further. What was life like aboard those first ocean-racers? Certainly everyone wanted to know, and to tell, because *Yachting World* published not just one but four accounts of it. So we have a picture of the race from the decks of *Jolie Brise*, *Fulmar*, *Bamba* and *North Star*, over fifty per cent of the field, all but *North Star* taking not just one but two editions in which to tell the story. Just imagine fifty per cent of the three hundred or so that enter for the Fastnet these days each writing up their logs for the yachting magazines!

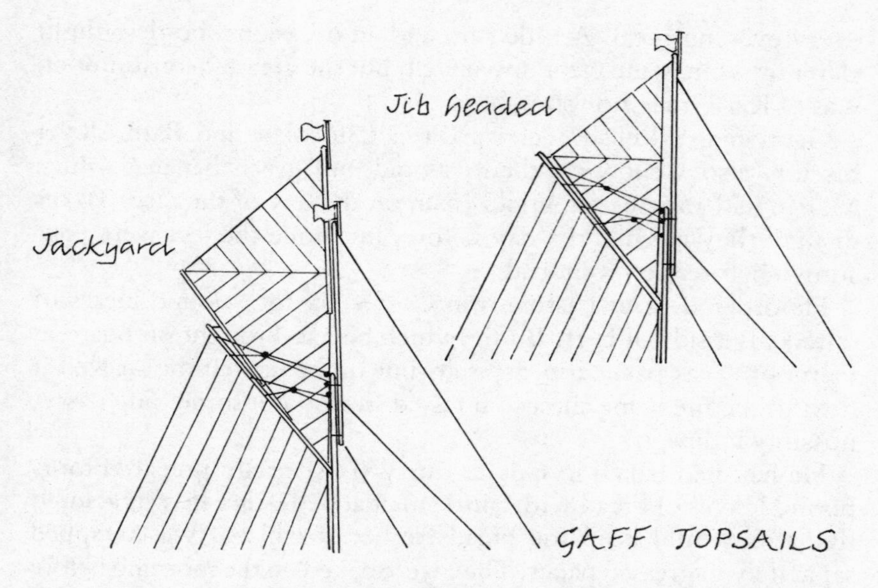

Jolie Brise, we learn, had her bottom scrubbed at Flushing when she visited Falmouth on 6th August and used Holzapfel's Racing Light Brown composition for anti-fouling. She took on board 240 gallons of drinking water, ample for six men on a 600-mile race. Fortunately Martin's cook had overcome the sea-sickness which he had suffered from earlier in the season, and it was planned that throughout the race breakfast at eight would generally consist of eggs and bacon or sausages, or potatoes and bacon after the eggs were finished.

Martin decided to have lunch at twelve, since this was the time that his men had their dinner and it seemed sensible for the whole ship's company to feed together, particularly as they were eating practically the same food.

They had tea at about four, as by then the gentry would be getting peckish after their unfashionably early lunch, and then dinner at seven thirty, in time for the change of watch at eight. That generally consisted of soup, then some fairly sustaining dish, followed by tinned fruit, cheese and coffee.

At four a.m. they had hot Bovril and later an early morning cup of tea. Martin happened to go into the forecastle after they had been at sea for four days and was delighted to see in passing how clean and tidy the cook was keeping his galley.

They had on board a mixed case of whisky, rum and a bottle of most excellent old brandy which they drank ceremoniously after every evening meal. A little rum and an occasional bottle of light claret or white wine went down well, but the greatest consumption was of Kia-Ora lemon squash.

Gentleman's Relish, Terry's Bitter Chocolate and Bath Oliver biscuits also went with them, as did 140 green bananas which Martin had anticipated would ripen on the day of the race. To his dismay they ripened the day before, but none the less were consumed before they went bad.

He ordered from Eastmans in Cowes six four-pound pieces of salted silverside of beef. Butter which he had brought on board at Falmouth was packed in dry salt, but unfortunately he stowed it next to the medicine chest so it tasted strongly of something nasty, possibly iodine.

He had had baked in Cowes thirty-six specially prepared four-pound loaves of bread with a little malt added, since he was assured that this would keep the bread fresher. Each loaf was wrapped separately in greased paper. They were baked on the morning before the race, but they were not really cold when they were stowed, which probably accounted for them eventually going mouldy.

During one of the race's many calms Martin was asked to prepare an onion soup, for which he was famous. His recipe is as follows:

> First, get someone else to peel fifteen large Spanish onions and cut them into quarters. Then take a large saucepan and put into it about an ounce of Bovril. Add a little water to dissolve the Bovril, warm this up and stir in about a quarter of a pound of butter. Then add a dessertspoonful of Worcester sauce and a small wine glass of sherry, or a large wine glass of white wine. Then put in the onions and add about three pints of water. Allow to simmer until the onions are perfectly soft.

This went down well, as did a special baked apple concoction for the preparation of which a suitable gouge was found in the tool locker. The apple cores were taken out and a mixture of rum and sugar poured into the holes.

The Irish crew of *Gull* were rather less fastidious about their victualling, which they seem to have done ashore in Ryde on the morning of the race. A complete surprise, since Donegan's writing style is breezy and life aboard seemed distinctly jovial, is that *Gull* did not have a single drop of alcohol aboard. By contrast, *Fulmar*, with her crew of cheerful engineers, was to invent a variety of revolting drinks in the course of the race. They had eaten ashore on the preceding night and had thus made certain that they were as well victualled as their ship. As they eventually rounded the Rock they celebrated with a "*Fulmar* Cocktail", the known ingredients of which included gin, vermouth, whisky, beer, rum and brandy, with a little condensed milk added and a raisin, in default of a cherry.

Moving to other culinary matters, one of the two Scotsmen in their crew turned out some scones, and as he staggered aft with them the ship sank appreciably by the stern.

On board *North Star* the cook was nearly keel-hauled since only just round the Fastnet Rock they had run out of fresh water, which he had been using for washing his teeth and washing the dishes and all sorts of unspeakable things. But *North Star* in any case only had an eighty-gallon-capacity water-tank, compared with *Jolie Brise*'s 240-gallon one.

Stomachs, heaving or otherwise, always loom large in an ocean race and this first Ocean Race was no exception.

Other charming details emerge, most remarkable of which perhaps was that this was the first time that *Jolie Brise* had really been raced and that, in the entire fleet, Weston Martyr was the only man who had ever been in an ocean race before. But his account, later published in *The South Sea Man*, of how the schooner in which he sailed in the Bermuda Race totally failed to find Bermuda, was, in any event, not one to inspire confidence.

Remarkable too amongst all the boats was a propensity for everybody to jump in the water and have a swim whenever the weather fell calm.

Either that or they were rowing in dinghies, taking photographs. The famous zephyr, which wafted *Jolie Brise* away from *Gull* and finally clinched her lead, indeed so much took her crew by surprise that they had to row fast to keep up with her, before they could clamber aboard and continue the race.

There was certainly an informality and a readiness for enjoyment which today's ocean-racers might do well to emulate.

The professional crews must also have had their moments of quiet amusement and pride. On *Jolie Brise*, Briggs walked up and down the deck when they were at last ready to sail and pronounced with cockney satisfaction that she was "just like *Britannia*" as his beloved cutter was towed from Cowes roads by motor-boat to drop anchor off Ryde, ready to start the race. He and his fellow companion in the forecastle, Green, the cook and steward, must have watched with mingled respect and amusement their amateur companions, Martin himself, J. R. K. Warneford, he of *Vanda*, Weston Martyr, and R. Maclean Buckley, who comes again and again into this tale.

One of *Bamba*'s paid hands was a Brixham man and off Land's End they had a brisk conversation with a trawler skipper. Had the trawler got any Brixhamites aboard? The skipper replied, "Dozens of them, and what the hell are you doing here?"

The hand explained the eccentricities of the Ocean Race, but the next question gave him still greater problems.

"Who have you got with you?"

This produced a rather ominous silence until he called out, *sotto voce*, "A lot of bloody amateurs."

Fulmar, the soldiers' boat, was probably the only contestant which could boast of having "no bloody professionals".

The little fleet encountered more or less remarkable vessels on the way. Brixham trawlers and crabbers under sail from Newlyn were worthy of only passing notice, though such working boats under sail would be ghosts today, as too would have been the French barquentine which *Gull* passed in Lyme Bay. However, there are still sharks about in plenty, such as the one *Fulmar*'s skipper tackled ineffectually with a brace of pistols, the sight of which sent his crew cringing in the scuppers.

The happy disorganization of the race is evident in that *Fulmar* was unable to gain details of the racing instructions from the Royal Victoria Yacht Club, the host club at Ryde. It seems that the only instruction was simply that of rounding the Fastnet Rock. *Bamba* was particularly annoyed because the official measurer refused to visit her on the morning of the race, taking fright, one suspects, at the problems of measuring such an obvious outsider. Thwarted as she was at the beginning, so again at the end, for arriving at the breakwater at Plymouth she duly sent up her flare to announce her presence, but the official picket boat failed to put out to meet her.

Fulmar too was in total ignorance of what was her handicap, though *Gull* explained it all with stentorian shouts during one of the periods of calm.

But possibly, as always, those to get the most amusement out of the affair were the keepers of the Fastnet Light. Appropriately, they waved a pilot jack at *Jolie Brise* as she rounded to indicate that she was the first in line. Poor old *Bamba* again got some stick because she had to fly as her identification flag the letter L, which also serves as a plague flag, to which the keepers responded, "I should like to know the nature of the sickness, if any, before I send my boat."

But the happiest tale of all, to those of us who follow the wake of *Jolie Brise*, is the response by the lighthouse men to *Fulmar*'s question, "When did *Jolie Brise* pass?" The answer came in two sections, "7.00." Cheers from the crew who now felt themselves reasonably close behind, quickly dampened by a second string of flags which read, "Yesterday evening".

Yes, that erstwhile pilot cutter and tunny fisherman had certainly proved herself a doughty ocean-racer and won a place in yachting history, that evening of 19th August 1925 when she first led the way round the Fastnet Rock.

So it was all over. Possibly what amazed the partakers most was how undemanding it had all been. There must have been the regret that I always have in *Jolie Brise* when a long passage is over. But there was also a surprise ingredient. This was the bond set up amongst the participating crews.

Gull's log spoke of "missing *Jolie*" who had been close by her every morning of the race up until the day she rounded the Fastnet – and she was missed *not* because she was ahead and winning (good luck to her for that) but for herself as good company in an empty sea.

It had been more of a happy cruise in company than a race. Everyone went as fast as they could, of course, and *Jolie Brise*'s was a notable win, but even there one had the feeling that Martin thought more in terms of pressing on to be in Plymouth to welcome his friends as they arrived, than actually winning the race for the sake of competition. And welcome them he did. That tall, courteous figure was standing in the picket boat to escort in every yacht bar one.

That one was *Bamba*, and she crept in unnoticed, because Martin was at that very moment presiding at a meeting in the dining-room of the Royal Western Yacht Club of England, at which was founded the Ocean Racing Club. He was elected the first Commodore, so that *Jolie Brise* then became the first and best-known yacht to fly the Commodore's broad pennant, with its white sea-horse, now so familiar and so respected the world over.

The sea-horse motif itself was Martin's own creation. Who knows, he may have carved the wooden model from which the pattern was taken by the light of the oil lamp in *Jolie Brise*'s saloon, with Briggs at hand to sharpen the knife and sweep up the chippings.

Weston Martyr must have viewed with modest pride the realization of his dreams. Britain had her Ocean Race and her Ocean Racing Club. Martin made a fine figurehead and *Jolie Brise* a fine flagship to carry the idea further.

However, Martyr's dreams had had their nightmare aspect too. Before the race he had written,

> "I have never been to *sea* with a single big mainsail and my terror of the rig may be all nonsense. I hope it is, for next month I am sailing from Ryde to Plymouth via the Fastnet in a fifty foot cutter. I journeyed to Southampton some little while ago, and my friend, the owner of the cutter, believes I made the pilgrimage to have a look at the boat, whereas I really went to take some careful observations of her boom. I saw it – a mile of it – lying on trestles in the yard, and ever since I have been trying hard to invent an excuse plausible enough to enable me to back out of the Ocean Race without arousing the suspicions of my friend. My friend is counting on me, he is a difficult person to deceive, and he is very large and very strong. So I think I shall have to break a leg."

He had not broken his leg, nor in the event did the boom break him, but that boom, particularly in hard weather and under racing conditions, still engenders a deadening in the pit of the stomach of many a bold man, even to this day.

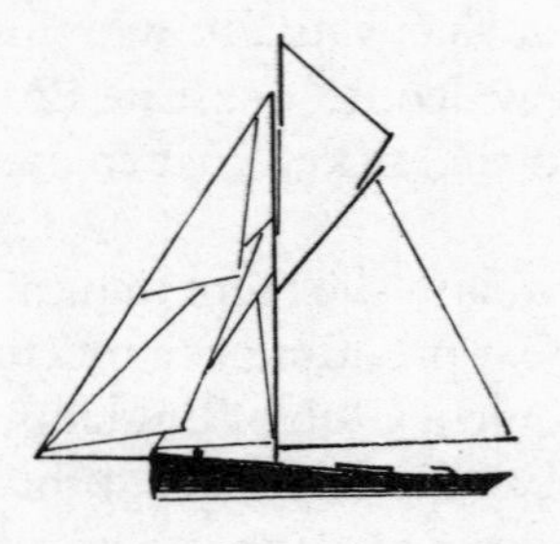

CHAPTER ELEVEN

To the New World

Today there is a steady flow of small boats following the trade winds to America. In the 1950s it was rare and the nineteen foot *Sopranino* made news indeed when she made the passage, as we shall see. But in the 1920s the concept of Atlantic voyaging, even in a boat as reasonably sized as *Jolie Brise*, was redolent of adventure.

The 600 miles of what we now call the Fastnet Race was a long way in those days. A boat of under a hundred tons or so would have little reason to venture further. Only such as Captain Slocum had been minded to take small boats further. Just as ocean racing was a new concept, so too was ocean voyaging in a small boat. This, then, was *Jolie Brise*'s next challenge.

In the New Year of 1926 Martin conceived the idea of not only crossing to the States but, once there, partaking in the Bermuda Race and sailing home again in time for the second "Ocean Race".

While there was nothing in this that a thirteen-year-old, well found, fifty-six foot cutter could not take in her stride, as we now know, the timing was none the less impressive. To take part in two of the world's most challenging off-shore races in the same short season, *and* voyage between the two, would be hard to emulate even today.

The voyage out is well chronicled. It features in E. G. Martin's classic book, *Deep Water Cruising*, and in his articles in *The Yachting World*. It is also chronicled by Weston Martyr, who came too, and was, as always, the inveterate professional writer with an eye to the next book. And it is recorded yet again by the faithful Warneford, Martin's navigator, in his letters home to wife and daughter Molly.

So we have those three threads – the practical, the romantic and the family man's – three men's view of the same voyage.

They were busy, those weeks of preparation in Falmouth, close by the Warneford house. And they were expensive. Martin's enthusiasm was outstripping his resources, but was infectious enough to bring Warneford to the rescue. Commander Warneford was a man of depleted means, having had to leave his property in Ireland to the fates and the revolution, but a new suit of sails was needed, and clearly the cause was good. He took his daughter Molly upstairs to her bedroom where he had laid out some of the family silver on her bed.

"This, by rights, should come to you, but *Jolie Brise* really should have a new suit of sails, you will agree."

And agree she did, but though Martin's praise of her father's navigation was always fulsome, the sacrifice of heirlooms to keep *Jolie Brise* sailing at her best never earned a mention. The glory of the boat herself was surely reward enough?

As departure day grew near, the boat's adequacy was never in question, but the inevitable testing of friendship cast its shadow before. Martin had a predilection, like Sherlock Holmes, for playing the violin – though it was a later owner of *Jolie Brise*, not he, who was to have a Baker Street address. Banished to the deck, such daily playing could be endured. What was not to be permitted was a ship's upright pianoforte, which Warneford arrived just in time to see being lowered through a hole in the deck where the skylight had been temporarily removed. The prospect of the owner playing "The Lost Chord" *ad nauseam* in mid-Atlantic was too ghastly to contemplate.

"Either that piano stays ashore or I do," threatened Warneford, and he won.

Where he did not win was in the matter of two passengers who, it appears, took no part in the sailing of the vessel, however amateur. Martin murmured something about them "helping with the finances". They may indeed not have come. Certainly all mention of them is studiously avoided in all accounts. However, certain unexplained figures do appear in the photograph albums beside the yacht's official company of Martin, Martyr and Warneford, the amateurs, as well as Briggs (skipper) and Green (cook and steward).

One final factor, though, seems to clinch the fact that there were no passengers, at least on this outward voyage, for the simple reason that the little ship's company had confessed to no one where they planned to sail. That is, not until the afternoon of 1st April when they were hauling up the anchor with the prospect of 6,000 miles ahead of them. Then it was that Martin spied a figure rowing towards him from a twenty-nine ton cutter which had just arrived.

It turned out to be John Blackmore, who had been his skipper from 1905 until 1920, war permitting, presiding over his master's triumphs sailing six-metres for his country, as well as being a guiding light in the days of Martin's ownership of the beautiful thirty-five tonner *Chance*. Blackmore was a Brixham trawler-man who Martin confessed had taught him all he knew. Martin now told him with pride of the plan afoot. Blackmore wished them well and rowed back to his new master's boat, *Tern III*. That new master, possibly watching his man rowing over to the black cutter weighing anchor, was one Captain Warren Ferrier. He was not to know, until his man came back with the news, that *Jolie Brise* was setting out on such a high adventure, nor indeed was he to guess that his future and hers would shortly be entwined.

However, it was the present which concerned *Jolie Brise*'s little crew as she put out past St Anthony's Point from Falmouth Bay. They prematurely, but for the first time, tried Martin's new invention, a great squaresail, which she was to use during her days to come in the Trades.

Martin had been puzzled, down in Teignmouth, as to quite how they could contrive adequate running sails in waters where a square-rigged ship had all to gain and a fore-and-after could but be at a disadvantage. Of course all the cutters of the Napoleonic Wars and before had had their vestigial squaresails, but Martin had wanted something bigger, over which he could set a raffee – a triangular sail set from the truck down to the top of the yard, so high up as to tickle the toes of any passing angel and, let it be said, to test the patience of any saint who tried to set it.

A squaresail on a cruising yacht was not unusual in the 1920s, as witness *Bamba* in the Ocean Race. Possibly Captain Ferrier's *Tern III*, at anchor astern of them in the last anchorage they were to see for forty-five days, sported her own squaresail. Certainly she had belonged to the legendary Claude Worth, champion of the Royal Cruising Club's objection to the concept of ocean racing. Worth was a great advocate of the squaresail and all his *Terns*, I feel sure, must have set them.

However, Martin's concern had been with the problem of the

handling of a yard of sufficient size for a squaresail on *Jolie Brise*, if it were to be easily stowed – for such a sizeable spar would be a liability indeed in the sort of weather they were likely to encounter, at least twice, in the voyage ahead. The solution had come to him on his way back to London on the train from seeing Briggs and *Jolie Brise* at Teignmouth. It was a solution which was perhaps triggered off in his mind by the memories he had of the *tangons* or great fishing whisker-poles which *Jolie Brise* had sported in her tunny-fishing days, and which Martin had been so quick to scrap. Those *tangons*, as you will remember, were hinged from the foot of the shrouds and were controlled by block and tackles from the hounds, so that when not in use they could be stowed vertically up the mast and secured chock-a-block beside it.

Martin's solution was the reverse of this, and you can imagine him perhaps drawing a sketch of it with his finger in the mist on the railway carriage window. It was this. His squaresail yard would be in two parts, hinged, obviously not near the foot of the mast like the *tangons*, but at the other end near the hounds. When not in use they would be folded not upwards but downwards to stow snugly on either side. However, when the squaresail was set they would project at right angles on either side of the mast but, and here was another advantage, the starboard whisker could be set at a different angle from the port whisker, should this be of advantage, to control the sail.

Furthermore, the squaresail was made in two parts so that the starboard wing might be set independently, if need be, of that to port. Or, conversely, the two could be laced together to form a single sail. It was an unorthodox idea but on that April afternoon it seemed to work, and with that discovery they seemed even better set for the long passage ahead. Indeed, only poor Green's seasickness seemed to cast any doubt upon the proceedings as they handed the squaresail and settled down to reach past the Manacles and out into the Channel.

Green was not alone, it transpires, for Warneford was to report, "All more or less sorry for themselves. Myself all right."

There is a big swell and very little wind and with her fine new set of racing sails safely stowed below, they lollop along with the trysail, which is at least quiet, having no boom to crash about. Time passes uneventfully and they feed well despite poor Green's continuing queasiness.

In the middle of the Bay of Biscay they sail close to a tunny-man, and photograph her. Perhaps she is one of *Jolie Brise*'s fellow berth-mates from Concarneau days.

Five days out they sight Cabo Villano Light and sail close by as they close with the Spanish coast. Fifty-three years later *Jolie Brise* and I were to be becalmed off that same headland at sunset and I put the boys off in the dinghy to take photographs. Did the old boat remember that she had been there before? I like to think that she did. But on this occasion our fivesome bowled on along the Spanish and Portuguese shores in high spirits. "Rather like the west of Ireland, but loftier and more rugged," reports Warneford.

They took their departure from the mouth of the Minho River, heading south-west to Madeira. A shark was sighted and Warneford, a sharkophobe, wished he had some means of attacking it.

By noon that day, 10th April, it was beginning to blow hard and they hove to. Then followed a night of calm but by the early morning a south-east breeze had quickly freshened and a big sea was rolling in from both the southward *and* the west. By breakfast they were hove to again with seas of between thirty and forty feet. The wind tore through the rigging as she gained the peaks and left her becalmed in the hollows.

"Like a switchback," says Warneford. This was Martin's first experience of heaving *Jolie Brise* to in deep water. He was thrilled at the results.

"The motion is so easy and the ship so quiet down below that one cannot tell whether it is really blowing or not, until one takes a look round from the companionway."

Weston Martyr reports, "7.20 a.m. sea milk-white . . . went below and had a shave. Everything very neat and dry in the cabin."

The next morning found them storming along under trysail and topsail with a strong north-easterly wind, as Martyr reports, "tearing off the tops of the old seas, which were still running as high as our lower mast-head".

And then, incredibly, they found that they were already in the Trades. They went south between the Canaries and Madeira before turning westward so as not to lose them. They were now eighteen or nineteen days out from Falmouth, with their eccentric style of squaresail and raffee set – something of a mixed success, as theirs was not an idyllic progress. The wind was strong at times, the raffee was a pig to handle and, sad to report, with massive rolling motion engendered by the squaresail, *Jolie Brise* herself could only be described as pig-like too.

"Certainly the average summer day's sailing in the Channel is pleasanter than an average day in the north-east Trades, as we found them," the disillusioned Martin reports.

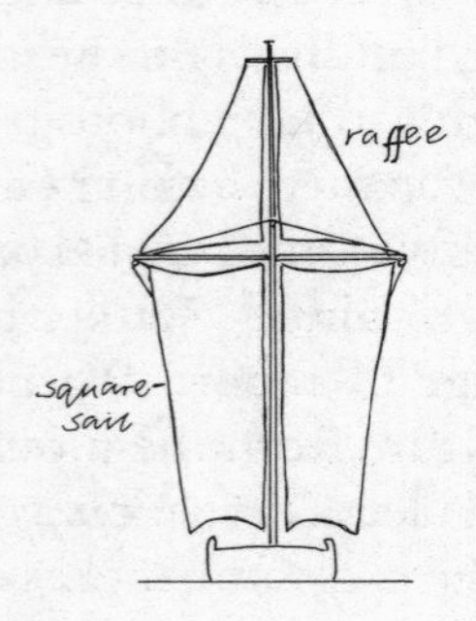

They passed Madeira about eighty miles to the eastward. The wind was freshening from the north and this was Martyr's finest hour. He and Briggs went up aloft to try and bring in the squaresail. They unhanked it from its hoops with such difficulty that in future the squaresail was only set flying. They put a strop around its head to the staysail halyards. Briggs smothered the thrashing sail with ties and the brute was subdued.

They then set trysail, jib and staysail, a lower, more modest rig which Warneford secretly preferred, but which Martyr felt, if anything, increased the yacht's endless rolling.

Should *Jolie Brise* embark again on such a transatlantic trade wind passage, I would hope that she might have twin inboard headsails with lines running back from them through blocks to the tiller head. That, I believe, would be the happy medium between the lower sails which gave her six knots and the big squaresail and raffee which gave her eight on this, her first transatlantic crossing. That, or the rig adopted by a later owner on her next transatlantic adventure, could be the solution.

But hold hard, as Martyr himself might say, let us skip the technicalities and romanticize for a little. Martyr writes, "We had picked up the Trades sure enough. And what is more, we held them for twenty-three solid and consecutive nights and days. Twenty-three days of fair winds, three weeks and more with the breeze blowing constant and true over the stern, a steady slide down-wind of 3,500 miles. Think of that! you sailors who trim your fluttering sails to the shifting fickle breezes of the Channel and the Sound."

Having made the reader in his armchair back at home envious, he then seeks his admiration as he continues,

"It was bad enough when steering in the day-time, to feel an endless succession of mad avalanches rushing up behind and trying to climb over the stern; but at night one trick at the helm was enough for anyone."

More prosaic, Martin was content simply to observe that the rolling was so bad that "no trousers could withstand it for long".

They crossed between latitudes 19 and 20 North. To the rolling were now added the hazards of heat and glare. They rigged up a canvas awning over the helmsman and wore "smoked glasses". Now they were settled in to a daily routine. Briggs and Green in the galley tickled their palates with some amazing cuisine, as well as choice titbits of foredeck humour, while Martin, Warneford reports, would strut around the deck in the most extraordinary attire and practise his violin every day. Martyr is nicknamed "Capstan" and keeps a pet cheese in a locker next to his bunk, much as any other man might have a pet parrot.

It was as well they had these little diversions, but the chief work in hand was navigation. Warneford is a wizard with the sextant and takes endless sights, trying to catch the sun on the horizon while defying the roll of the ship and protecting his instrument from salt water. Martin assists the operation by keeping the chronometer on time and mastering the mysteries of the splendid four-valve radio set, which has an aerial on a precarious whisker stuck up the back stay.

"We had GMT to within .5 of a second during the whole voyage," Martin reports with pride. The product of their joint labours was that they sighted the westernmost point of the Canaries on a misty day after a run of 1,100 miles exactly where and when expected.

By 24th April they had been 2,000 miles, with 4,000 or 5,000 to go. Warneford predicts an arrival at Long Island Sound on 18th May and a change of course northward on 28th April. They are doing six to seven knots, and the day before had had a record so far of 172 miles run in the day.

Jolie Brise was in the tropics now, and the advent of new stars in the southern hemisphere gives Warneford fresh opportunity for his celestial navigation. However, as she turns northward and shakes off the following wind at last, they are to encounter calms and the weed of the Sargasso Sea. Weston Martyr picked up one lump of weed with a boat-hook, "and found it was made of weed, three yellow shrimps, two pink crablets, one tiny blue lobster and a golden fish about an inch long". Then comes a moment of unreasoning panic when a bank of weed looks for all the world like a sandbank in the waters of *Jolie Brise*'s native Seine Estuary, until reason reminds them that they can but be in 3,000 fathoms of water.

The noon positions on the chart are close together here as *Jolie Brise* idles her way northward. Green is making excellent bread while Briggs makes fine rock-cakes and curries, and they have duff on Sundays and Wednesdays.

The West Indies are temptingly close now but such landfalls are to be resisted if they are to meet their pressing time-table, with the Bermuda Race in the States and the Ocean Race back home. Weston Martyr looks wistfully westwards, but it is to be on another voyage and with another owner that *Jolie Brise* is to make such an enchanted landfall.

As they enter the Gulf Stream the passing of those days of steady following winds is regretted, as well as even the sail-slatting days of calm. Only in Martyr's mind and from his pen come now the images of "the tip of her bowsprit cutting through the blue while from it two white jets like graceful feathers splay up and out". Or of her bow, "a black wedge ploughing through the gleaming azure and throwing magnificently outwards two gleaming wings of snow", or, again, of looking astern at "the round sun shining through the thin, translucent top of a great blue wave". No, such sailing was just a memory now as they entered that inevitable part of their passage which certainly gives most pause for thought to any who plan such a trip.

The abrupt change in water temperature as you enter the Gulf Stream gives rise to sudden squalls, rain showers and then mountainous seas, followed by unnerving windless conditions.

Warneford enjoyed himself in these circumstances. There was the extraordinary sensation of a following sea behind, but with the wind ahead. He was pleased to be rid of the squaresail and trysail as they set the proper mainsail and topsail, jib topsail, balloon staysail and big jib. At last she feels like a proper cutter again. And all goes well until they are caught in a sudden squall and Briggs is unable to get the topsail off her, as it jams in the peak halyards. Martin was frankly disturbed by the proceedings. He reports, "I got the tiller hard up but for a time she would not pay off." The tiller, all ten foot of it, and made of solid oak, began to bend in an alarming way. They tended to sail in traditional pilot fashion with a rope from the tiller head to the bulwarks which the helmsman could play with one hand, while actually handling the tiller with the other. On this occasion Briggs hurries quickly aft and adds a second tiller rope, for fear the first would break, and at last they swing her round before the wind and like a wild horse she runs away with them. With far too much canvas jammed aloft to hope to heave to, ever present is the fear of being dis-masted or knocked down flat, broaching before the following waves.

So much, then, for spreading her more accustomed wings. These were quickly replaced with her passage-making sails. This runaway dash was the prelude to a thoroughgoing gale, and as Martyr writes,

"That savage wind, blowing across the current of the stream, raised the sea so steep and high that it seemed absurd to hope that any little boat could live in it. And then, when you watched the boat, it seemed absurd to think any sea could kill her! Make no mistake – she had to fight hard – very hard. But she fought with such gaiety and cheerfulness that it hardly seemed to be a fight at all. *Jolie Brise* was very French just then." And he pays tribute to Martin, who, instead of lashing the tiller, lashed himself to the steering bench and eased her along through every motion of the waves while oil bags were hung over the weather rail and oil was pumped through the lavatory, and the seas were marginally smoothed in the immediate vicinity of the ship – (I must confess *Jolie Brise* carries no oil bags today!).

The gale pushes them back seventy miles, but at last they shake off the Gulf Stream, fortunately just a hundred miles wide at the point where they hit it.

And how are the crew, that little floating village on that sturdy island of oak? Warneford professes to being in good order, despite a punitive lack of sleep, for between watch-keeping and navigating there has been little time to get his head down. Martin has not shaved for some time and steers with a towel round his head, wearing a funny hat and goggles. Warneford reports that "he looks just like Mrs R. Foster", and one can only imagine that if that was the case Mr R. Foster must have a very hirsute wife. Martyr is less happy. The endless tiring motion has frankly got him down and his predilection for cheese has given him nagging indigestion. How Briggs and Green are faring before the mast is not reported, but one hopes that by now Green is feeling no longer quite as green as his name. At last, over a month from sighting Palma, Martyr sights land on the port bow from the mast-head. It is 20th May, just two days later than Warneford's predicted time of arrival.

These are the days of Prohibition in the States, and the strains of days of confinement, likely to tell on the best of chums, are further exacerbated as Martin throws overboard their last bottle of rum as what looks like an Excise boat comes towards them. It is a tribute to Warneford's excellent navigation that he had placed them precisely where they were intended to be after 5,832 miles, which Martyr claims enthusiastically as "the longest non-stop run ever made by a small boat".

By today's standards, *Jolie Brise* was a big yacht, but hers was a small crew and the achievement of those five men, undertaken with the aid of oak, spruce, canvas and sextant, casts in the shade those who voyage today, relying on plastics, aluminium, terylene, self-steering gears and satellite navigation systems.

CHAPTER TWELVE

In the Sound

"America opened its heart to us today and welcomed us in. It was well worth sailing 6,000 miles to find this great goodwill and kindness at the end."

So wrote Weston Martyr, while the press on both sides of the Atlantic reported the arrival of the black cutter from England. On the front page of *The Yachting World* were the jubilant words, "*Jolie Brise* crosses the Atlantic", and the editorial goes on to say,

"We feel sure that all British yachtsmen will greatly admire the pluck and endurance of these gallant Corinthians, who, without any undue fuss or public announcement, quietly slipped away on 1st April to cross the Atlantic to America with the object of taking part in the popular Ocean Cruiser Race from New London to Bermuda."

Heroics apart, *Jolie Brise* was now pleasure bent on just over a month of cruising and hospitality among the harbours and yacht clubs of Long Island Sound, a place of sheltered sailing and friendly people.

Aboard *Jolie Brise*, only Martin and Green had not been there before and to them it was a delight to find this sheltered water so like the Solent, but with inlets and islands as varied as a Danish fjord.

Past Montauk Point and through the race *Jolie Brise* creamed at seven knots, now wearing all her best party clothes in the shape of her racing suit of sails. But night came and with it a full moon and a glassy calm. Martin, who had felt no strain over the past few days, went below to look at the chart, leant forward to check a detail and fell at last blissfully, happily and deeply asleep.

All the next day they had a cheerful sail up some eighty miles of the Sound. Small wonder, they thought, as they scurried along in the lee of the island, that the prosperous of New York should have their estates there, commuting by express motor-cruisers to their offices in New York or, in the case of Mr A. Curtis-James, the still greater status symbol of *Aloha*, a barque with all sails set, possibly the finest commuting vehicle ever conceived.

They had a day, those five men, to accustom themselves to smooth water and the sight and smell of land and other boats, before calm at evening and the splash as they dropped anchor in the bay off Larchmont, a short train-ride from New York itself.

Immediately the captain of a nearby schooner yacht, *Carol*, rowed over to greet them and to tell them that to clear the doctor they would have to sail next day to City Island. He returned again with provisions from his own stores. And so, one suspects, not over-anxious to set foot on shore after so many days at sea, the crew of *Jolie Brise* finally went below to a feast of new bread, fresh butter, eggs and vegetables, pork, bacon, grapefruit and apples. Meanwhile, news had got to Mr H. L. Stone, organizer of the Bermuda Race. The black English cutter could not be incognito much longer.

The next day they sailed the five miles eastward to City Island which, Martin hazarded, held the same role in relation to New York yachtsmen as Southampton did (but no longer does) to those from London. There they were all given a clean bill of health and sailed back again to Larchmont, which, since they had dropped anchor there twice, was beginning to feel almost like home. By now the flags were out in full style and the club launch of the Larchmont Yacht Club came out with a cheerful bunch of members, each one of them in his mien giving the lie to the effectiveness of Prohibition.

They brought with them an invitation to dine with the Commodore. This was to be the opening night of their sailing season and they were having a stag party. Somewhat bemused, since this hardly seemed to be the "dry" land they thought they had come to, the ship's party quickly tidied up and were duly swept ashore in the launch again half an hour later.

The scene which met them in the club was convivial indeed. Some two hundred members, all clad in white butchers' aprons, were keeping up a great wave of jovial sound.

"Some," says Warneford, "were making a shot at eating but most were drinking."

The Yacht Club at Larchmont was a sort of Swiss-cum-Norman waterside mansion complete with gables, turrets, verandas and dormer-windows, and round this building a cordon of amiable police kept guard to make sure that the distinguished members of this ancient club could pass their evening without interruption.

The bar was certainly a thoroughgoing affair with straps to hang onto, like those in a railway carriage, and cuspidors just to give the authentic Wild-West effect in this civilized East Coast *milieu*. The English sailors in their best shore-going shoes could not help feeling that they should have worn their sea boots. However, the welcome was certainly enthusiastic, as all-embracing as only Americans, or perhaps the Irish, could have contrived and, as undeniably, it was overwhelming. The little party was showered with invitations to various yachts to continue the night's revelry, but they slipped back to *Jolie Brise*, pleading the need for sleep. Was it always, they wondered, like this? And they were reassured to find that the anchorage the next morning was very quiet indeed.

Happily, the Larchmont Yacht Club's reputation for hospitality lives on. Just a year ago a Canadian visitor was instantly given honorary membership when he casually mentioned that his son sails with us today in *Jolie Brise*.

That was just the beginning. Next came a dinner in New York itself, at the New York Yacht Club, in the dining-room set to look like a ship's cabin, where Martin made a speech recalling their voyage, before lingering longingly in that yacht club's famous model-room.

Then back to City Island again. They were by now a little in awe of the great expense of all things in the States.

"1½ dollars," Warneford reports, "for a hair-cut in any go-down." Martin observes that everything to do with yachting is twice the price of what it is in England, and so the former pilot cutter seems even more of a cheeky interloper in a glistening company. But when they get up on the slip at City Island for only twenty-five dollars and clean some extraordinary but harmless worms off her bottom, her underwater lines get admiring glances from those who know.

They set sail across the Sound to Huntingdon Bay on the Long Island shore. The Cruising Club of America is holding one of its famous meets or rallies, but *Jolie Brise*, not for the last time, because of her great draught has to anchor on the edge of the party. With over ten feet beneath the water, she was unable to join the rakish, shallow-draught schooners which most members favoured. The situation brings to mind my own experience last summer (1980) when I took *Jolie Brise* to our own Royal Cruising Club's Centenary Meet in the Beaulieu River, and had to arrive last and anchor furthest down-stream. On that occasion we were not short of visitors, nor indeed was *Jolie Brise* on this, for a twenty foot sloop called *The Great Republic* – big name for a small boat – acted as a ferry-boat between *Jolie Brise* and the fleet. The two boats, greatly dissimilar, had an affinity in that *The Great Republic* had herself crossed the Atlantic, eastwards to England, but home again on the deck of a steamer.

Another small boat – a cruising cat-boat called *Nancy Lee* – sailed around *Jolie Brise* too, and she has a special part in our saga because at the tiller was her young owner, Charles H. Vilas, and as I write now my desk is covered to an impressive depth with helpful letters from him, because he is today the genial and helpful editor and historian of the Cruising Club of America. He is still as active, it seems, as *Jolie Brise* herself, though she must have seemed old to him even when he first saw her through the shrouds of his boat, far back in that summer of 1926.

Jolie Brise's pottering and socializing could not last for long. The Bermuda Race and the passage home were beckoning, much though they might all, by now, have preferred to stay. Martin, for instance, was mastering the language and soon discovered that he should call somebody's cabin "homelike" rather than "homely", the latter word signifying that he thought his host's cabin plain or almost ugly – the reverse of what he intended. Nor could he resist scouring the waterside for interesting sailing boats, and another pilot in particular took his eye. She was a Boston schooner of around the 150 tons which he now swore was essential if one was to enjoy the Trades in any degree of comfort. Yes, and she was for sale, for the simple reason that her rum-running owners were in prison. She had an engine – of sorts – but it seemed that her fuel-tanks were more accustomed to liquor than anything which might be expected to drive a propeller.

And so as June wore on they worked their way back up the eighty miles of Long Island Sound to New London, the gathering point for the Bermuda Race. And where is New London? On the Thames, of course.

CHAPTER THIRTEEN

Bermuda Race, 1926

Saturday June 20th 1926 was the finest day of *Jolie Brise*'s life, and I doubt if we shall see finer in years to come. There had been, were to be, and perhaps will be, days which were more heroic or more triumphant, but it was this summer day, at the start of the 1926 Bermuda Race, which saw her at her finest and loveliest.

The evening before she had anchored in the Thames with the other eighteen competitors. The scrutineers, finding her fully laden for her voyage back to England, passed her without question, other than requiring the carrying of three extra lifebelts. All the fleet dined to the full that night and after dinner Mr Sherman Hoyt gave the owners their instructions and handicaps. *Jolie Brise* had the heaviest displacement of all the fleet. Most of her fellow competitors were auxiliary ketches or schooners. Only she had no engine and, with her single mast, was penalized in her handicap on both counts. To cap it all, she was two and a half inches deeper in the water than she would normally have been in unladen racing trim.

Admiring *Jolie Brise* as a cruising yacht and, frankly, as a museum-piece, her American hosts and indeed her own master and crew thought her to be hopelessly outclassed. Indeed, were it not that Bermuda was on the way home for her, some might have wondered why she was entering at all.

The day dawned beautifully fine and there was a pleasant sailing breeze from the north. The crew aboard *Jolie Brise* went quietly about their business and hoisted the main and jackyard topsail. Her great yankee jib topsail ("Briggs' pet") was also hoisted in stops, ready to be broken out smartly when needed. As they sailed down the river towards the starting line, the spinnaker was got ready on the port side. They inspected the line and found it uncomfortably short. The water was abuzz with motor-boats but Martin, nothing daunted, sailed back well up-wind of the line, reckoning that, in a boat with double the displacement of most of her competitors, his chance lay in building up a fine turn of speed before crossing. He timed it to a nicety and aimed her bowsprit through the covey of schooners and ketches, crossing the line just as the gun fired.

Jolie Brise's great jackyard topsail, set at over eighty feet above the water, sent up a gasp of admiration. At first, as she cut through the fleet, there was no room to send out her long spinnaker boom, but by swinging across the stern of two schooners *Jolie Brise* found a gap, set the spinnaker and was soon slipping ahead. Better was to come because it is a peculiarity of Long Island Sound that breezes generally seem to begin high above the water. Often the lower sails may still be full, while the burgee of a tall ship indicates a head wind. Running with the northerly behind them, Martin could see a south-easterly breeze making into the Sound ahead; and so it was that *Jolie Brise*'s racing flag, "of the thinnest possible silk", confirmed this changing direction and was vital early warning. They hardened in their sheets, handed their spinnaker and, with a further gasp from those now astern, broke out the great yankee jib topsail from its stops. Meanwhile many of the schooners and ketches were caught aback, their spinnakers a positive hindrance in what had so suddenly become a windward race.

Jolie Brise tacked southward towards Long Island while the schooners, *Malabar IV* and *Trade Wind*, and the ketch *Dragoon*, favoured the eastward tack. As soon as Martin thought that he could clear the Race, which is a feature of the entrance of the Sound, he came about. *Jolie Brise* was showing her remarkable propensity for moving fast in light airs and smooth conditions while her master, a stranger to these waters, showed helmsmanship and foresight of true brilliance. Never were master, ship and conditions as well matched as upon that day.

Except for lunch, Martin never left the helm. They held the yankee and jackyard topsail throughout the afternoon. They tightened in the boom but let off the out-haul of the loose-footed mainsail, itself an anachronism, and so achieved the perfect flow for the sail.

If the glory of that day was to be shared with anyone, it should be with Tom Ratsey, doyen of sail-makers back home, and with

Molly Warneford, whose future inheritance had been diminished in order that *Jolie Brise* should have such a gorgeous racing suit.

Now clear of the Sound, with the stretch of Long Island shore dropping astern, its low profile relieved only by the finger of Montauk Light, *Jolie Brise* led the fleet into the open sea, a lead confirmed as she tacked and crossed ahead of the bows of *Dragoon*, fastest and longest ship in the race, sailed by Mr Bravier, one of America's crack helmsmen, and manned by a picked crew. That was a crowning moment and when, a little later, the schooner *Blue Water* passed close under their lee and gave *Jolie Brise* a great cheer and a shout of "Well done", the seal was set on a triumphant day.

Back home it must have been with some excitement and surprise that readers of *The Yachting World* saw the headlines, "THE BERMUDA OCEAN RACE. *Jolie Brise* LEADS AT THE START", and reading on found that Lt. Cdr. E. G. Martin's *Jolie Brise* took an early lead in the race to Bermuda.

"The schooner, *Countess*, was the first over the line at the start but before Long Island Sound was cleared, *Jolie Brise* gained the lead." And then, as they scanned the entries, they would have found her to be the only cutter and by no means the largest boat.

The triumph of that day was a deep-rooted one because it was the triumph of the traditional European cutter, with its ancestry based on pilot boats and similar craft, over the traditional American schooner, deriving in their turn from the fishing boats of the Grand Banks. There had been rivalries between these two very different types in both peace and war. The rakish American schooners often eluded Britain's warships, while Britain's cutters had always played an important role, briskly serving her fleet.

But it was a peace-time encounter which I believe was vindicated on that summer day in 1926: one which had rankled with every English yachtsman since 22nd August 1851. That was the day on which the schooner yacht *America* had beaten the English racing cutters in their own waters of the Solent. The clear lead which *Jolie Brise* showed the American schooners in their own waters seventy-five years later must surely have settled that ancient score far more appropriately than the long and continuing line of unsuccessful match races between "J" Class and twelve-metre yachts, which persists to this day.

So much for the view astern. The view over the bow was equally encouraging to would-be ocean-racers back home, who had feared ridicule in their own waters, should American competitors choose to enter England's own Ocean Race. To them *Jolie Brise* had shown that American competition was not overwhelming; and that there was nothing to lose and all to gain if the two nations were to race together off shore.

However, the last laugh lay with a Frenchman, Monsieur Paumelle. Yacht designers might develop refined versions of work boats for their clients, but his boat, designed for work rather than amateur amusement, had shown them all just how it could and should be done.

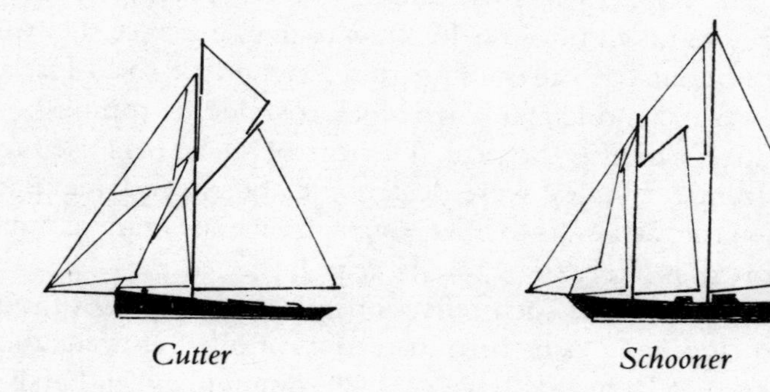

Cutter *Schooner*

Sadly, triumphant though she was that day in American waters, *Jolie Brise* was to fare less well on the high seas and in the British waters of Bermuda. None the less, in the end she came a creditable fifth.

What was it which stole the race from her? It was her old enemy, the Gulf Stream, without which the Bermuda Race would be no more than a 600 mile passage from A to B. Many a yacht, such as the one Weston Martyr had previously sailed in, actually misses Bermuda due to difficulties of navigation stemming from the Stream's irregular north-easterly set.

But *navigation* was not *Jolie Brise*'s problem. With Warneford aboard how could it be? It was instead the confused seas which she met crossing the Stream which, with the fullness of her bow, tended to stop her more than it did the lean schooners with which she was competing. That and the failure of a shackle. On the transatlantic passage the only short-comings of her gear had been the chafing of the mast-head strop securing the after shrouds and the problem of setting up the lanyards on her dead-eyes, both faults inevitably stemming from her constant rolling. But now, engaged in a private contest with the large racing ketch *Dragoon*, a shackle on *Jolie Brise*'s weather topmast back-stay snapped. The topmast gave a fearful jerk, but the helmsman flung the boat round on to the other tack and saved the spar.

It was on this tack that she and *Dragoon* parted company and it could have been that tack which cost her the race, much as *Gull* may have failed to win the first Fastnet of the year before through as small a factor as the failure of her jackyard topsail halyard. By such misfortunes are ocean races lost – not so much in themselves but by the shaking of confidence which must accompany them. Later in the race, as they bore down to Bermuda, Martin concedes that he should have driven his *Jolie Brise* harder, but the breaking of shackles loomed large in his mind. Less lucky was an experience she was to have in her present-day sail training guise. In the 1978 Oslo-Harwich Tall Ships' Race, a hidden fault in a block cost her her topmast – and of course any chance in the race. The loss of such spars used to be relatively frequent. They were designed to be expendable. Sadly, today, when the fashion is to have your whole mast made as a single spar, any break is likely to be totally crippling.

However, enough of such reflections on the dangers of modern fashions in rigging. Let us turn instead to another mishap aboard *Jolie Brise* in that Bermuda Race of 1926, one which can befall any boat at any time. It certainly gave rise to a little levity. After a day of perplexing breezes and calms in the Gulf Stream, and an amusing contest with the schooner *Windjammer*, a strengthening following breeze had given Martin fresh hope, but this had been combined with a contrary sea and, dipping constantly into it, *Jolie Brise*'s spinnaker was finally ripped. Nothing daunted, however, it was shortly the subject of a most picturesque repair effected by Briggs, who appended a patterned counterpane to Mr Ratsey's best light-weather cotton. What is more, there is a photograph to prove it.

Jolie Brise's crew had been augmented for this race by Herbert L. Stone, who was to write appreciatively of the cutter from the stance of a hitherto dyed-in-the-wool schooner *habitué*. It is amusing that time has shown that neither the gaff cutter nor the Bermudan schooner is ideal for an ocean race. Herbert Stone and E. G. Martin wrote many pages for and against the two rigs in their time. In fact, neither was right and neither was wrong, since in our racing fleets today it is Bermudan cutters which predominate.

The faithful Maclean Buckley was on board too. Was it he or Martin who had put *Jolie Brise* so smartly about when the topmast back-stay snapped? Reports and memories differ, but one man certainly saw the shackle part and gave a timely shout. This was another of *Jolie Brise*'s augmented crew, Cyril Holland-Martin, E. G. Martin's cousin, and with him we reach a milestone, since he is the first that I have mentioned of those connected with *Jolie Brise* who is fortunately still with us, alive and well.

Defeated she was in that Bermuda Race of 1926, but loved and respected she was too.

"Coming down from the North-East Breakers Buoy was the British entry, *Jolie Brise*, her full jackyard topsail gleaming white as the westering sun hit it," or so the August edition of *Yachting* for 1926 reports.

And so the winners of the race watched her heading towards the line. It was small consolation that *Jolie Brise* won in Class C, the class reserved for those not originally built as yachts, even though her only other class-mate was well over a day behind her. Little consolation either that a large proportion of the field were to suffer a strong blow in the Gulf Stream and were to arrive much later, bloody but unbowed. But she *was* in cruising trim, taking the island in, as it were, on her way home to Plymouth, and if the earlier promise in Long Island Sound had not been fulfilled, a little comedy could but bring a smile to both crew and boat alike.

Two pilots put out to show her into port. A stand-up fight ensued between the two, eventually conceded to the one who had, by a whisker, arrived alongside first. The ghosts of the pilot men that still walk her decks must have chuckled too.

CHAPTER FOURTEEN

The Royal Mail Under Sail

There followed a British Colonial interlude full of pleasing civility, pomp and circumstance. They anchored that first night in Georgetown Bay, with white houses reflected in the water, and the scent of cedars seeping across the Sound to those who sat on *Jolie Brise*'s deck.

The next day their chosen pilot rejoined them for a ticklish tack between the dockyard on Ireland Island into Hamilton itself, to join the main part of the racing fleet.

There was prize-giving at the Royal Bermuda Yacht Club – faithful to the old girl in years to come – and the next day a party at Government House. The Governor himself and his wife, Lady Asser, sailed later in *Jolie Brise* back to the dockyard. *Jolie Brise* flew the Governor's flag proudly from her mast-head, a Union Jack bearing the initials G. R.

And so it was that HMS *Wistaria*, HMS *Calcutta* and others of His Majesty's ships, dipped their ensigns in salute to the English yacht rather than vice versa. But though the first, this was not to be the last time that a sovereign's ship was to initiate rather than simply to return salutes with *Jolie Brise*.

The two Commanders, RNR, were in their element in the dockyard, and Martin reports that the Navy was kindness itself in getting his little ship ready for sea again, with the word "forthwith" smoothing away all possible delay.

A week later they were ready for sea, with their racing sails stowed away and the yard sent up to take the squaresail as required. The American, Herbert Stone, had returned to the States, as had

Cyril Holland-Martin. There remained on board Martin, Warneford, Martyr, Maclean Buckley, Briggs and Green, as well as an addition, Mr G. Gallowhur, owner of the schooner *Harlequin*, which had just sailed in the race.

The spirit of Britannia and the British Empire graced their stay in this little colony to the last, for on 4th July they set out from the dockyard accompanied by the Captain of the Dockyard's steam-launch, with the Captain himself and various other officers in *Jolie Brise*. They bore with them too a couple of bags, one yellow and one brown, carefully sealed. These were probably the last of His Majesty's mails to be carried under sail by sea from Bermuda, or indeed perhaps from anywhere. At midday, clear of the channel, their guests left them in the steamer and they were on their own again, heading home once more.

There is a tale, perhaps apocryphal, but charming, that at dinner some American millionaire's wife had asked "dear Commander Martin" to take her "little boy" with him on this passage "because it would be such an adventure". Warneford, so the tale continues, viewed the callow rich youth with considerable distaste. Hardly were they clear of Bermuda than a passing steamship was encountered and the mother's darling sent home in her.

There is no reference to this in Martin's account. Warneford too is silent, for there are no letters to be sent home on this homeward leg. But the tale is like something out of Kipling's *Captains Courageous*, and appropriately so too, for on this 3,000 mile "Great Circle" passage back to Plymouth, *Jolie Brise* was to pass close by the Grand Banks and the waters of Kipling's story of the Grand Banks' Schooner Fishing Fleet.

The first third of the passage was characterized by fickle winds and calms; the second third by passing shipping in the transatlantic steamer lanes, and here they keep to the thirty-mile-wide central area, particularly as for a considerable time they are in fog. Martin had had a war-time experience of his ship being sunk in collision in thick fog, clearly leaving as much of a mark on his mind as was left on the mind of a future owner of *Jolie Brise*, whose own war-time command had exploded. However, Martin put great faith in his fog-horn; a wooden box and trumpet with a handle, rather like a hurdy-gurdy. And, as I read his description of it, I realize with a sudden flash of recognition that this is precisely the same contraption as we have on board today, and that while he was faithfully honking it in mid-Atlantic in that summer of 1926, I too found myself relying upon it, if with rather less faith, in the North Sea in this last summer of 1980. It thrives, Martin observed, by being kept damp, otherwise it opens up; and this I note for future reference. On passage they see the *Mauretania* and speak to the *President Roosevelt* requesting with their signal letters that their position be telegraphed back home.

Then comes the final third of the passage, with winds now blowing more or less fresh from the north. There are periods when the boat is almost being driven too fast, and Martin experiments with what seems, after squaresails, to be his next greatest obsession, that of oil bags. The Wolf Rock is sighted precisely as expected, and is a final tribute to Warneford's excellent navigation. They cream up-Channel past familiar coves and downs with a fair tide and at a steady eight knots in smooth water.

So at last came Plymouth breakwater, twenty-three days out from Bermuda. They drove her hard up the harbour with water washing in the scuppers, broke out their signal letters before the Royal Western Yacht Club of England and, in the lee of the Hoe, shortened sail before making up to their buoy under Drake's Island. Here Martin confesses, and one knows the feeling, to a certain stage-fright when, after such a long passage, he is suddenly obliged to think in terms of close manoeuvering and the effect of fickle winds and difficult tides in confined waters.

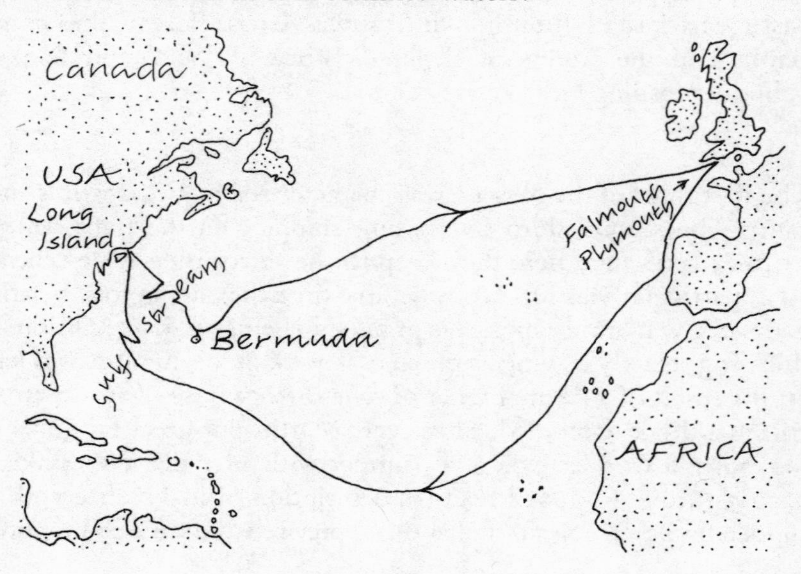

For a week last month (June 1981) I too had to handle *Jolie Brise* in those same waters – not with an Atlantic passage behind me to make me soft, but with Clare Francis on board to keep me on my toes, and wind and tide to sneak at me from those opposing shores of rival Devon and Cornwall. I am glad to report that I came to no grief then, while of course neither did Martin back in 1926.

They circled the buoy and came up to it again. The pennant was made fast without mishap, the sails stowed, customs cleared, and the party and His Majesty's mail went ashore, leaving the boat to herself after completing ten thousand miles within the space of four months. It was as proud an achievement as on that occasion less than a year before when *Jolie Brise* had arrived in Plymouth, victor of the first Ocean Race.

CHAPTER FIFTEEN

The 1926 Fastnet Race

Hardly ashore again, Martin's thoughts now turned to the second Ocean Race, now, more often than not, referred to simply as the Fastnet. It was to start from the Solent on 14th August, hardly a fortnight after *Jolie Brise*'s return from Bermuda.

It would be pleasant to report that the same crew sailed her round the course to victory as a kind of lap of honour after their great ocean circuit, but alas, this was not to be. For, as with the Bermuda Race, so with the Fastnet, *Jolie Brise* was to come fifth in that summer of 1926. Martin's navigator was "a member of Lloyds", and with them they had a "Major from the Royal Marines", a Naval Lieutenant, Eric Bush, and two cadets, Cayley and Cockburn. Of these, Eric Bush and Johnny Cockburn, both retired Captains RN, are still very much alive and well today.

So then, for *Jolie Brise*, a change of faces on board and no triumph at the end of the race. However, by now she had about her an aura of legend and success which all respected, and they respected too the fledgling Ocean Racing Club, of which her master was Commodore and whose broad pennant she flew.

In this year of 1926 the Club achieved added respectability because the start, instead of being from Ryde, was from the Royal Yacht Squadron line at Cowes. It attracted as well a more distinguished gathering of yachts, for the rules had been altered so as not to ban yachts built to the International Rule as in the previous year. On the Thursday before the race there was a dinner held by the Royal London Yacht Club at which Martin made a speech, as did Major Phillip Hunloke, who had been elected Admiral of the Ocean

Racing Club. Hunloke brought to the proceedings all the distinction of his post as Sailing Master to His Majesty. In his speech he referred to members of the Ocean Racing Club as "keen sportsmen and thorough sailors". He said that many people who went in for yacht racing just jumped into their boat and sailed round the course, leaving their men to do everything. Those who took part in the Ocean Race were sailors, because they had to do practically everything themselves and rough it. A man was not a sailor until he had roughed it. And then the members, sitting back with their cigars and brandy, must have felt brushed by the skirts of the greatest when Hunloke referred to his own charge, His Majesty's Yacht *Britannia*. She had been absolutely unmanageable off Ryde the previous day, and he said that it was of great credit to his Master, the King, that he had decided to lay the vessel up forthwith. From mention of kings came mention of presidents and a toast was drunk to none less than the President of the United States, and the reason? Partly *Jolie Brise*'s sojourn in American waters but, principally, the presence there of Mr F. L. Ames, who had sailed over from Boston with a crew of four undergraduates in the little schooner *Primrose IV*. Her appearance here for the Fastnet Race was as significant as *Jolie Brise*'s had been in that to Bermuda just two months before. The American presence in English ocean racing had begun, and it came in the form of one of those highly typical thoroughbred American schooners such as Martin had met in the Bermuda Race. That race had been won by *Malabar*, owned and sailed by her famous designer, John Alden. *Primrose* was just another such schooner and the first of several from that distinguished drawing-board to challenge the English Fastnet fleet.

At 11.30 am, Mr Algernon Maudsley and Major Malden Heckstall-Smith fired a cannon from the Royal Yacht Squadron battery and, as *The Yachting World* has it, "despatched the voyagers on their long journey". There were eleven that year including *Jolie Brise*'s old friend *Gull*, the Royal Engineers' Yacht Club's new acquisition, the Nicholson-designed *Ilex*, and the new and magnificent Fife-designed *Halloween*. Another was *Altair*, built by Lucas of Hamble, owned and sailed by a lady, Mrs Aitken Dick, the first of the fair sex to take part in an ocean race in English waters (I wonder if she took note of the article by "A Woman" in *The Yachting World* of the previous year?). *Bamba IV* was there again, surely the most unlikely Fastnet competitor ever to take part in the race, and one of the most sporting. French like *Jolie Brise*, but from

St Malo rather than Le Havre, came *Penboch*. So Martin joined some old friends on the line and made some new, among them, stiff and distinguished opposition, which he could only expect in reply to his boldness in inaugurating an ocean race the year before and founding an Ocean Racing Club. It is the fate of the pioneer to be quickly overhauled by those who follow and develop his example.

However, whatever the outcome of the race, that Saturday morning in August of 1926 is a special one for me because it was an occasion when the great Beken, marine photographer of Cowes, captured one of my favourite pictures of *Jolie Brise*, in which she is running under all light racing sail, past the grounds of Norris Castle, pursued significantly enough by the squaresail of the little white American schooner, *Primrose* (see the back of the dustcover). *Jolie Brise* had been first across the line but, keeping close in by the island shore, she had been quickly overhauled by *Gull*, *Saladin* and *Halloween*. There was indeed another fine picture, later to appear in the press, of Mr Donovan looking pleased with himself at the tiller of *Gull*, with *Jolie Brise* very much astern. However, *Jolie Brise* was just behind *Halloween* at No man's land Fort, with *Ilex*, *Saladin* and *Gull* astern of her again. She did well to hang close to this new Fife fifty-tonner as she beat down-Channel in short tacks close in shore. The two were becalmed off St Albans that night, but at the Lizard, *Halloween* was six hours ahead of her, or so the signal station reported. Martin assumed that *Jolie Brise* was lying second, but *Ilex* had stood far out into the Channel and was to be second round the Fastnet.

It was a fine reach out to the Rock from Land's End, and so it was disappointing that as *Jolie Brise* turned for home, so the wind began to freshen and back to the southward. This was no weather for her as she pitched close-hauled into the seas. *Primrose*, yet to round, passed standing upright and making good time in weather which well favoured a schooner, or would do, until she herself turned. A little further on they saw their old friend *Gull*, but sadly she was making for Baltimore, just five miles away, leaking badly, having sprung a plank in her bow – sailing to safety and out of the pages of this book. By six o'clock the wind was rising and they hove to on *Jolie Brise* for five hours, as did *Penboch*, seen in the distance, and *Bamba IV*, both still *en route* for the Rock. Meanwhile Mrs Dick had followed *Gull* into Baltimore in her little *Altair*, adding to her notoriety as the first woman in the race by being the first Fastnet competitor not to report a retirement. She thus caused consternation at home, sufficient to call out two destroyers to search for her.

The next day the wind came round to the west and *Jolie Brise* got under way again, and from thence it was plain sailing to Plymouth. *Halloween* was first home, clearing the breakwater on that wild night five days out from Cowes, but the cup went to *Ilex* and the hard-sailing engineers, three of whom were washed overboard in the course of the race and miraculously pulled back on board again. Those two boats, then, were the heroes of the race, as was the American schooner *Primrose*, next in on Thursday morning, well justifying her transatlantic challenge; after her came *Saladin* and then *Jolie Brise*.

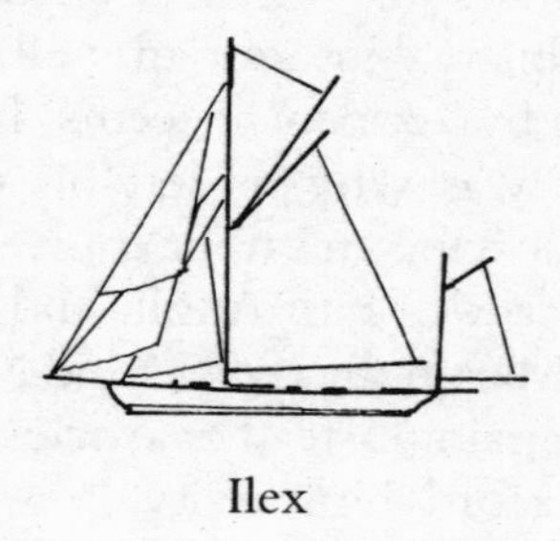

Ilex

Could *Jolie Brise* have won? The waters of the Fastnet are littered with "if onlys". By his own admission, if only Martin had jogged her quietly on during those five night hours, he might have won the cup a second time. But, with him, seamanship outweighed competition, as it should always do. The memory of a broken shackle in the Bermuda Race, an unwillingness to tempt the fates so near the end of the ten thousand miles sailed by his cutter that season, perhaps most of all an uncertainty about the experience of his crew, had prompted him to heave to. One of the youngest of them, Johnny Cockburn, confesses that they were a very amateur bunch. He was fascinated by Martin, "a huge man who wore black brogue shoes at sea and on shore did up the collar of his shirt with spun yarn instead of a stud".

Characteristic to the last, during those five hours they were hove to, Martin brought out his fiddle and played wild music to the accompaniment of the gale. To the last, I say, for it *was* the last, because after that astounding season, master and boat parted company.

To Martin's everlasting credit was his finding of *Jolie Brise* in France and the way in which he saved her for us all to have, even to this day. His place as founder of the Ocean Race and of the Ocean

Racing Club is secure too in the annals of yachting history. But what became of him? He still remained Commodore of the club he had founded, spoke at its dinners and raced on occasions in its races. But his writings to *The Yachting World* became fewer and fewer. While every other page during the years of '25 and '26 had seemed to have been about *Jolie Brise*, new stars were now appearing on the yachting scene. Conor O'Brien and his *Saoirse*, and Mulhauser with Martin's old *Amaryllis* were earth-girdling names which were now catching the imagination of the fireside yachtsman.

Martin, in the parlance of the Empire, "went native". Member of many yacht clubs, founder of one, and virtual inventor of a whole new yachting sport, his real interest after all was with work boats. That was why, quite by accident it seems, he bought *Jolie Brise* in the first place. That was why he left his old skipper Briggs at Teignmouth and, following an earlier course in Briggs' life, headed eastwards to the estuaries of East Anglia and signed up as first mate on a Thames barge. Martin the recluse and Martin the literary man had come to the fore again. Instead of articles, he now wrote books, published by the Oxford University Press. A small treatise on helmsmanship likened the helmsman's art to that of the violinist; another slim book, beautifully illustrated by his own pencil, *Sailorman*, dealt with great literary finesse about the technical niceties of the Thames barge; and a third, *Deep Water Cruising*, became as much a classic of the yachtsman's library as Eric Hiscock's *Cruising under Sail* was to become a few years hence. In this was embodied all that he ever learnt from and felt for the greatest heroine in his bachelor life, his greatest love, *Jolie Brise*.

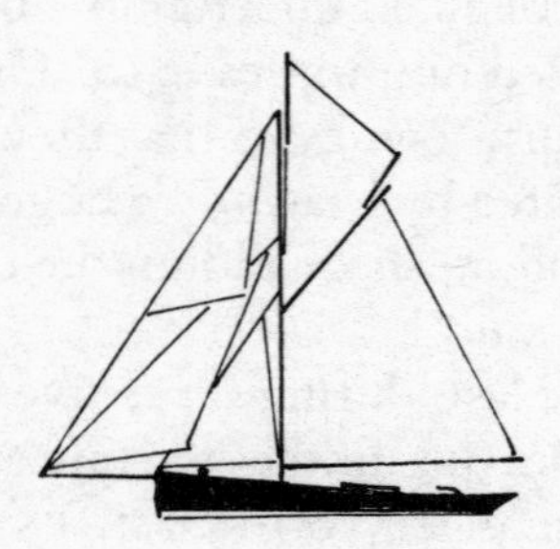

PART FOUR

1926–1928

CHAPTER SIXTEEN

Marriage of Convenience

And that might have been the end of the story.

Week after week from November 13th 1926 to February 5th 1927 *Jolie Brise* was advertised in *The Yachting World*. No mention was made of her great successes or her voyagings. She was simply described as a "a Havre Pilot Cutter, price £1,900, for particulars apply E. G. Martin, 40 Dover Street, W.1".

However, the photograph which accompanied the advertisement told all. It showed her cutting her way through the schooners at the start of the Bermuda Race with her spinnaker just lifting, and her jackyard topsail towering over all. There was no need to boast of her successes for any prospective purchaser would know and, of course, even as she was being advertised, Martin's accounts of her summer cruising were appearing regularly in the same magazine. None the less, famous and beautiful though she be, there seemed to be very few people who would contemplate buying her, as that monotonous parade of twelve weekly advertisements so sadly demonstrated. The fact was that on the one hand £1,900 was a very fancy price indeed for those days and, on the other, as an ocean racer such a boat could only have a dwindling future, while in any event her spartan accommodation would not appeal to the average yachtsman – and certainly not to his wife.

Just above that first advertisement appeared another, which was as much a pointer to the future as this was a symbol of a passing age. That advertisement read simply,

"The Fastnet Race, 1927. Suitable yacht for this competition now building; early acquisition ensures having rig and other details exactly to owner's liking." In under three years from the inception of the race which she had more or less invented, yachts were now being specifically built to take part in it. *Jolie Brise*'s days as an ocean racer must surely be numbered.

It must have been depressing for Martin, both spiritually and financially, to find so few buyers for his beloved boat. This indeed was the time that the dark haired girl from our first chapter was going backwards and forwards on the Gosport Ferry just to see *Jolie Brise* lying at her mooring. But there were few others so inclined, and certainly none with cheque-books at the ready, for *Jolie Brise* was, and is, the epitome of the sort of fantastic boat which it is always splendid for somebody else to own.

As the weeks went by, mention of price disappeared from the advertisement and purchasers were referred either to Camper & Nicholson at Gosport or Morgan Giles at Teignmouth, rather than to her dispirited owner. However, someone equally dispirited must have been Sydney Briggs, about to be dispossessed of his darling. But there was to be a happy end to this part of the story, which has so many endings. We last saw Captain Warren Ferrier eyeing *Jolie Brise* from the deck of his own yacht *Tern III* in Falmouth Harbour. His man Blackmore had rowed over to have a word with his former master Martin, just as *Jolie Brise* was weighing anchor for her transatlantic crossing. That same Captain Warren Ferrier now came forward at last, together with a partner, Dr Brownlow Smith, and bought *Jolie Brise* and, more important, with her "acquired" Sydney Briggs as his skipper.

Several marriages of convenience were involved and, like many such marriages, they were not to survive for long. Captain Ferrier owned many boats in his time and was an active and respected member of the Royal Torquay Yacht Club, both before and after the last war. The name of Dr Brownlow Smith, on the other hand, does not appear in Lloyds Register of Yachts before or after his brief joint ownership of *Jolie Brise*. Not for the first, nor the last time, *Jolie Brise* needed the enthusiasm of one man and the finance of another if she was to be kept in commission, and I just hazard a guess that Dr Brownlow Smith had more money than heart in the project. And money there needed to be because, if *Jolie Brise* were to become a conventional yacht, she must have those two things most abominated by her former master – an engine and a ladies' cabin. These were fitted at the yard of Morgan Giles in Teignmouth, and so that huge after area of sail-locker became sub-divided into engine room and sleeping cabin, as indeed it remains today, though both cabin and engine have changed, the latter twice over.

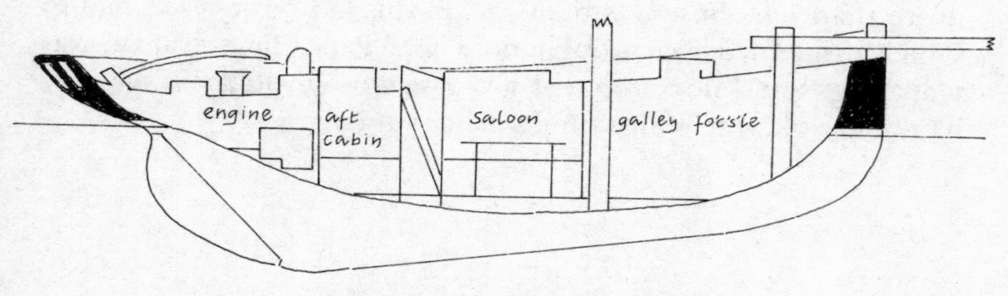

(Compare with drawing on p. 51)

There was, then, a marriage of convenience between the partners, but so too was there between them and Sydney Briggs. To take on a skipper with a boat has mixed advantages. Inevitably, time and time again, "Commander Martin and I did this", and "Commander Martin and I did that", must have come into the conversation. Indeed, with Briggs as oldest inhabitant, Brownlow Smith and Ferrier must on occasions have wondered just whether they owned the boat or he. You can add to that the dubious privilege of owning a famous boat. Scrap Batten still finds himself being referred to as the new owner of *Dyarchy*, twenty years after he bought her from Roger Pinckney. How much more, then, must these brand-new owners of *Jolie Brise* have suffered from people coming to see the boat rather than themselves. It is something which we who sail *Jolie Brise* today are very used to, and accept as part of the privilege of sailing in her, but I suspect that, back in 1927, Ferrier and Brownlow Smith hoped that they had bought a yacht and not an institution.

Tales of those times come to me from Albert Broom, previously mentioned, who served as mate under Sydney Briggs for her new owners. Not surprisingly he had a proper disdain for white flannels and jaunty yachting caps and a marvellous regard for the degree to which Briggs and *Jolie Brise* were in accord, even if the rest of the ship might not have been. He tells of how they were sailing into her birth-place, Le Havre, one day and the newly fitted engine refused to start – much consternation between the owners but ill-disguised pleasure from Briggs. Broom was kept busy on the foredeck as they sailed in between the breakwaters with Briggs at the helm. Briggs rounded up inside, called to Broom to let go the anchor and douse the jib, while he himself ran forward and triced up the main. The cutter checked to the anchor, her counter slipped back to just a couple of feet from the quay, so that "even a lady might step ashore". It was a matter for pause then and recollection now, but no more than *Jolie Brise* was built for, in this her birth-place, and to which Briggs had been brought up. I hope Paumelle, still alive, was watching, and I hope too that just every now and again we may handle the old ship with a similar felicity today.

CHAPTER SEVENTEEN

The 1927 Fastnet

However, do not let a tale of an engine-scorning skipper amazing his owners mislead you, for neither Warren Ferrier nor Brownlow Smith were duffers (to borrow the slang of the day). They had the courage to enter their ship for the third Fastnet Race, which neither, I believe, had sailed in before; and their courage was not so much physical as moral. Every eye in the fleet would be watching them to see how their antics compared with those of her previous owner, founder and Commodore of the Ocean Racing Club and inventor of the Fastnet Race itself. A newcomer might slip in unobserved in a strange boat, but to arrive in one so famous would be regarded by some as verging on the pretentious; and so the need to do well would be all the greater. To enter the race on such terms could only be to their disadvantage. If they were to win, doubtless it would have been the old boat and their skipper Briggs who would have had the credit rather than themselves, but, if they were not to do well, they alone, of course, would be responsible.

As it happened, the duo acquitted themselves admirably and, dare one say it, displayed greater courage in so doing than Martin, who, like all sensible sportsmen, had quitted while the going was good.

As in 1926, so in 1927, the Fastnet Race was bedevilled by bad weather. A very considerable westerly gale struck the fleet before they had cleared the English Channel. *The Yachting World*'s account of *Jolie Brise*'s part in the race is short, anonymous and to the point, probably from the pen of Warren Ferrier himself.

The starting gun was at 11.30 am on August 13th. With High

Water Dover at noon, they had a foul tide until they turned westward. The weather was overcast and raining, with poor visibility, and from that day we still have a very fine photograph of *Jolie Brise*. All her crew are standing dripping rather than enduring sitting on the top of wet bulwarks, a discomfort familiar from wet days sailing in her today. They cleared St Catherine's Point at 3.10 pm. Visibility by now was very poor with a heavy rain and a big sea. They stood into the Poole Harbour Buoy, which they made at 6.00 pm with no other competitors in sight. Deciding against tacking out into the Channel and the steep seas, they short tacked against the strong tide but with smoother water along the Dorset coast, only weathering Anvil Point at 11.30 pm. Portland was rounded at 3.00 am and then they stood into the Bay, making the best of the tide and the smooth water.

At 8.00 am on the 14th they were off Exmouth, wind south-west-by-south Force 5, still with very heavy showers. Berry Head was abeam at noon and from there they short tacked round the coast until at 7.15 am on the next day (August 15th) they left the Lizard with a westerly wind Force 7–8 in confused seas.

They hove to and shifted to the second jib. The weather they described as "O.C.B.G.", the meaning of which, be it rude, technical, or both, eludes me, but one can guess! They had then to decide whether to go on, to remain hove to or to take shelter. Going on meant close reefing and, with the heavy seas running, a grave risk of not being able to go about. Staying hove to appealed to no one, for they had not even a violin on board to while away the time. There was not a dry rag between them and no one had had any appreciable sleep since leaving Cowes. And so it was that they turned and ran for Falmouth, coming up to *Nicanor*, the schooner which had been their only sparring mate in the earlier days of the race, and *Ilex* with her usual doughty crew of Royal Engineers. But they saw too Lord Stalbridge's *Tally Ho!* and the Alden-designed schooner *La Goleta*. *Ilex* and *Nicanor* were shortly to turn tail too and follow *Jolie Brise* to shelter, while only *Tally Ho!* and *La Goleta* were to complete the race in a classic duel between an English cutter and an American schooner, in which for once *Jolie Brise* played no part. So again she dropped anchor in Falmouth, where Ferrier had seen her set out on her transatlantic voyage just eighteen months before.

Ideas of continuing the race, as and when the weather moderated, were abandoned because, unlike perhaps in previous years, some of *Jolie Brise*'s crew "could not stay indefinitely".

The laurels then in 1927 went to *Tally Ho!* and her aristocratic owner, and to *La Goleta*, still to be seen in Lymington, and her owner Mr R. Peverly from across the Atlantic.

However, there was much scope for consolation among *Jolie Brise*'s company as they dried out their gear in the welcome shelter of Falmouth Harbour. The entire fleet but two had retired, including not just their own boat, with her transatlantic triumphs, but also Mr Conor O'Brien's earth-girdling *Saoirse*. But most remarkable, and cause equally for congratulation and speculation as to how she would have been placed had she continued, *Jolie Brise* had been leading the fleet by *five* hours when she had reached the Lizard and had decided to retire. This was no mean feat for a heavy boat of outdated design, moderate windward ability and new owners, new to the sport.

Looking back at that wild Fastnet of 1927, we wonder how it compared with that tragic race in 1979 when the fleet was so brutally diminished. Certainly I believe that there was a tendency to over-dramatize the severity of the weather in the old days. When old men shook their heads and said that the fault in 1979 lay in newfangled design, they were only partly right. No, the severity of the gale which hit the Fastnet fleet on 13th August of that year was without precedent in the history of the race. But I *can* confirm that *Jolie Brise* met similar conditions on that wild night with a remarkable degree of equanimity. It so happened that I was bringing her home from Spain when that same gale hit us suddenly and viciously just south of Ushant. Once she was knocked down, but she merely shook herself like an old Labrador, and, with all the assurance of a heavy, deep, long-keeled boat, picked herself up and went on her way. All that night her massive rigging hummed and sagged before the wind, till I felt that something must go – but it never did. In its flexibility lay its strength. To the north of us, albeit in still more severe conditions, light-displacement boats with short keels and highly tensioned masts had a sadly different tale to tell.

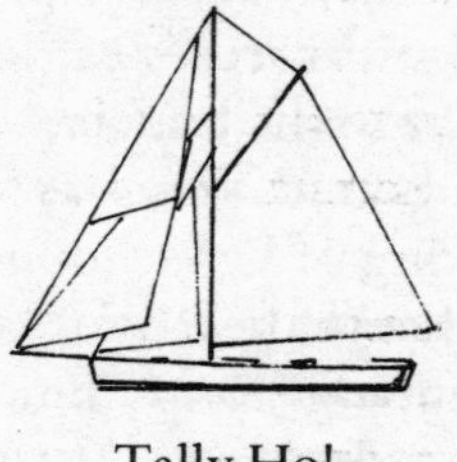

Tally Ho!

CHAPTER EIGHTEEN

The 1928 Fastnet

Warren Ferrier was an inveterate buyer and seller of boats, but 1928 finds him still with *Jolie Brise*. He and Brownlow Smith bring her again to the starting line in interesting company. There is *Amaryllis*, in which Mulhauser had sailed round the world, and which had been George Martin's last big boat before he bought *Jolie Brise*. And there is *Nina*, the American schooner designed by Burgess as the ocean-racing yacht *par excellence* of her day, and nine more besides, undaunted by the fracas of the previous year.

The little fleet had a fair wind eastward down Spithead, and a windward beat down-Channel towards Land's End. *Nina* was far out ahead with *Mohawk*, another American schooner, just astern of her.

Nina's skipper was Sherman Hoyt, first met by us briefing the Bermuda Race skippers over dinner at New London in 1926. He took the schooner first round the Rock with *Jolie Brise* next, followed by *Mohawk*, *Neptune* and *Ilex*. The indomitable engineers had broken their topmast, replaced it with a spinnaker pole and then re-rigged the topmast, duly repaired with a very professional-looking scarf. But for this mishap and stiff breezes earlier in the race, *Ilex* would probably have been closer to the leaders.

However, homeward bound *Nina* was favoured with a southerly wind far more to the liking of her schooner rig than the following wind which had driven her to the Rock. That leg back to Plymouth found the schooner romping home, nine-and-a-half hours ahead of her fellow American *Mohawk*. *Neptune* came third, a large

Norwegian-style double-ended cutter, *Jolie Brise* fourth, and her old sparring partner, *Ilex*, fifth. *Jolie Brise* saved her time on both *Mohawk* and *Neptune* and was second on corrected time.

This was not a startling result but better than the last race, from which she had retired, and the race before, in which Martin had hove to.

But *Jolie Brise* had been close enough up to the leader for those aboard to appreciate the shape of things to come. *La Goleta* had nearly taken the cup the year before and now another American schooner, Bermudan and extreme in design, had taken it home with her across the waters to America. *Jolie Brise*'s owners of two years' standing could understandably be discouraged.

However, there was one young man aboard *Jolie Brise* who one day was to buy that controversial American schooner which had snatched the prize. He was to be a close friend and shipmate too of her skipper of that year, Sherman Hoyt.

But all this is to anticipate. Deck-hand Albert Broom chiefly remembers this amateur newcomer to *Jolie Brise*'s crew as one who very much took matters into his own hands. He did so with such enthusiasm that, rather than don cumbersome oilskins in freshening weather, he would strip down and, lithe and naked, shin to the end of the bowsprit to take in the jib topsail.

He must have been well pleased with that lovely view aft from the bowsprit end, for it seems that then and there he resolved to make *Jolie Brise* his own, undaunted by her comparative antiquity.

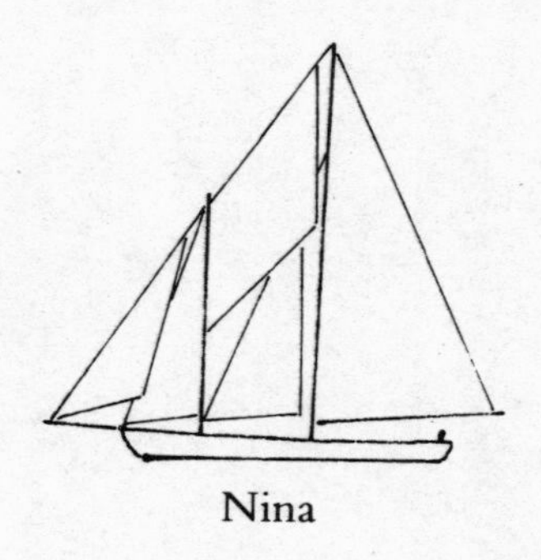

Nina

PART FIVE

1928–1932

CHAPTER NINETEEN

A New Champion

The young man was Henry Robert Somers Fitzroy de Vere Somerset. When he bought *Jolie Brise* he was just thirty-one. Imagine him pacing her decks as Briggs looks on with a mixture of admiration and regret at the dawn of this new golden age of *Jolie Brise*, of which he will not be a part. Somerset is a man of outrageously good looks, with slightly drawn, vulpine features. He smokes a cigarette with casual elegance, and the defiance of a man who lost half a lung and gained the Distinguished Service Order, where so many of his teenage contemporaries lost their lives, in the trenches of the First World War. Who can deny this arrogantly attractive survivor an element of the devil-may-care buccaneer as he enjoys to the full the life he so nearly lost? He has about him everything that a man like Briggs would respect, everything too that a mother ambitious for her daughter would approve of – Eton, Sandhurst and the Grenadier Guards; and not just one but two grandfathers who were Dukes, on his mother's side the Duke of St Albans and, on his father's, the Duke of Beaufort. There is also the intriguing knowledge that only something perhaps as simple as a fatal fall out hunting lies between him and a dukedom of his own, and with it the ownership of some 52,000 acres, because Somerset is the heir-presumptive to his cousin, the tenth Duke of Beaufort, two years his junior and happily still very much in charge today.

However, when we first met him, such speculation by prospective mothers-in-law was a thing of the past, because Somerset had married very suitably and happily at the age of twenty-three.

Since the day he bought her, the name *Jolie Brise* was to be equally linked with Somerset as with Martin. "Martin and Somerset" rolls off the tongue with the ease of, say, "Rodgers and Hammerstein" or Marks & Spencer. It is as if theirs had been a partnership, rather than what it was – two glorious reigns divided by a brief interregnum.

Everyone called Martin Commander, sometimes George, but more frequently just Martin, or E. G. Martin. The initials "E. G." made up a name in themselves – as with A. J. P. Taylor or A. P. Herbert. But Somerset had so many initials that it is not surprising that we do not similarly remember him.

To refer snappily to H. R. S. F. de V. Somerset would be beyond most of our capabilities. Indeed, Lloyds Register of Yachts were so bemused by this avalanche of initials that they assumed he was not one man but two. To have called him simply Somerset would sound grand enough if he were a peer of the realm; Mr Somerset would somehow seem inappropriate. Captain Somerset is how Debrett refers to him, but, a sign of a new generation, *Jolie Brise*'s new owner was, more often than not, known simply as Bobby.

So on an autumn day in 1928 Sydney Briggs watches as *Jolie Brise* sails out of his life. On board, his place is taken by a new dynasty of professional crew, that of the Crossley family of Antony Passage, just off the Tamar River. Fred Crossley was Bobby Somerset's skipper and Jack, his younger brother, who is still so happily with us, sailed with her too, while their father Abram Crossley was to keep both the boat and his boys in order, since it was he who was to be in charge of her fitting out and general well-being at her home moorings.

And where was this new home that *Jolie Brise* was heading for? The cutter rounded up behind Drake's Island; sheets were hardened as they tacked up the Tamar on the flood. A critical eye from the shore would probably have observed that all hands knew what they were doing, be they amateur or professional, because Bobby Somerset's other boat was also a French gaff cutter, older and smaller, built on pilot boat lines and hailing from near St Malo.

This brings one to an endearing aspect of the man, which appeals to those of us less handsome and less highly born than he; it is that Bobby Somerset was not particularly well off – no spanking new yachts for him, at least at this stage of his life. He not only had to make do with old converted work boats, but he took a pride and showed an enviable skill in doing so. Fred probably took the helm from his master and expertly pointed her bows through the narrows of Antony Passage where the River Lynher flows into the Tamar.

He would probably have waved to his Dad by the little group of cottages on the quay on the northern shore; Bobby in turn might have looked up on the southern shore towards the great house at Antony, wondering whether his neighbours, the Carew Poles, were watching the arrival of his "new" yacht.

Above Antony Passage the river widens and the deep wooded shores give way to placid meadowed slopes coming down to what, at high tide, is like some huge lake and, at low, reveals shining flanks of mud, criss-crossed with the footprints of waders. The fields on the starboard side were Bobby's, and, crowning them, now comes in to sight his house, Ince Castle, four-square, with its distinctive pyramid-roofed Georgian Gothic towers at its corners. Ince is as much a romantic novelist's dream of a house as Bobby Somerset himself fulfils the novelist's dream of a hero.

And so, on that autumn afternoon that I am imagining, that ideal trio of *Jolie Brise*, Bobby Somerset and Ince Castle come together. Over the fields beneath Ince a small landing-stage had been built out across the mud and, taking careful soundings because the channel is narrow here, Abram Crossley had laid a new mooring for this new arrival.

Back in the castle, Bettine Somerset will have been watching from the drawing-room windows, as she was to do so often and for so long in the years to come, for sight of those high setting sails. I can imagine her now, ringing for Ted Platainey, the chauffeur, and asking him to get the Austin 12, to bring it down to the landing-stage, for there would be many bags to bring up from the dinghy and the Crossleys to take home to the village. But she herself I can see walking out across the fields, standing and waving at the water's edge, and waiting patiently as her husband puts his new toy to bed. Down comes the gaff, steady and horizontal to the boom as the Crossleys stow the mainsail, not without wonder and a curse at its great size. Then finally everything would be lowered into the dinghy and Bobby would sit in the stern sheets, passing a critical eye over his new acquisition, being as well pleased with the sight of that as with the sight of his wife, as the dinghy's prow reaches the shore and her welcoming hand. Imagine them now, bouncing up the rutted track in the back of the Austin and along the long, autumn tinted avenue to the waiting castle, husband and wife looking beyond the chauffeur's neck and down the bonnet to where first the central section of the house, with steps rising to the *piano nobile*, come into view and then the two flanking towers. The car pulls up on the gravel and Bobby and Bettine jump out and up the outside steps to the first floor and, for Bobby, every yachtsman's first thought on coming home perhaps, a warm bath before tea.

So it *may* have been on that first homecoming in *Jolie Brise*, certainly so it *must* have been on many homecomings to that quiet anchorage. I have said that Bobby Somerset was not well off, and I suppose, with all this talk of chauffeurs and castles, to say nothing of skippers and mates, you will not be believing me. But remember, in those days Fred Crossley's pay would only have been some three pounds a week, and the chauffeur's much the same. The placid acres sweeping down to the estuary would have been worth very little in those times of profound agricultural depression, while the castle itself had for many centuries been some great man's subsidiary house, not particularly comfortable, nor in particularly good repair. No, it was all idyllic but you did not have to be a millionaire to live like a Duke's grandson or a Duke's heir – or did you?

CHAPTER TWENTY

Plans

And what did Bobby Somerset plan to do with *Jolie Brise*? Cruising, yes, and a little duck shooting in the winter months, but principally his aim and his passion was to ocean race. For, you see, it so happens that Bobby Somerset has been several times already in the pages of this book – and not just in that last race with Brownlow Smith and Warren Ferrier. He was a founder member of the Ocean Racing Club and he sailed on that first Fastnet Race in 1925 as navigator in Michael Tennant's heavy Norwegian double-ender *North Star*. She it was, you will remember, who, two hundred yards from the finishing line, retired from the race in order to get in in time for dinner and, as it happened, in time for the inaugural meeting of the Ocean Racing Club. That was probably the first time that Bobby had cast an appraising eye over *Jolie Brise* though, as a member of the crew of the slowest-but-one in the fleet, he could have had little chance of seeing her in action.

Bobby has come again into this story before we find him now at the centre of the stage, so to speak, for he also owned *Penboch* – hove to, you will remember, close by *Jolie Brise* during that wild night in the Fastnet Race of 1926, and taking shelter, as you will again discover, flipping back through these pages, in Dartmouth in the Fastnet Race of '27 when *Jolie Brise* herself ran back to Falmouth. So, over the years, the destinies of man and boat have been drawing closer together and the practicalities of Bobby Somerset's purchase of *Jolie Brise* in 1928 revolve round two factors. The first is the undoubted respect for the French working cutter which he had, for *Penboch* after all was very much the miniature of *Jolie Brise*, and second there was a change in the Fastnet Race rules following the fracas of 1927, when all but two of the fleet retired. A limit of waterline length was now placed on boats which might enter for the Fastnet. *Penboch*, only thirty-one feet on the waterline, was no longer eligible. Such smaller boats now had their own race, the Junior Ocean Race, a Channel race from the Solent to Cherbourg. To borrow phrases from two different sports in explanation of a third, Somerset had acquired for himself horses for courses and his brace of yachts moored beneath the castle were just that, for with *Penboch* he could enter the Channel Race and, with *Jolie Brise*, the Fastnet.

Three things are extraordinary here, first that there had only been one, and now just two, ocean races in the ocean racing season. Again, to draw a horsy analogy, they were more like hunter trials than races, those early contests, for just as a man who hunts tries his hunter over a hunter trial course at the beginning or end of the season and probably never competes with him again, so the cruising man was competing against other yachts just once or twice in the year. How very different from the highly tuned, specially built ocean-racing fleet of today with its brim-full calendar of events!

The second factor which is remarkable is that a boat of thirty-one foot on the waterline should be considered too small for the Fastnet Race, when today such a competitor would seem quite sizeable.

Third is the extraordinary idea that, with just two races in the calendar, one should be for the smaller boats and the other for the larger. The number of entries was small enough and the chances to ocean race so infrequent that it seems incomprehensible why this should have been so, other than that the 1927 experience had given the Fastnet Race organizers cold feet. But what was most remarkable was that a man should take the trouble to keep and maintain one yacht for one race and the other for the other and that, going to such lengths, the yachts he should choose should be both so eccentric. For of those two cutters lying off his landing-stage one had been built in 1901, this the faithful *Penboch*, and the other, *Jolie Brise*, as we know in 1913. Neither had been built as yachts. Both, to the yachtsman's eye, were antiquated in the extreme. However, there was nothing antiquated about Bobby Somerset, and in that summer of 1928 he would teach the ocean-racing world a thing or two, and learn one or two things himself. With *Penboch* he won the Channel Race while with *Jolie Brise* – but then, that is another story, and one which nearly never came to pass.

CHAPTER TWENTY-ONE

"King George Will Provide"

Allow me, first, a little digression. A few years ago I visited the then Commander-in-Chief Home Fleet at Portsmouth, Admiral Sir Terence Lewin. I was concerned at that time with the future of the frigate *Foudroyant*, Britain's oldest ship afloat, beside which *Jolie Brise* is quite a chicken. I was handed with some ceremony from WRN secretary to aide-de-camp and, finally, into the Commander-in-Chief's inner sanctum, to find a rather donnish figure informally dressed in a "woolly-pully". His knowledge of and interest in the history of ships is formidable and he gave me sound advice, but he ended by saying with a twinkle in his eye, "but you do realize that this is just my own personal suggestion. I can pull no rank at all, you know. I am just Commander-in-Chief; it isn't as if I were First Sea Lord . . ." The next day I opened my *Times* and saw under "New Appointments" in the Court Circular, "to be appointed First Sea Lord from Commander-in-Chief Home Fleet, Admiral Sir Terence Lewin".

This, then, was the man that I had found approachable, interested, and with a sense of humour. So a couple of years later when we were seeking finance for the restoration of *Jolie Brise*, I sought his help again. The First Sea Lord wrote back, his letter typed with a green ribbon and his signature in green ink, in which colour, as everyone knows, all First Sea Lords conduct their correspondence. He courteously explained that, in his position, while interested in all restoration projects, he could not be seen to support one or another in particular, and then went on to say,

"You might not know that the Royal Navy entirely refitted *Jolie*

Brise some years ago when she was in the hands of Bobby Somerset. Apparently he could not afford the winter refit and tried to pay off the crew. However, they were having none of it and assured the owner that King George would provide. They then spent the winter pinching everything they needed from Plymouth dockyard, and she sailed like a new pin the following spring. So you see the Navy has already helped."

I later discovered that this delightful tale had come to him via his flag officer from Jack Crossley, and in more detail it runs thus. Very soon Bobby Somerset had decided that he had in fact bitten off more than he could chew by buying *Jolie Brise* (how well one knows the feeling). So it was with a long face that he told the Crossleys that sailing days were over. Indeed, with the stock-market the way it was, he could not be so sure that his days at Ince Castle were not numbered too. But, as we have heard from the First Sea Lord, Abram Crossley would have none of it and in that classic phrase said, "King George will provide". "Pinching" is not quite the right word in this context. Abram Crossley ran a barge in and out of the dockyard and worked for the Navy in a civilian capacity, and in those spacious days it was accepted that such a man, a master unto himself, should be allowed to help himself to more or less what he required. And so, over the winter, the materials were transferred across the Tamar from the dockyard to Antony Passage, where *Jolie Brise* was undergoing her refit in the hands of the Crossley family.

The four coats of paint on the deck serve as the best illustration as to how the Navy "helped". The first coat was a dark grey, described as "Home Fleet". The second coat was a shade lighter, described as "Middle East", and the third coat was lighter still, designed for the Far East fleet, while discreetly covering all this battleship grey was a fourth coat, described as "Mast", an agreeable putty colour.

While all this activity was going on, Bobby's spirits rose and he celebrated the prospect of another ocean racing season by writing to Ratsey's and ordering a complete new set of sails for his new boat, brown this time, as a change from Martin's predilection for white.

So the spring of 1929 came round and Abram Crossley, the father, and Fred Crossley, his skipper son, looked on with mild interest as Somerset loaded his new sails on board.

"Well I'll be damned," was the general feeling. "We have just about done this refit at the King's and our own expense, and here is the boss spending money like water."

Somerset was unabashed.

"Things are looking up again, and what's more, I think we shall change the iron ballast for lead."

And so, shaking their heads at the strange ways of the gentry, the Crossleys were press-ganged into driving a Morris Cowley tourer round all the scrapyards of Plymouth, Devon and Cornwall, acquiring £200's worth of lead, which they melted down themselves into pigs, to replace the larger and less efficient iron ballast with which *Jolie Brise* had originally been fitted.

"Well, all I can say is I hope it's worth it, sir," came the comment. "£200 is a lot of money."

"I know, I know," Somerset replied, and then, disarmingly as ever, said, "When we have raced in the Fastnet we will compete in the new race to Santander – and we shall win. The Queen of Spain has offered a cup and a £200 prize, and that should pay for our lead."

Whether *Jolie Brise* did or did not win that first Santander Race, and whether or not the lead was paid for is another story, but the answer I think you will have already guessed. However, be patient, for first we have another Fastnet.

13 Making sail at the start of the 1926 Bermuda Race; all six foot seven inches of E. G. Martin strides down the deck as they prepare to hoist the famous jackyard topsail, complete with racing flag, left of picture, out of focus. Briggs in peaked cap; Warneford, in felt hat, stoops to hoist. The time? The clock says twenty to ten. (Warneford's album)

14 Where it all began: winning the first Fastnet. Left to right: Briggs (peaked cap), Green (noddy hat), Dick Maclean Buckley (with pipe), E. G. Martin at the helm, and Weston Martyr. J. R. K. Warneford (inset, 15) took the picture.

16 Who was who? Ship's company say farewell to their pyjama-clad friends at English Harbour, Antigua in 1932. (The O'Mahonys' album)

17 Jim and Lillian Worsdell take tea with the press when their dream voyage was still full of promise.

18 Owners, pre-war and post-war, dining together in Lisbon. Somerset, third from right, Lobato next to him (fifth from right). Second from right is David Somerset and (sixth from right) the faithful Dick Maclean Buckley, the pipe-smoker from the first Fastnet Race (see plate 14). (Collection Lobato)

19 "Crow's nest" view of a Lobato boatload of friends. (Lobato)

20 Swordfishing days. (Lobato)

21 Glossy paintwork: dried out for a scrub in Lisbon. (Lobato)

22 Down below: looking forward through the galley to the forecastle. Portuguese racing trophies overhead. Falmouth church chair by the table. (Payne, 1981)

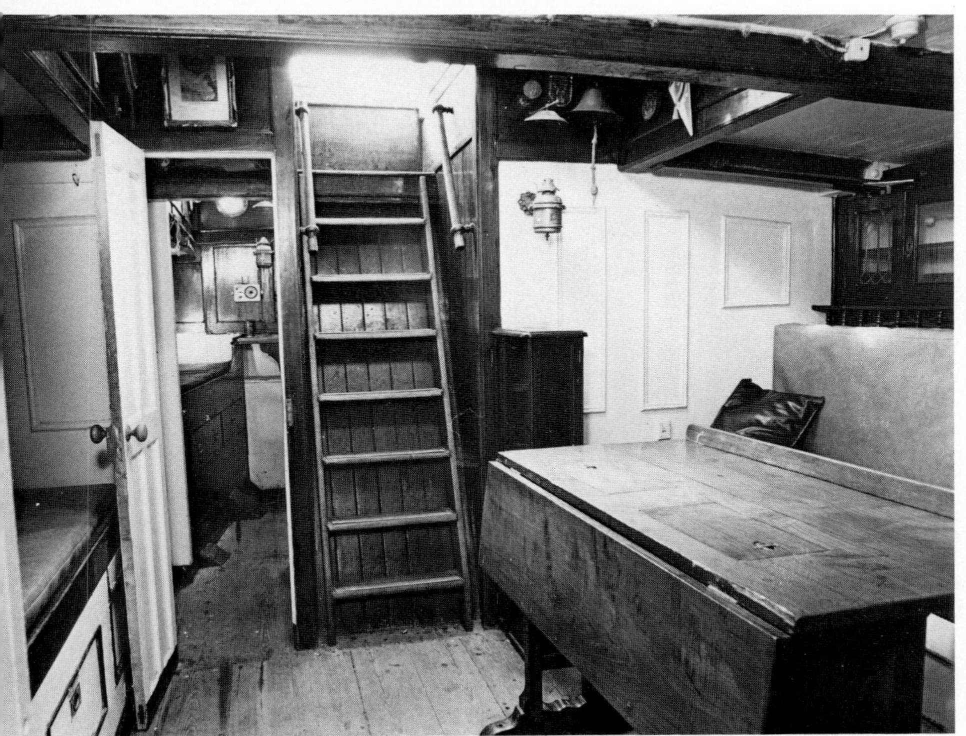

23 . . . and aft. The companionway and a glimpse of the Captain's cabin. (Payne, 1981)

24 In miniature: from France, J. P. Dole Robbe's fine model of her in pilot cutter livery. (Dole Robbe)

25 Somerset's own model, given by him to Lobato. (Bryer)

26 Under construction: from Holland, J. P. van den Heuvel was anxious to get every detail right. (J. P. van den Heuvel)

27 Ian Procter and members of the Dauntsey's School Sailing Club made this model for instruction purposes. (Parish)

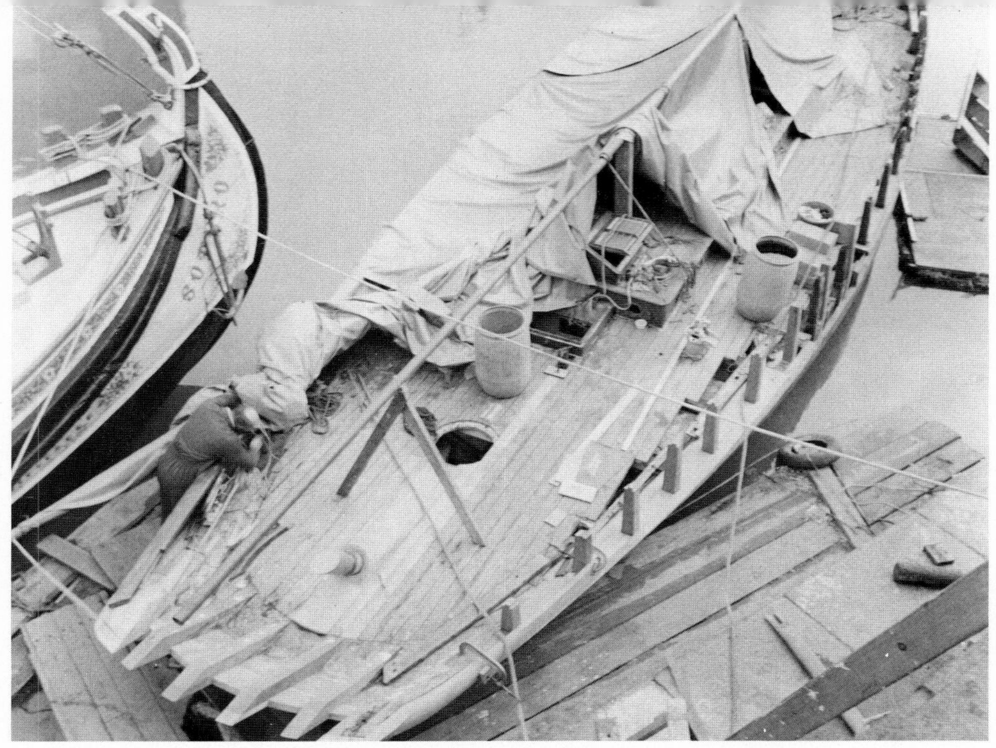

28 The Exeter Maritime Museum undertook major reconstruction works in 1979–80 and 1980–81. (Goddard)

David Goddard, Director, Exeter Maritime Museum.

30 Bill Parish, Commodore, Dauntsey's School Sailing Club. (A. Parish)

31 Sailing today: members of Dauntsey's School Sailing Club – Tessa Whitley (at the helm) and Fraser Rush – enjoy a beat out of Loch Ewe. Summer 1981. (Bryer)

CHAPTER TWENTY-TWO

The 1929 Fastnet and the first Santander

August at last and the Fastnet again, with *Jolie Brise*'s new owner at the helm. Ten competitors run down eastwards towards the Forts, meeting the twelve-metre class tacking up towards them. It is a patchy, light-winded race down-Channel and *Jolie Brise* scores with her remarkable skill of moving with no wind at all in calm conditions. Once round the Lizard, with a stronger wind just forward of the beam, she thrashes her way up to the Rock, leaving others still becalmed somewhere astern, much indeed as on her first victorious Fastnet. The north-easterly falls light as she rounds, but it is a south-easterly course home and a pleasant enough sail. Winds are so light off the Lizard that *Ilex* has to resort to kedging, but *Jolie Brise* is first home and winner of the Fastnet for the second time, the only boat to win twice in the race's very short history. She certainly showed them that her day was not yet finished. Bobby had reason to be proud.

True there had been no American schooners that year in the fleet, but there was the very modern *Maitenes II* and the French bermudan schooner *Vega*. So *Jolie Brise*'s win was certainly a distinguished one and ample justification for Bobby Somerset's preoccupation with ballast and trim. The mainsail, too, was two panels shorter than Martin's had been, and she must have been correspondingly better balanced and lighter on the helm. Indeed, it all seemed so effortless that there is hardly a tale to tell, except one of triumph and a new confidence as she comes to the line of a brand-new race.

The background to the Santander stems from an idea mooted by an RAF officer called Square, who had married a Spanish girl from

Santander – it sounds like the start of a limerick, but it was in fact the start of a great race. Square had approached the Ocean Racing Club on behalf of the Real Club Maritimo. Somerset and two other Ocean Racing Club men, Rose-Richards and Hunloke, had taken the matter further.

It was supposed to be very much a Royal affair and an international one, and our own Navy decided to send two destroyers as guard ships. The Ocean Racing Club had to presume to suggest that instead they send HMS *Royal Oak* as being rather more of a size with the ships which the Spaniards and the French intended to lay on. Another regal aspect in this race was that there was a big class and a small class, the "big" girls racing for the King of Spain's Cup and the "small" ones for the Queen's, and in that bigger class was Lord Stalbridge's huge three masted schooner *Cetonia*, a far cry from his *Tally Ho!* But the largest boat of all was the ex-Kaiser's ex-*Meteor IV*. *Jolie Brise* races regularly today with the Tall Ships' fleet and has become accustomed to finding herself among the giants, but to arrive at the starting line with such huge yachts was for her a new experience on that day in 1929.

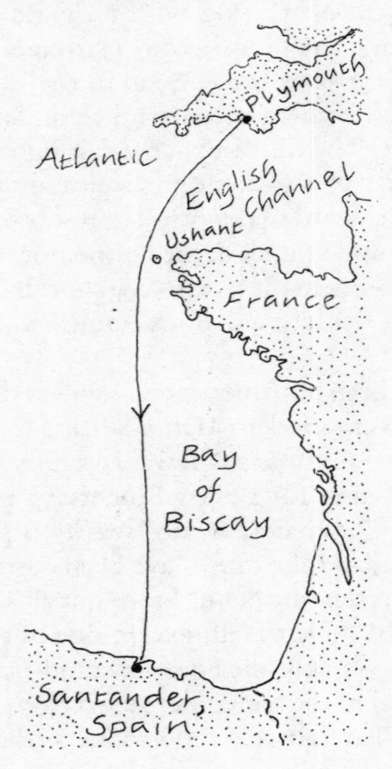

But Bobby Somerset's eyes were on his fellow class-mates, as *Jolie Brise* crossed the starting line at Plymouth. In particular there was her old rival *Ilex* with her engineer crew, and *Neptune*, with whom she had had close contest in the Fastnet the year before. But largest of the small class was *Maria del Carmen*, a schooner bearing somewhat confusingly the same name as that which the old *Meteor* now bore. Theirs is a tale of blissful fair days spent sailing across the Bay of Biscay. It was indeed the kind of ideal passage which one always hopes to have but seldom gets. If anything, it verged on the tedious as the weather was hot and the winds were light. *Jolie Brise* won her class ahead of *Ilex*, who, arriving in the dark, added her unfailing touch of humour to the occasion by signalling to HMS *Royal Oak* first in Spanish, then French and then in Latin, before realizing that she was British. And so indeed *Jolie Brise* sailed home with the Queen of Spain's Cup as planned and the Queen's £200 to justify the extravagance of the lead.

CHAPTER TWENTY-THREE

Forecastle Tales

However, *Jolie Brise*'s sailings in these days were not just restricted to the summer or to racing. As Bobby Somerset had a castle ashore, so too he had a castle afloat, and what luckier a man could there have been than he who walked down to his own river shore to row out to that black cutter waiting for him? And in those winters the ocean racing would give way to the pursuit of duck. *Jolie Brise* was, and still is, a magnificent boat in which to remain snug on a dark winter's night. Bobby and his friends and the Crossleys would lay duck punts on her deck and sail out into Plymouth Sound and along the coast to Salcombe, which could be a blustery sail on those short winter days, but once across the bar the steep sides of the bare-treed estuary would provide shelter enough. He would point her bowsprit up towards the Bag, that wide reach of the river between Salcombe and Kingsbridge, and there they would drop anchor in the early evening, launch the punts and go to shoot duck flying home at dusk. And then back with their bag to a pleasant supper around the cabin table and a pipe and conversation far into the night.

However, this ideal picture of a yachtsman at his winter sport was not always without a flaw. One night Bobby came back on board with his dogs and a bag which they had retrieved from the marshes which looked all too distinctly domestic. The next morning Bobby had to go ashore with profuse apologies and promises of replacements. Needless to say, as always he fell on his feet. The owner of the ducks turned out to be an old friend and all, apart from his reputation as a discerning wild fowler, was finally made well.

On another occasion, *Jolie Brise* lay anchored in Lulworth Cove, where the great chalk cliffs enfold the harbour and the boats within like the arms of a benevolent madonna; that is, unless the wind is in the west, whistling through the entrance, making the cove a hell on water. But on this occasion the morning was peaceful and calm; you could see the anchor on the bottom, and Somerset was in his accustomed sailing gear, a large pair of khaki shorts and nothing else, setting off his deep-tanned, barklike skin, and leaving revealed the scars where his lung had been removed.

It was after breakfast.

"Who's for a swim?" he said. The crew had completed their duties of chamois leathering the dew from the varnish work. The brass work was polished, down to Jack Crossley's special task of keeping the pipes on the engine, down below and out of sight, agleam.

"Not me," said Fred. "Water is for fishes and no one else."

"How about you, Jack?"

Jack was game and stripped down but not before his master was already standing on the capping rail, preparing to dive. But instead of entering obliquely, Bobby slipped and plummeted vertically into the calm water.

"After him, Jack," shouted Fred, "he has gone too deep for him," remembering his single lung. Immediately Jack jumped in, plunged beneath the surface, caught hold of Bobby and brought him up.

Later Bobby confessed,

"I couldn't have stood that for long; I reckon you saved my life."

Jack had an extra ten bob in his pay packet that week – a small sum maybe, but a man as bold as Somerset probably valued his life at no more, as his eventual end would indicate.

Once, though, it was not so much Bobby's life but that of *Jolie Brise* herself that was in danger. It was a wild night, gusting Force 10 down the Lynher River. There was a dance in the village hall, from which Abram summoned his boys immediately to the quay at Antony Passage. There, out in the dark and the flying spray, was the silhouette of *Jolie Brise* drifting steadily and relentlessly backwards towards the rocks on the little headland they call Point.

The brothers put out in a rowing boat from the harbour, but were almost immediately swamped, abeam as they were to the relentless waves. They gained the harbour again and waited for the old ship's inevitable end.

But suddenly, from up-river, skimming through the dark, down-wind on the crest of the waves, came her owner in a light pram dinghy.

He had pursued her the mile or so from the landing beneath Ince Castle, perhaps having wandered down there after dinner before turning in in the safety of his own bedroom. Certainly, if that was so, his wife Betty waited in vain for his return that night, for as he came abreast the cutter he grabbed the bulwarks and swung himself aboard, leaving the pram dinghy to charge on to be splintered to matchwood on the rocks, perilously close just a hundred yards or so down-wind. Bobby started that engine which he hated so much and all through the night kept *Jolie Brise* just jogging there in Antony Passage, clear of the rocks which would undoubtedly have been her end had he been just a few minutes later. Whatever the frictions, whatever the rivalry, the Crossley brothers' respect for their Master was sealed that night.

Just this year I visited Ince Castle, drove down the drive where Platainey used to navigate the Austin 12, and was met by the castle's present owner, Viscount Boyd of Merton. As Lennox Boyd he had been one of this country's finest Colonial Secretaries, and indeed he has on his walls, hanging inconsequentially, photographs of himself in Cabinet groups under various distinguished Prime Ministers, where another man might hang group photographs of himself in rugger teams. He and his wife can be proud too of their garden at Ince, "finer than it has ever been", and also, amazingly, of one of the finest collections of walking-sticks in the country.

But all these reasons for pride – small and great – in that amiable man were eclipsed, that afternoon when I visited him, by his pride in living in a house and on a river associated with Somerset and *Jolie Brise*.

"Where did Bobby Somerset store his sails in the winter?" I asked.

"Here," replied Lord Boyd, pointing at the floor of his elegant drawing-room (in fairness, be it explained, on the ground floor of the castle beneath the main rooms).

Soon he drove me down to the landing-stage on that cold February afternoon, a large man shivering just a little in the tropical suit which he had yet to shed, having just returned from Kenya. At the end of the landing-stage, standing with happy incongruity with their feet in a glistening sea of mud, were two tall white posts with gold onion tops.

"Like something from Venice," I said. "Did Somerset put them there?"

"No," said Lord Boyd, "they came from our hotel in Venice, but over there," pointing up the estuary, "was where *Jolie Brise* used to lie" – or lay until that fateful night when she dragged her moorings down-stream past Jupiter Point and Antony Passage, nearly to end her days on the rocks; because from then on fresh moorings were laid for her opposite Antony Passage in deeper, more sheltered water, where the Crossley family could keep an eye on her.

Bobby, always an innovator, acquired a specially built high speed tender with an outboard motor, capable of fifteen knots. He might have one of the most antiquated of vessels afloat, but at least his yacht's tender was *le dernier cri* and quite the envy of the most up-to-date yachtsmen. It was certainly a far cry from the heavy dinghy *Jolie Brise* had in tunny fishing days. Amusingly, today we carry no outboard motor – and gladly so, noisy things that they are, because we received a generous cheque from a donor on condition that we never would.

However, the happiest days of all must have been when Betty Somerset was aboard, because she chose her weather carefully and the crew could be sure of no buffetings at sea. And, on one such of many days, Bobby's son Johnny caught his first mackerel. Joy reigned supreme, but Jack Crossley unknowingly came on deck to fetch a fresh bucket of water – and tossed the bucket, complete with trophy, into the sea. Johnny was inconsolable and Jack at his wit's end. *Jolie Brise* by now was creaming along at eight knots and certainly at no speed for fishing. In desperation Jack promised to catch Johnny another fish and, with little prospect of success, tossed the line over, but miraculously, even at that speed, succeeded in hooking one.

So life became serene again – at least on deck. Down below Platainey grumbled and groaned at his press-ganged role as ship's steward. What a job for a chaffeur indeed! He cooked and cleaned but when it came to making up beds he drew the line, although he would grudgingly supply the sheets, none too clean or dry, for the gentry to make up their own.

Happy days, family days. But all dipped beneath the horizon now. Johnny was to be killed in the Second World War and only Jack Crossley survives from those summer days at sea.

CHAPTER TWENTY-FOUR

Regatta Time

This picture of an ocean racer off duty omits the framework which held it together. *Ocean* racing maybe did not occupy *Jolie Brise* all of the time, but racing in some form or another was the incentive for her summer cruising. As in the days when Martin in *Jolie Brise* and Warneford in *Vanda* sailed from regatta to regatta, so too in Somerset's day. There would be quite a coastwise traffic of yachts sailing from Cowes to Torquay and on to Plymouth; and it was the regattas of those rival sailing centres which were the spur.

It is hard to appreciate today quite how such an individual boat as *Jolie Brise* could become a part of inshore racing. She was at her best, when racing in sheltered waters, either with a lot of wind or none at all. However in other conditions she would be just as likely stubbornly to refuse to come alive. There were days, even weeks, when she would not even leave her mooring, serving simply as a floating residence for her master while he raced in twelve-metres.

This his crew welcomed. A week in Cowes with no racing and just the brass to be kept polished was a holiday to be cherished. *Jolie Brise*, had she a heart (and she has), would have welcomed it too, for it was in class racing round the buoys that Bobby Somerset's tiller hand and his eye for a lifting sail learnt their cunning – cunning put to good use whenever he brought his heavy long-distance ocean racer to the starting line. One Cowes week he helmed *Evaine*. He was known for only racing in a boat if he could helm. Arrogant perhaps, but justified when one day in Plymouth he brought home first a member of the twelve-metre class known for being last.

Distant days those regatta days, times when sailing almost achieved the status of a spectator sport. Postcards of pilot cutters like *Jolie Brise* racing off the beaches of Normandy resorts, the occasional line of Marcel Proust, like a breath of marine air through a hotel window, Wilson Steer's out-of-focus canvases of yachts at Cowes, Dufy's brilliant dashes on bright blue canvas – all evoke regattas on both sides of the Channel in which *Jolie Brise* at one time or another had taken part.

Cowes alone remains with any degree of style, the style which Somerset set so much store by, but which was thwarted on one occasion. They had arrived in the Solent one wet windy morning in time for the start of Cowes Week. They dropped anchor smartly in Cowes roads and Bobby ordered, "Lower the main." The halyards were let loose but nothing happened. With the wet, the manilla ropes had expanded in the blocks and the sail refused to budge.

Something of these days came back to me when, a month ago, we sailed in from Plymouth up the Needles Passage with all sail set, one windy but sheltered Sunday afternoon. Jack Crossley sat at the helm like a cat with cream as we overtook everything in sight. He had not sailed *Jolie Brise* for fifty years, nor been to the Solent since. The Solent had changed most certainly, but the old boat not at all.

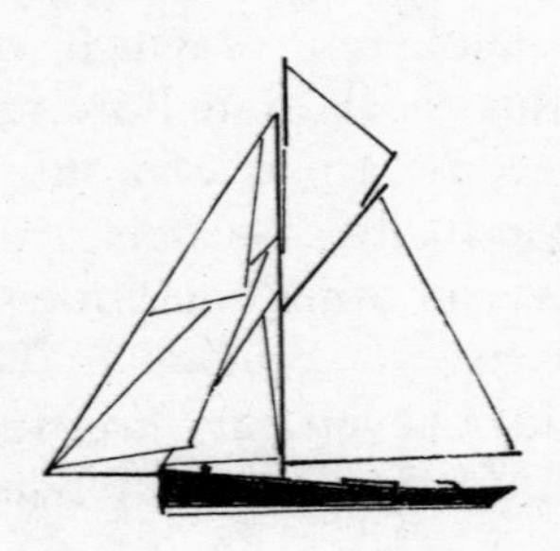

CHAPTER TWENTY-FIVE

The 1930 Fastnet

1930 brought ocean racing quite as exciting for *Jolie Brise* as had been her double win in 1929. The Fastnet of that year saw her at her most glorious. Her crew were: Bobby Somerset, Rose-Richards, Maclean Buckley, Jack and Tom Ponsonby (who had sold *Penboch* to Bobby), Eric Bush and the two paid hands. Eric Bush, you will remember, was with her in the 1927 race, with Martin at the helm. He is still with us today and it is to him that I am indebted for this crew-list. It is rare to know precisely who was on board for one of Somerset's races, so it is good, in this instance, to have the record more or less complete.

It was as eccentric a gathering as ever at the race's start at Cowes. There were just nine yachts: *Ariel* from France, and *Lelanta* from America, the big *Viking*, then *Magnet*, *Maitenes II*, *Amaryllis* (Martin's old boat) and the two redoubtable old rivals *Ilex*, with her engineer crew, and *Jolie Brise* herself. They had a spanking run eastward down Spithead to the Forts, but from the very beginning fresh winds from the west were gathering momentum. Within the first hour both *Jolie Brise* and *Neptune* had their spinnakers blown out, but they were to have little further need for them in the days to come. The first casualty was *Magnet*, who put back to port before clearing the western end of the island. *Maitenes*, still sporting her despised Bermudan rig, kept close in to the coast, short tacking westward before putting into Newlyn for repairs to her mainsail slides. Double reefed, *Jolie Brise* tacked deep into Mounts Bay. The thought was in everybody's minds, should they go on?

"What do you think?" said Bobby to skipper Fred Crossley.

"She can take it if we can," came the famous reply – so true, so often, in so many ocean-racing situations, for it is always the crew that is weaker than the ship. And so that dogged bowsprit bucketed its way out of Mounts Bay.

Clear of the troubled waters of Land's End, they could just lay a course for the Fastnet, close-hauled with a fresh breeze. In pursuit behind them were *Ilex*, *Maitenes* (out of Newlyn again), and the large, graceful *Amaryllis*. Fred's optimism was soon rewarded with a free wind and sunshine.

Jolie Brise was twelve hours on the long run home as *Ilex* rounded the Rock with a soft off-shore breeze. *Maitenes* was less fortunate, but by the time all the four survivors rounded, a gale from the north-west had sprung up, giving all the problems which a helmsman dreads, particularly if he has a large gaff mainsail and a delicate helm to nurse home.

Maitenes trailed warps and buckets and had her oil bags out to control her speed in relation to the chasing seas. *Ilex* unbelievably had no reef in her mainsail, too unwieldy an operation perhaps, with her great boom hanging out over the water and problems of rounding into the wind. Instead they scandalized her gaff, that is, dropped the peak to reduce the main's effectiveness, while two men fought her kicking tiller, before at last they had to take the mainsail down completely and replace it with a staysail set as a trysail.

Amaryllis, now in Admiralty hands and therefore something of a rival to the soldiers on *Ilex*, carried away her topmast, but, unbelievable to weight-conscious modern-day ocean racers, she had a spare spar on board which she duly had in place and active again, just fifty miles short of Plymouth.

And what of *Jolie Brise*, romping ahead, apparently with no problem? She was first across the line and first on corrected time. To say it had been her race and her weather is not altogether true; it had been a hard beat down-Channel in a boat far from ideal for windward work, but that phrase, "She can take it if we can", had won the race for, the hard beat over, from Land's End to the Rock and home again had been her race all the way.

Somerset had won two years running in a boat built for work and not play and deemed to be hopelessly outclassed. It was a major achievement. To have won, as she had now, the Fastnet Race three times placed *Jolie Brise* in a position which is still unique in the history of ocean racing and which, in these days of rapid evolution, is likely so to remain.

CHAPTER TWENTY-SIX

The 1930 Santander

But enough of home waters – and back to the deep sea. The second and last Santander found *Jolie Brise* again at the Plymouth starting line. Could she win the Fastnet and the Santander in the same year yet again? There was a strong wind from the south-west and the hulls of the fourteen starters were often lost deep in the swell which built up off the Plymouth breakwater. Indeed, conditions were probably identical to the start of the 1981 Transatlantic Race, which *Jolie Brise* attended in the role of elder statesman. Not knowing quite what to expect, Bobby Somerset had put up the topsail set over a reefed mainsail, a familiar trick, since the topsail can be far more quickly handed in the lee of the main than can a second reef be taken down. *Ilex* had no reef but had her ear-rings reefed in preparation. It seems that, as in the 1930 Fastnet, her soldier crew were either too buccaneering to consider shortening sail or a trifle shaky at the thought of the complexities of the operation. *Maitenes* was smug and snug with two reefs in that Bermudan main of hers.

Ilex was proud of her jockeying position at the start and let draw with one minute in hand, heading for the line but, as an observer on board her reported, with just forty yards to go, *Jolie Brise* "looking black and sinister" sailed through her lee. Of all Somerset's skills, that of making a clever start, simulating a move to decoy others, lurking where not expected, made him paramount as a helmsman in this most demanding of all aspects of the race.

Jolie Brise was soon 200 yards ahead and to windward of *Ilex*. *Neptune* and *Maitenes* were astern of *Jolie Brise*, *Uraba III* well down to leeward with *Karin* astern of her, and the bigger boats *Lelanta* and *Avocet* only now coming up to leeward.

Somerset on *Jolie Brise* had resolved to point as close to the wind as possible, even though it was within his grasp to lay a course for Ushant. A pessimist, he was anticipating a more southerly turn in the wind, and he wanted to establish himself in a strong windward position. However, *Ilex* was already on course for that wild island which marks the turning point between the English Channel and the Bay of Biscay and which opens wide the course to Spain and Santander. Others of the fleet had decided to sail further westward still, gambling for a favourable change in the wind.

When evening came, Somerset had a little bit of fun. The wind had eased and *Ilex* had her great jackyard topsail up. *Jolie Brise* by now had slipped to leeward of her, surer at last of a wind to take her round into the Bay. But a squall blew up from the west and those on *Ilex* saw *Jolie Brise*'s jib-headed topsail coming down. Quickly, before the wind reached them, they handed their more unwieldy jackyarder. The squall passed, *Jolie Brise* set her topsail again but, and here was Somerset playing tricks, very shortly afterwards the crew of *Ilex* were to see *Jolie Brise*'s topsail come down yet again. Expecting more wind but puzzled at not seeing any other sign of it, they yet again pulled down their jackyarder and no sooner had they done so than *Jolie Brise*'s far handier jib-header was sent up yet again. The trick had worked, and rather more successfully than perhaps Bobby could have hoped, because *Ilex*'s exhausted soldiers totally failed to set their jackyarder a third time. As one of her crew remarked, "It didn't see why it should be hauled up and down the mast merely to keep time with a paltry jib-header on *Jolie Brise*. It just wouldn't move. We stroked it, kicked it, tried everything in vain, but it was no use and we just walked away and left it. We kept going back and pretended to fumble with the rigging. Suddenly we turned round, gripped it and forced it up the mast before it had time to realize what was happening." Fortunately Somerset's games were at an end, because the same eye-witness reports that otherwise *Ilex*'s crew would soon have been lying in a state of exhaustion all round the deck.

Lighter winds saw the fleet heading into the Bay, with *Jolie Brise* over to the west in a favourable position, but *Ilex* had the stronger tide close by the shore and, with lucky flukes of wind, she drew ahead.

However, by the afternoon of that second day both *Ilex* and *Jolie Brise* were drifting backwards towards Plymouth, rather than forging ahead, Santander-bound.

In the evening a Spanish destroyer came to talk to them both and grudgingly conceded that *Ilex* was in the lead. Later the wind backed to the south-east and there was a strong tide running in both yachts' favour. Ahead lay bright blue seas speckled with tunny fishermen, redolent of *Jolie Brise*'s earlier life. However, as so often, all was not sweetness and light and by the evening of the Tuesday the wind boxed the compass not once, but twice. Wednesday was misty and found *Jolie Brise* sailing into a shrouded Santander, guided by the high inland mountains rising above the mists. The Club Maritimo is a stately place in its tiny off-shore castle and it was still a place of Royal welcome with destroyers in attendance and sea-planes fussing round. *Jolie Brise* was first home. Was this to be a second triumph – the Fastnet *and* the Santander in the same year? *Jolie Brise*'s crew looked out from the bar of the yacht club across the rock-strewn estuary to the guard ships, skinning their eyes for the next sail to come. It was a relief when the larger *Neptune* proved to be the next across the line, but a little worrying when next out of the mist came *Ilex*. And so that second Santander Race was not to be a triumph for *Jolie Brise* after all but for the smaller *Ilex*, who had won on corrected time, by just four minutes. No one could, from now on, say that ocean racing was an inexact and undemanding sport.

Ilex's crew came ashore to be plied with champagne and the congratulations of *Jolie Brise*'s company, whom they found the most cheerful losers they had ever met. After all, what is four minutes between friends over a distance of some 500 miles? Nothing indeed beside the outliers of the gathering clouds of war. For this, just the second, was to be the last Santander Race of those inter-war years. With the impending Spanish Revolution, Royal patronage and Royal prestige and Royal hospitality could no longer be offered to that little band of sportsmen setting out in their ocean racers from Plymouth Sound.

Jolie Brise was not to return to Santander until 1979, when I met her there with a relief crew, steamer-borne from England towards those selfsame cloud-piercing mountains. For the first time as her skipper I pointed her seawards, sailing out past the castellated University on a sparkling afternoon, and I wondered if those oak planks beneath me remembered those two Santander races so many years before.

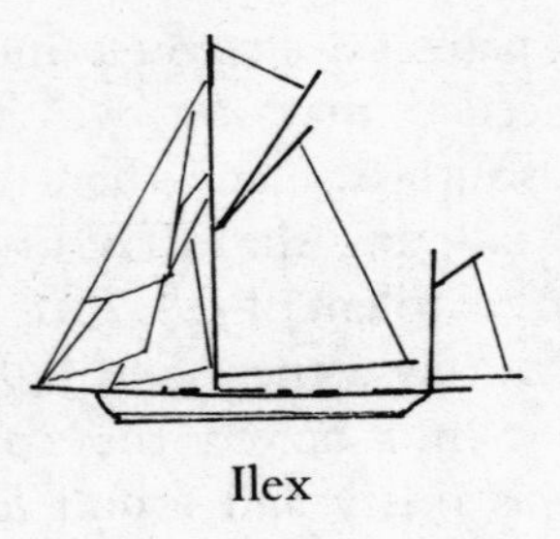

Ilex

CHAPTER TWENTY-SEVEN

The 1931 Fastnet

My pursuit of *Jolie Brise*'s fortunes in the 1931 Fastnet Race took me this summer to the Royal Thames Yacht Club in Knightsbridge, where I met David Laurent Giles, having a drink on the quarter deck with a Dorset neighbour of mine who was contemplating building a new yacht; and I felt how reassuring it was that such conversations in such comfortable surroundings still continue. The age of the yachtsman is not dead.

But my reason for a word with David was not concerned with the 1980s and motor yachts, but with the 1930s and gaff cutters. David's father was the famous Jack Laurent Giles, designer of the revolutionary *Myth of Malham*, a remarkable evolution in the design of ocean racers. But he had, too, an eye for tradition, though he hated, as I do, the term "old gaffer". From his drawing-board came *Dyarchy*, perhaps the last flowering of the gaff cutter, or should one simply say "cutter", for according to Lloyds Register of Yachts, a cutter is still assumed to be gaff unless otherwise stated. Sailing in *Dyarchy* with Roger Pinckney, her owner, had first introduced me to sailing with a gaff rig and had induced a reverence both for the boat and for her designer. *Dyarchy* was built in 1939 as briefly before the Second World War as *Jolie Brise* had been before the First. The two boats are superficially dissimilar. *Jolie Brise* has a straight stem, *Dyarchy* a spoon bow; *Jolie Brise* has a counter and *Dyarchy* a transom, and *Jolie Brise* has twice *Dyarchy*'s displacement, but the family likeness is there, for there is an echo of *Jolie Brise* in *Dyarchy*'s sections. Jack Giles had measured *Jolie Brise* in 1928. He had "lifted her lines", perhaps much as Palladio would have measured some classical building in ancient Rome. It was perhaps this fact which gives rise to the myth that *Jolie Brise*'s lines had never been on paper before, when as we know, just a letter to Monsieur Paris in France could well have brought a copy of the original plans by return of post.

But it was not this first encounter of Jack Giles with *Jolie Brise* that interested me when I met his son David on that day in London. What interested me far more was his father's manuscript log of the 1931 Fastnet Race, for which he formed part of *Jolie Brise*'s crew. He handed it over with promises from me that I would treasure and return it, and inside I found the race-card for the seventh Fastnet Race, still headed just plain "Ocean Racing Club", for the R.O.R.C. was yet to achieve its Royal charter. Twenty starters are listed. The race is stated as being open to yachts of more than twenty-five feet and not exceeding sixty feet. "The preparatory flag 'Q' will be hoisted at 10.50 am and a gun fired. The Blue Peter will be broken out at 10.55 am and a gun fired. The starting gun will be fired and the Blue Peter hauled down at 11.00 am."

But after that final gun very little happened. It was a hot, calm day and for half an hour no yacht moved. On board *Water Gypsy* somebody played a guitar, a member of the crew of *Ilex* lounged round the deck in a loud pair of pyjamas, another was wearing a turban, while aboard *Jolie Brise* a large Mexican straw sombrero was seen nodding above the bulwarks. With such informality and inactivity did the Fastnet fleet affront the dignity of Cowes upon the Squadron starting line. But among that motley gathering was the new fifty-foot waterline Nicholson-designed cutter *Patience*, and at her helm, looking nostalgically at his old black cutter, was none other than E. G. Martin, sailing her for her owner, H. E. West. But it was to be a backward view that Martin cast at his old love, for throughout the race *Jolie Brise* was to be in the rearguard, as was his still older love *Amaryllis*.

Jolie Brise was eighth round the Old Castle Point Buoy and was well behind at the Bembridge Ledge. The light head-winds made them tack across to the Guernsey shore, praying for a change of wind. There was a complete flat calm until a long awaited southerly took her off on course for the Long Ships. It had been a tactical error making for the French shore and others of the fleet, short tacking down the English coast, fared better both with tides and winds.

They rounded the Fastnet on the Thursday evening. *Water Gypsy*,

Dorade, *Patience*, *Mistress* and *Highland Light* were ahead of them, but it was comforting to be in company with *Amaryllis*. Jack Giles' log notes become sketchy here: "Night dark and threatening. Wind working up gradually. Took in medium jib topsail and later topsail. Reefed as soon as light. Wind freed slowly to allow us to lay southerly course fairly comfortably, making for Seven Stones."

They rounded the Seven Stones in a vicious squall and freshening weather which was to punish the smaller yachts still astern. From thence the run to Plymouth was uneventful, but Jack Giles said sadly in his log that "at last the redoubtable *Jolie Brise* had met her match. Of the six yachts already home, two were receiving many hours from her, and those bigger than herself had saved their time comfortably.

"She had not, of course, had her own weather, but I doubt whether the old-timer could have hoped to leave her modern competitors under any circumstances. True, she had held onto *Mistress* when the wind was light and ahead, but off the wind her maximum speed is probably two knots lower than that of other vessels of her size in the race and, whilst the leaders averaged some eight-and-a-half knots from the Fastnet to the finish, *Jolie Brise* never touched that speed."

Perhaps the young naval architect was being a little harsh and certainly another comment of his that "In *Jolie Brise* you have to send below for gum-boots when wind increases above Force 3" was totally inaccurate. But none the less the message was there loud and clear, the "old-timer" (then just eighteen years old compared with her present age of sixty-eight!) was outclassed at last. It was a hard pill to swallow and the pill really came in the shape of *Dorade*, not a traditional American schooner, such as those with which *Jolie Brise* had more or less held her own, but a relatively small yawl, designed by a man called Olin Stephens, whose name was to be as much a one to conjure with in the United States as was that of Laurent Giles at home in Britain.

It was *Dorade* who won on corrected time by an enormous margin. She came in astern of E. G. Martin in *Patience* and the American *Highland Light*, who in their own way stole the show. The two cutters were identical in size but Martin was able to nudge his boat across the line just one minute and eighteen seconds ahead of *Highland Light*, some achievement in a race of a distance of 615 miles.

But while *Jolie Brise*'s star was eclipsed by these newcomers, the darkness which fell on her was nothing beside that which fell on all the fleet when *Maitenes* finally made port. She had to tell of the loss of her co-owner, Colonel Hudson, the first fatality in this great ocean race, which *Jolie Brise* had helped to inaugurate and which, since 1931, she has not raced in again.

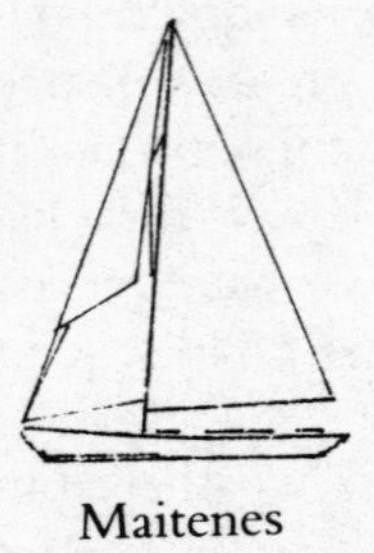

Maitenes

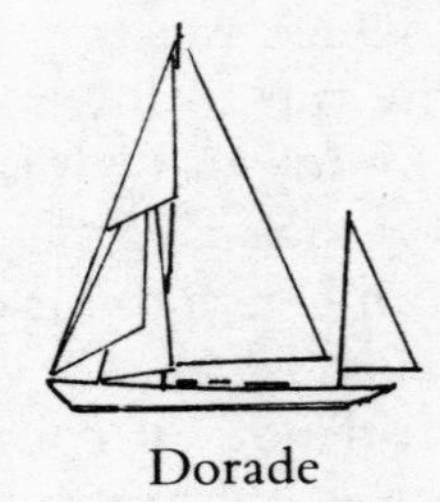

Dorade

CHAPTER TWENTY-EIGHT

The New World Again

Done? Finished? Of course not – even though *Jolie Brise*'s dull showing in the 1931 Fastnet would not be forgotten. Had Somerset been a pilot or a fisherman, he might have run his outmoded boat ashore and set a match to her the moment she ceased to serve her purpose. But he was a yachtsman and *Jolie Brise*, despite her ancestry, was a yacht. So, then, what was to be her fate? That decision at least could be delayed, because it had been decided that the Fastnet Race should become biennial rather than annual, and there was to be no Fastnet in 1932. But in the immediate future, what was in prospect? Gentle family sailing round the coast? Just a little cruising and picnics? No! Bobby decided to point her bowsprit across the Atlantic and to be cheeky enough to enter her in the 1932 Bermuda Race. She had been a strange enough entry, albeit vindicated by her showing, when Martin had brought her to the starting line in 1926. How would she seem in 1932 after six of the longest years in the history of yachting development? No matter, Bobby's sights were set. He had won the Fastnet in two consecutive years where Martin had only won once. Martin had taken her to America; so too would he. Martin had entered her for the Bermuda. Somerset would enter her for the Bermuda too. There must be a sense of *déjà vu* as in our mind's eye we follow in *Jolie Brise*'s wake across the Atlantic for a second time. However, it is to be a rapid trip because records are sparse. Unlike E. G. Martin, Somerset was reticent about putting pen to paper. But he was rather bolder in saying where he was going. Martin had slipped out of Falmouth six years before without committing himself to his destination, whereas in 1932 the *Yachting*

Monthly sported a beautiful full-page photograph of *Jolie Brise*, stating that she had been entered for the Bermuda Race and was expected shortly to leave England for America in company with another entrant, Major Rose-Richards' *Lexia* (Rose-Richards, you will remember, was a frequent and popular amateur member of *Jolie Brise*'s own crew).

On that outward voyage with Bobby were Francis Festing, later to be a Field-Marshal, Reggie West and David Robertson, who shortly afterwards repeated the trip in his own much smaller Norwegian double-ender *Escape*.

Relations on board seem to have been marred by just one incident. Half-way across the Bay of Biscay, Bobby Somerset took skipper Fred Crossley on one side and said that, in future, he and his mate were not to use the ship's lavatory but were to leave it for himself and his guests. The paid crew, he said, must content themselves with a bucket in the forecastle. Even in a relatively small boat with the shared rigours of a transatlantic passage, social distinctions were to be observed. Fred acquiesced, but told his Master that once returned to Plymouth he would never sail with him again.

However, all was sweetness and light as they picked up the Trades and set their running canvas, not this time the hinged yard, squaresail and raffee beloved of Martin, but hated by all others for the violent rolling which it induced. No, Somerset had contrived instead two small double spinnakers, one to starboard set upon a gooseneck and the other to port, set above the stowed mainsail, simply tethered to the mast by jaws. This arrangement was reasonably conventional, but not so the balloon spinnaker which surmounted all, set from the top of the topmast with an eighteen foot yard, tethered at its foot at a level just beneath the cross-trees with a jack-stay to the bowsprit end, a tack-line to the stemhead and braces aft. Particularly incongruous, on such a traditional ship, were three holes set in the middle of this miniature sky-scraping spinnaker, as was the latest fashion in the racing world for keeping spinnakers steady.

The venerable Mr Ratsey, white hair streaming in the wind, had come aboard *Jolie Brise* at Plymouth, from his equally famous cutter *Dolly Varden*, to inspect this ensemble himself. Like a Savile Row tailor, he had on many occasions paced these decks to see how his sails set and, with a few deft strokes of the chalk, sent them back to the cutting-room for improvements. Quite what he thought of this

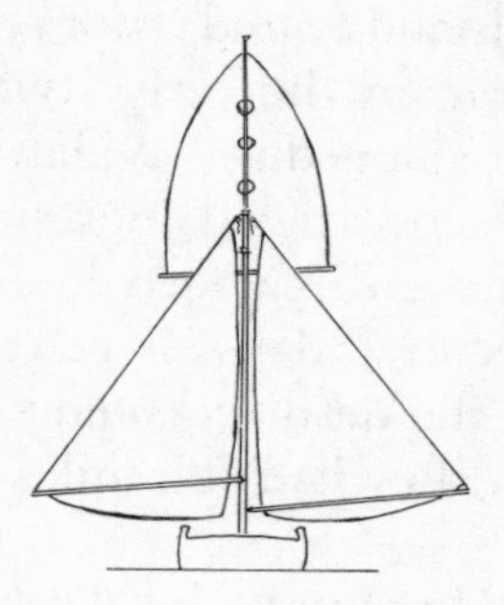

new running rig is not recorded, but if holes in spinnakers were good enough for the "J" Class yachts, they certainly were for *Jolie Brise*. Even young Jack Crossley happily induced the opprobrium of longshoremen at Saltash by improvising holes in the running sail of his own little dinghy.

From great to small the fashion ruled, and as *Jolie Brise* settled herself into the way of the Trades, it turned out that the fashion served her well. With spinnaker to port, spinnaker to starboard and spinnaker aloft, she rolled hardly at all and, in one period of seven days, ran for 1,226 miles at an average speed of 175 miles a day, in considerable seas, with an average wind-speed of thirty miles. Major Rose-Richards in *Lexia* used the same arrangement but was less ecstatic about it.

Weston Martyr had yearned to visit English Harbour, Antigua on that first Atlantic crossing in 1926. In 1932 *Jolie Brise* was to do so. She arrived on 10th May, reputedly the first yacht to discover this, one of the world's loveliest harbours. She found a derelict dockyard hardly touched since Nelson's day and it could be that she was the first boat to enter there under sail flying the white ensign since Nelson's time. And that little band of Englishmen were greeted by Dr and Mrs O'Mahony, recently posted there and the only white people in that deserted ghostly paradise.

It was the sort of landfall and fleeting friendship which was to leave a memory to last a lifetime – certainly in the mind of Mrs O'Mahony, who writes to me from Eastbourne. She and her husband, clad in their pyjamas, saw *Jolie Brise* off early on the morning of 13th May. Now English Harbour is much visited, well known and well restored, but the image of those cheerful young men, moored among the ruins in a black cutter from England, is still crisp in the lens of memory.

How *Jolie Brise* made her landfall at Montauk Port and how they were received in Long Island Sound is not recorded.* Somerset had made the same crossing in the early 'twenties in the schooner *Diablesse*. He had been shipped as navigator. His experience then had extended only to the occasional noon sight in fishing craft. The crew had more and more disparaged his work with the sextant when, on three consecutive days, it placed the yacht's position quite at variance with the dead reckoning. But when at last they found Montauk Point, they had 800 miles on the log on a course of only 620.

Somerset's sights had been right, but *Diablesse*'s loss of three days' sailing remained a mystery – until the Admiralty Hydrographer explained that she had probably found unusual outlying south- rather than north-going eddies in the Gulf Stream. So as Somerset now sailed *Jolie Brise* towards Montauk Point, he must have done so with the circumspection bred of that earlier experience.

The social round in Long Island Sound must have been as gay as ever, and *Jolie Brise* herself something both of an old friend and a celebrity – winner not just once but three times of the now internationally established Fastnet Race, and with not just one but three transatlantic crossings under her keel. The younger, more gregarious Somerset could hardly have been less welcome than was Martin in his time.

And so *Jolie Brise* mustered with the rest of the Bermuda fleet yet again. How would she fare on her way to Bermuda? Would she be placed, or would it just be a first step on the long voyage home, having shown the flag and been comfortably placed somewhere half-way down the fleet?

* – or so I thought. A letter to the O'Mahonys from Francis Festing has been found since going to press. It reads, "From English Harbour we had a very good passage to the Virgin Islands . . . from there we were nine days to New York. We were lucky in our weather and only had one squall, which caught us with spinnaker and topsail set. However, we only broke the spinnaker boom, so we were lucky. We had a wonderful time in New York and it was great fun living like a millionaire, if only for a day or so."

CHAPTER TWENTY-NINE

The 1932 Bermuda Race

I have found no report of that summer day in 1932 when yet another Bermuda Race began. Doubtless *Jolie Brise* jockeyed for position, "dark and sinister", a gaff cutter among the schooners, and doubtless too on that day she sailed close by the huge schooner *Adriana*, too large to enter the race and, after some argument, permitted to sail in a class of her own. On board *Jolie Brise* were two Americans, Paul Hammond and Sherman Hoyt. It had been Hammond's schooner *Nina* that Hoyt had raced against *Jolie Brise* in the 1929 Fastnet and so now the two were getting a taste of the old cutter. It was Hoyt, too, who had given Martin and his fellow competitors their racing instructions in 1926. At the helm of *Adriana*, Clarence Kozlay would have spared a look, and perhaps a wave, at Bobby Somerset, sitting on his helmsman's bench, planning his position at the line. How *Jolie Brise* fared on that first day again is not recorded, but in the early hours of the next morning she was reaching with a strengthening breeze, well ahead of some of the big schooners, as well as the biggest of all – *Adriana*.

They were shortening sail when Hoyt looked astern and saw flares climbing into the sky some miles away. *Jolie Brise* was sailing well and it was tempting to dismiss these as simply Yankee high spirits. But Bobby Somerset decided to put the boat about and he set off back – reeling off preciously gained miles, jettisoning his place in the race for what might yet prove to be a trivial cause. But, as the two ships drew closer together, flares were replaced by the sight of flames leaping from what proved to be *Adriana* in the grips of that most terrible of hazards – a fire at sea.

Imagine the terror upon that schooner. Her paid crew were off watch asleep in the forecastle and her fireplace in the saloon had been banked up. Situated on the bulkhead behind it was the ship's oilskin locker, in a sensible place, one might think, for drying wet clothes. But on that fateful night, at a time when oilskins were literally oil skins, and not the plastic of today, that bulkhead over-heated and the oilskins caught fire and dropped into a coil of manilla rope. The fire fanned rapidly throughout the ship. Many below were asleep while those on deck had no warning until it came licking through the hatchways. Before the days of ubiquitous radio, self-inflating life-rafts, radar and all our other life-saving aids, the man who sent up those flares must have done so with little hope either of help or survival. As the flames reached the deck, so the freshening reaching wind made them roar at the rigging and the sails. As the halyards burnt through, sails fell to the deck, to add both to the confusion and the flames.

As Bobby approached this tragic sight, reaching down the schooner's weather side, he could see people struggling to launch a boat, putting out spinnaker booms, anything that would carry them away from their floating furnace.

The prospect of bringing his own boat alongside *Adriana* in a sizeable swell was hazardous enough – after all, even the French pilots never brought their boats alongside ships at sea – but the idea of entangling the two ships and catching fire as well was still more horrible to contemplate. Much must have raced through Somerset's mind as he mustered all his courage and his experience to the task. Just after the war he had suffered dismasting in a winter gale in a Lowestoft sailing smack, of which he was both the owner and the third hand – with, incidentally, the former boot-boy from his house at Eton as cook. On that occasion, a fellow smack had come to give assistance but, reaching under her counter, her head had been caught and only by rapid easing of sheets had a serious collision been averted. Closer contact then had been abandoned. But now, as Master rather than third mate, Bobby faced a similar situation, and one in which it was for him to play the role of the rescuer rather than the ship in need.

One thing was certain, however, an attempt had to be made. Once turned towards those flares the die had been cast. No lowering of dinghies or standing off would meet the occasion. There was no time for debate, the operation must be bold and swift. What would you have done, you at home, sitting in your armchair? Lowered the sails and started the engine? For those of us not obliged always to manoeuvre under sail it would have been tempting, but probably wrong. No, the drama which was about to unfold was to be in the true traditions of great encounters under sail.

So *Jolie Brise* came down on *Adriana*'s weather side, reaching fast, the crew sheeting in the mainsheet for all they were worth, and two men ready by the back-stays to bring the one forward and tension the other, as Somerset wound her round the counter of the stricken ship, sweeping through 180 degrees and rapidly letting out the mainsheet onto the reciprocal course. Momentum must be maintained, otherwise she would be in irons in the lee of the schooner and unable to pull away again. Many of *Adriana*'s sails were tumbled to the deck, presenting no screen from the wind, but none the less *Jolie Brise*'s headsails were set aback and with a sickening crunch the two hulls crashed together.

The cross-trees and rigging of the two ships fouled one another and the tarred lanyards on the dead-eyes of *Jolie Brise*'s main shrouds took fire. But there was nothing to be done, no order to be given because immediately *Jolie Brise* made contact the crew of *Adriana* leapt from deck to deck. The cook, it is said, a Peruvian Indian, was stark naked and brandishing a huge knife. As suddenly as she arrived, *Jolie Brise* was thrown away again from the schooner's side and sailed on from beneath her flaming lee. To the cutter's crew were added perhaps some fifteen terrified, relieved, certainly disorganized people and it was only then as *Jolie Brise* pulled away that a solitary figure was seen making his way round the flaming schooner's mainmast – *Adriana*'s helmsman, Clarence Kozlay. How different had been his part in this great encounter than his helming of the schooner across the start in Long Island Sound, so few hours before. It was he who had kept *Adriana* on a steady course, so that Somerset could have a hope of plucking her crew aboard. Screened by the tumbled mainsail and the boom sagging on the deck, he had not been visible from *Jolie Brise*; but now as he deserted the helm at last and made his way forward came the explanation of *Adriana*'s steady course and, with it, a large proportion of the reason for the success of the operation. Having made the leeward rail at last, he jumped as *Jolie Brise* slipped away. His fingers clasped the capping rail but he fell short. Sherman Hoyt threw him a line which he briefly grasped, but as the sails filled and the cutter gathered momentum, leaving astern the all-too-contagious flames, Clarence Kozlay slipped away into the dark and the waves.

After the drama came sickening peace and a slow dawn. *Adriana*'s crew sat huddled below. Two life-belts from *Jolie Brise* dotted the empty waves, sad symbols of rescue for the lost man. With daylight came no sight of him, but there was the schooner, peaceful now, steadily burning, to the casual glance as fine and as elegant as ever, her sails perhaps a little strangely stowed and her boom at a drunken angle. But, flames apart, such strange normality would shortly disappear in this schooner doomed to die.

Lost, one ship, one man, one race. Dawn too had revealed *Jolie Brise*'s crushed port bulwarks and battered quarter. Sadly, Somerset set sail back to Montauk Point.

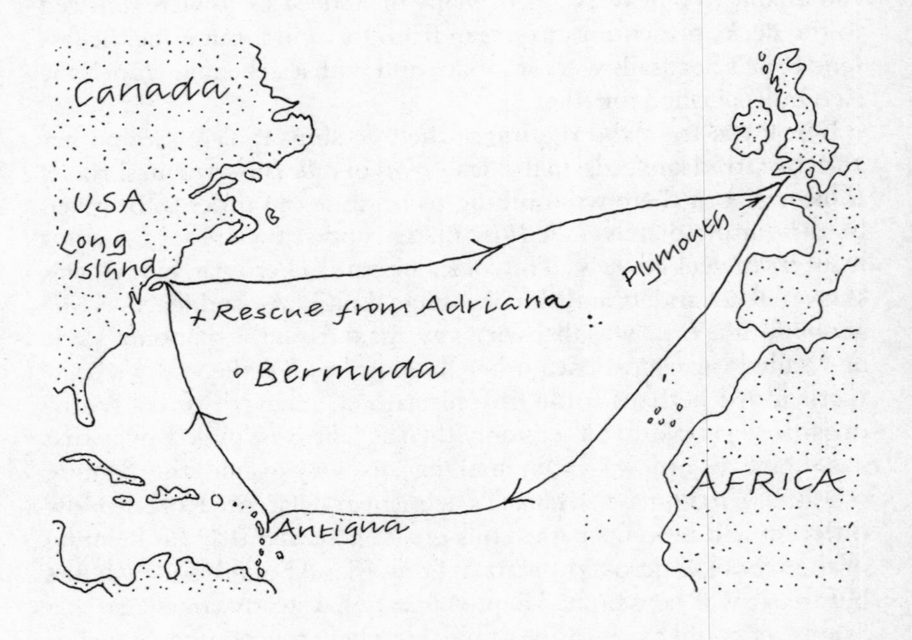

CHAPTER THIRTY

Homeward Bound and Farewell

They reported *Adriana*'s loss at Newport, and also *Jolie Brise*'s retirement from the race, before going to nearby Bristol for repairs. These included rebuilding a large proportion of her port quarter, which has subsequently been replaced again twice, for, like an old war-wound, it persistently gives trouble.

To Somerset and *Jolie Brise* came all the honour that a nation could muster. From the President of the United States, a gold watch. From the Cruising Club of America, the Blue Water Medal. Two years later, from the State Department, a special life-saving medal, and, from another quarter, a set of sheet winches. *Jolie Brise* was used to the Blue Water Medal, since Martin had been awarded it for his voyage in her in 1926. But she was not used to sheet winches, they were never fitted and she remains innocent of such newfangled devices to this day. She might have been placed in the Bermuda Race; she might have won. Certainly it had seemed to be her weather and her course, straight as a die with a reaching wind, but this, her retirement from her last great ocean race, was a far better thing than she had ever done, and they had every reason to be proud of her as she set her bowsprit homeward towards Plymouth.

Sherman Hoyt came too. A small man, like myself, he found the ten-foot tiller a heavy task and claimed to have walked many miles up and down the helmsman's duck-board. At times they hove to, taking the journey home gently. The voyage was enlivened by an encounter with the Cunarder *Berengaria*, who circled closely round them and courteously informed them of their position. Bobby knew precisely what it was in any event, or he thought he did, and with accustomed cheek signalled back, "Can *we* be of any assistance?"

The arrival in Plymouth and journey home to Ince Castle went smoothly, with Customs formalities waved aside. It was a genial return to home waters, until Sherman Hoyt set out to return to America again, to find that Bobby had not gone through the formality of having his American passport stamped, so that *Jolie Brise* was guilty of smuggling in, albeit unwittingly, an illegal immigrant.

Despite a happy homecoming, two eras were about to be closed. One of Bobby Somerset's reasons for going to America had been to see their ocean racers at close hand, and, while there, to purchase the schooner *Nina*, which the yachting press was already confidently expecting him to enter in the next Fastnet. His marriage to that notorious schooner was to be short-lived, and in fact he never brought her to these shores, but certainly his marriage with *Jolie Brise* was at an end, as was the long partnership between himself and the brothers Crossley. Though it had only been a storm in a lavatory, crossing the Bay of Biscay earlier in the year, Fred *had* said that he would make do with a bucket in the forecastle but, after that season, would never sail with Somerset again, and he was to be true to his word.

"Come across to the States with me and pick up *Nina*," Bobby had confidently said.

"No, sir, I stay here, I meant what I said," was Fred's reply. And he rejected too the normal ten-shillings-a-week retainer which he received during the winter, for he and Bobby Somerset were not to have another season together.

Once, sailing up the Tamar, a friend had asked Bobby's advice. He wanted to marry and he wanted to have a boat. He could not afford to do both. Which should he do? "Marry," came the reply, "because you can always say 'no' to a wife but never to a boat. If your boat wants something she must have it." Certainly, in her five years with Somerset *Jolie Brise* was never refused anything. Many years later Somerset was to devise a formula to arrive at the cost of maintaining any given boat. Could it have been applied to *Jolie Brise*? "Of course not, I kept accounts for the first few months and then gave up."

When he parted company with *Jolie Brise*, Bobby Somerset did not sail seriously again for sixteen years. Like Martin, he must have felt that any boat after *Jolie Brise* would be an anticlimax.

However, Bobby did create a memento of his racing years in *Jolie Brise*. The Jolie Brise Cup, which he presented to the Royal Ocean Racing Club in 1933, was originally intended to be awarded to the most successful boat which had entered the Fastnet Race with no chance of winning, due to the handicap system. It still features at the prize giving after each Fastnet Race, a happy reminder of a boat – and a man – not given to conformity.

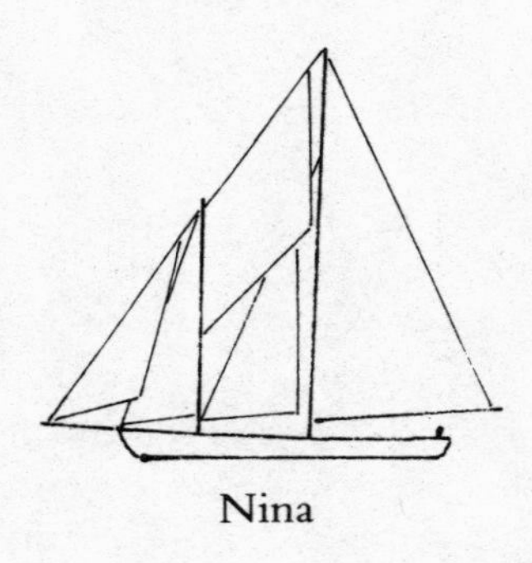

Nina

PART SIX

1932–1938

CHAPTER THIRTY-ONE

Brief Engagement

On a mellow autumn afternoon a neat, varnished carvel-built dinghy set a bright white lug sail main. A brilliant dot in the middle of Portsmouth Harbour, she was sailing inland towards the blue misty skyline of Portsdown Hill. There were two people in that little dinghy, one a girl and the other a man, well tanned from years abroad. Old "wooden-wall" frigates eclipsed the dinghy but, emerging into the sunlight again, the girl's hand on the helm and her other hand on the mainsheet took firmer grip as, now close-hauled, the dinghy headed towards Fareham Creek. In khaki shorts and woollen pullover, this was Joan again, a young woman now, with a book on sailing to her name; and that book had been read by an Air Force officer, far away on the North-West Frontier, who now sat amidships on the dinghy's thwart.

He had written to her, been asked to lunch that day and caused the rise of a maternal eyebrow when he had absent-mindedly wiped his knife and fork with his table napkin, as if brushing away Indian dust.

"Hardly necessary, Squadron Leader," had come Joan's mother's mild reprimand. But now they were alone in Joan's dinghy, exploring the Portsmouth creeks in the autumn sun.

"I do believe it's *Jolie Brise*," said Joan. There ahead of them, moored off Vosper's yard, was that distinctive black silhouette which had first so thrilled her when she saw it from the Gosport Ferry six years before.

"I have always had a crush on that boat," she explained. "She has won the Fastnet three times, crossed the Atlantic four, been first and second in the Santander and made a dramatic rescue from a ship at sea." Her companion was reassuringly enthusiastic too as they scudded past her and saw, first sight confirmed, the words *Jolie Brise* tucked beneath her counter, where really only fishes, mermaids and girls in small dinghies might hope to read them. Yes, *Jolie Brise* had come back to Portsmouth waters again. Bobby Somerset had sold her to one John Gage. His was to be an ownership of just over a year.

There is little printed evidence of this brief ownership. Lloyds Register of Yachts reads simply, "Lt. J. F. B. Gage, RNR," and gives the address, "Southbrook, Havant, Hants". No club is given after his name. In Sherman Hoyt's memoirs comes the simple statement that, in the Fall of 1932, Hoyt had joined Bobby Somerset aboard *Jolie Brise* in Brest.

"We returned to Plymouth for survey and to effect the sale of *Jolie Brise* to John Gage, and I sailed with him back to his home-port in the Solent." Thus, so far as I can find, run the only two printed references to John Gage's ownership.

But if you are expecting John Gage to have no more than a walk-on part in this long, well-peopled, drama of *Jolie Brise*'s life, his appearance, though brief, is none the less vivid. For it seems that Gage was a character who might, according to which angle you looked at him, have been created either by Dornford Yates or P. G. Wodehouse.

Imagine him, a large man, striding into a motor-car sales-room. He is married to Griselda, daughter of Sir Godfrey Payne, and, as a serving Army officer, had gained his Colonel's displeasure for marrying at an age deemed to be too young. He transfers to a more tolerant regiment and, thence, to the RNR. But in his easy way of life such problems matter little and uppermost in his mind as he walks round the car showroom are the problems of choosing the right car and finding a crew for his new boat. A Mr Bailey comes forward to help him and together they review the merits of the latest MG, Alvis, Fraser Nash, or a Bentley perhaps. Finally, imagine him installed behind a vertical steering-wheel and long, green louvered bonnet, with Mr Bailey on the seat beside him. Gage tests the model on the open road. Back at the showroom, almost absent-mindedly, Gage produces his cheque-book and says, "She will do well enough; how much do I make it out for?", and as Mr Bailey scurries round, adds, "Well, you say you sail a little, so come and join me on my new boat."

And so Bailey was press-ganged for duty on *Jolie Brise*, more or less willingly. His boss was quite prepared to give him the time off to help crew for such a good customer. Indeed, it seemed that whenever Gage wanted him to sail with him, the process would be repeated – the purchase of yet another car, the casual question, framed more or less as an order, "Come and sail with me", the questioning look at the boss, and the nod in return. In fact sometimes Mr Bailey was not so sure that he wanted to go sailing, but, "You must, my boy, it's good for business," came as something of a two-line whip to induce him to put to sea.

However, *Jolie Brise* was no hell-ship. Life aboard under new management was as pleasant as always. Sometimes Sir Godfrey Payne came, well provided with alcoholic refreshment for a gentlemanly trip to Cowes. Sometimes his daughter, Mrs Gage, would be aboard, sometimes indeed Mr Bailey's girlfriend and future wife Dorothy would be asked along too.

Skipper Briggs and Skipper Crossley, from the old days, were replaced now by Bill, who had served on the Shambles Light vessel. Bill controlled his impetuous master with the quiet authority of his calling. In place of Fred Crossley's catch-phrase, "If we can take it, she can," came Bill's oft-repeated quiet suggestion, "Time to get some sail off her, sir!"

There was racing round the buoys, but nothing which hit the headlines. On regular trips to France, John Gage, in good Dornford Yates tradition, would delight in his linguistic abilities and – much to the embarrassed amusement of his party – persist, in restaurants and cafés along the quay-side, in masquerading as a Frenchman without a word of English. It must have been particularly disconcerting when in contact with fellow English yachtsmen, who would patiently try to make themselves understood to someone they thought was a native. It was the sort of jape which was redolent of pre-war life. Perhaps we are all a little too serious now.

Back in home waters, Bill, poor man, had crushed his ribs and was unable to row the party ashore. John Gage was very solicitous of his well-being and wanted to get him to a doctor. He summoned a boatman, who quoted the outrageous sum of five pounds for the short trip from *Jolie Brise* to the quay, a price pretty steep even today, but positively mountainous at a time when a yacht's skipper had a wage of just three pounds a week. Gage said nothing and loaded his party aboard, but when on the quayside the boatman put out his hand for his fiver, Gage, still silent, simply picked him up, threw him in the harbour for his insolence, turned on his heel and walked away.

Conjecture, mere "cabin talk", tales from the forecastle? Perhaps, but it was all a long time ago and when no cups are won, no great voyages made, one summer's sailing merges into another and memories of a briefly known boat become indistinct. But certain trivia do stay in the mind of those who knew *Jolie Brise* in Gage's time: the zinc water-tank still occupied the centre of the saloon, under the cabin table; the insides of the bulwarks were painted red – as they are today – and the insides of the ventilators were painted pale blue, as we shall perhaps paint them next season. John Gage's son presides over the Edwardian splendour of a pub in Knightsbridge called Paxton's Head. Like a detective, I showed him a photograph of his father's old boat under full sail – as always, a stunning sight, and he was stunned at the sight of her, but could remember nothing, not even his father mentioning her. But that is not surprising; he was only just born when *Jolie Brise* sailed briefly into his father's life.

Dorothy, whose boyfriend Mr Bailey sold cars, is now his widow, and is happily still sailing her immaculate folk boat in Chichester Harbour. John Gage himself died seventeen years ago, but Griselda Gage looks out across the English Channel from her house on the sea-front at Hayling Island.

"It is such a long time ago," she writes, "that I have nothing but happy memories." What better phrase on which to end this brief chapter in *Jolie Brise*'s life?

CHAPTER THIRTY-TWO

Stars and Stripes

From Gosport, *Jolie Brise* went to Camper & Nicholson's at Southampton, She was sold to an American and from there she was lost to the researcher, somewhere upon the face of the globe.

In 1934, she appears in Lloyds Register of Yachts as belonging to "Mortimer", with no home-port and no address, but reference to the fitting of a new Gardner diesel engine. The entry in the 1935 edition of Lloyds is equally brief – as evasive, indeed, as Mr Tony Benn's entry in the *Who's Who* of today. But in the 1936 edition, we learn that Mortimer is, in fact, Mr Stanley Mortimer of 33 West 67th Street, New York, USA and *Jolie Brise*, formerly of Le Havre, formerly of Concarneau, formerly of Teignmouth, formerly of Plymouth and formerly of Gosport, now has emblazoned on the page her new home-port – New York, no less. Had she really crossed the Atlantic yet again? Was she, in those years, yachting in American waters?

I wrote to all the principal yachting magazines in America to enquire. I wrote to the New York Yacht Club – so prestigious that one wonders why it is not designated "Royal", until one remembers that America is no longer a colony – and had back a brief and courteous letter, simply headed "Secretary, New York Yacht Club", with no further address, in which Mr Vincent Monte-Sano II said that Mr Stanley Mortimer had not been a member of the Club and that he was sorry that he could not be of further help in my research.

I wrote too, despairingly, to "The Occupier" at that West 67th Street address and got no reply. Short of stepping on Concorde and showing, as I had in Knightsbridge, a photograph of *Jolie Brise* round the waterfronts of New York, there seemed no way in which I could hope to take the matter further. Fortunately I had an ally in Mr Charles H. Villas, Editor and Historian of the Cruising Club of America, who has already sailed into these pages in his cat-boat, admiring *Jolie Brise* on her first visit to Long Island Sound. Yes, he knew of Stanley Mortimer – son-in-law of Averell Harriman, statesman and financier, son of an early railroad king (Rudyard Kipling's *Captains Courageous* tale was rearing its head again). According to the Social Register, the American equivalent of our Debrett, listing America's untitled aristocracy, Stanley Mortimer graduated from Harvard in 1936, so it seemed that unless he was a very precocious young man he could not have taken on fifty-five tons of venerable French pilot cutter in 1934.

But, nothing daunted, Mr Vilas wrote to Mr Stanley Mortimer on my behalf and, oh joyous day! in due course I had a letter on my desk signed "Stanley Mortimer". But *Jolie Brise*'s Stanley Mortimer was not Averell Harriman's son-in-law, but that man's cousin. Stanley and Mortimer, it appears, are names that go together like a horse and carriage, and my letter had been passed from one bearer of that distinguished combination to another, there being one father and three cousins all bearing the same Christian name. The letter I had before me had the address "Normandy Farm, Litchfield, Connecticut "and it came from a man hale, hearty and eighty-four – a landscape-painter by profession, as well as a farmer who raised Corriedale sheep. That letter came into my grasp almost at the same time that I discovered an article in the Cruising Association library in London, from the 1935 *Yachting World* of September 27th, by Mr Stanley Mortimer's skipper, Michael Cumberlege. Combining the two together, the following picture emerges.

Jolie Brise had not returned to Long Island Sound and become a gentleman's conveyance to commute to New York City, but yes, she *had* flown the Stars and Stripes. Her official home-port *was* New York. But her keel slid now through the waters of the Mediterranean and, at the end of each season, back north again through the Bay of Biscay to winter in Southampton. It was from 1934 to 1938 that she flew the American flag and she came to do so in this way.

Still a legendary character in the harbours of the South of France is Admiral Cumberlege, who lived and sailed with his family on sizeable yachts. Indeed, one of his sons was born aboard (Mistral Cumberlege), to whom, also, I am indebted for information. He was named after that southern wind so characteristic of the French Mediterranean shore, because it was the mistral which had prohibited medical help getting aboard to his mother when she was giving birth to him, a tale irrelevant to our story but useful enough as an indication of the sort of man the Admiral was – he who had a quayside restaurant named after him in one of the ports which he frequented. The Admiral was a friend of Mr Mortimer, whose motor-yacht was a familiar sight. One day that yacht exploded. "I was in command of a submarine chaser in World War I when she blew up – I was not lucky with motor-boats," Mr Mortimer recalls today. We can imagine him and the Admiral discussing the disaster and the Admiral, in turn, recommending him to his son Michael.

A glimpse of Michael I have, amazingly, from the widow of a recent co-owner of *Jolie Brise* – Commander Newcombe Hoare. Pam Hoare remembers him as an old boy, returning to her prep. school (co-educational – very daring for those days) and being, from the great eminence of his teens, something of an heroic figure. From Chilgrove he had gone to Pangbourne, and thence into the Merchant Navy. As yachts were his life, having been brought up with them, and unable to afford the sort of boats he would like to own, he had taken to skippering – largely in the Mediterranean and, chiefly, for American owners. As such, he was one of the forerunners of the gentleman skippers of today. In the 1920s a gentleman's son would not have become a yacht's skipper, but these were the 1930s. An attractive Englishman, with a good background, could take on what was normally regarded as a servant's job with increasing ease, particularly when his master was American. He was the forerunner, indeed, of the classic English Gentleman type, who has exported himself to the States to serve an American master, mixing aristocratic self-assurance with the professionalism of the servants which his family themselves once employed.

Such social history apart, Michael's father, the Admiral, doubtless said to Mr Mortimer, as he bewailed the loss of his yacht and considered her replacement, that Michael would go to England and find him just what he required, and skipper it for him too.

The chances are that in *Jolie Brise* Michael Cumberlege found more what he himself fancied than what Mr Stanley Mortimer would have had in mind, had he been left to his own devices. Indeed, Mr Mortimer tells me that he had never owned a sailing boat before, and has never owned one since. When I mentioned this to the Editor of the American magazine *Cruising World* he made the sage reply that he was lucky to hit the right sailing boat first off and, clearly, any other boat afterwards would have been an anticlimax. But how could such a spartan ocean-racer-cum-French-work-boat be reconciled to the moderately comfortable requirements of an American gentleman with a penchant for cruising in Mediterranean waters?

In the summer of 1934, she was sailed south and plans were drawn up for her refitting. Mr Mortimer was either too careful of expense or not Croesus-rich enough for the work to be done at Camper & Nicholson's in England. Instead, she was to go to whichever port along the Riviera could handle the work most economically. But, even here, the prices were daunting for what amounted to a total stripping of the ship's accommodation and rebuilding.

Michael seems to have been alone on this jaunt, with his master safely back home in the States. He had with him two Breton sailors, crew enough to sail on to some of the Spanish ports, but the yards there, far from giving better estimates, refused to give estimates at all.

However, the early winter found *Jolie Brise* in Palma, Majorca. Here, at the yard of Señor Ballester, Michael Cumberlege made a bargain. He would employ the yard's carpenters at 12.50 pesetas a day, pay directly for all materials that they used, and pay Señor Ballester fifteen per cent commission plus insurance, for his own profit. There were two carpenters, working a forty-eight-hour week, with the "*Maestro*" to superintend – for in Latin countries a *maestro* is not a word which is exclusive to the concert hall, and indeed these men were every bit as masterful as any musical virtuoso, with their handling of adze and plane.

Someone who knew her in the 'twenties wrote to me recently, hoping that *Jolie Brise* had not been "tarted up".

What "tarting up" was done to *Jolie Brise* was done in that winter in Majorca, and next to nothing has been done to her since. But the work of Señor Ballester was as impeccable as were Michael Cumberlege's plans, every bit as worthy of the boat as the work done by Camper & Nicholson in the 1920s on the forehatch, Morgan Giles on the after cabin, Mashfords on the bulwarks and the craftsmen of Paumelle himself, in the Le Havre of 1913. The small amount of work done might have been so much more. She could have had a massive deck-house added. She could have been turned into a ketch, Brixham-trawler-style, her thirty-eight-foot boom being erected aft as a mizzen. She might have become a chugging motor-fishing-boat with next to no sail at all. But no, her rig and her appearance from the water remained absolutely the same. However, a coach-roof was added, marring, to the purist's eye, her uncluttered flush deck. The future removal of this has been in my mind ever since I first saw her and yet it is a comely structure, incorporating parts of her old skylight and companionway, leaving four foot six inches of deck on either side. It is comfortable to sit on, or to lay out drinks or food, and gives head-room to the after cabin, as well as off-deck storage for a water header-tank, sail ties, reefing gear and other paraphernalia which otherwise appears only to find a home in the dinghy stowed on deck. Indeed, so much of this new cabin top conceals stowage that only in part of the saloon and the after cabin does it serve its proper function of giving head-room. Yes, it is well built, useful and unobtrusive, and now I know of those men working on her in Majorca in the winter of 1934, I regard it as part of her history and her evolution, worthy of respect.

Down below, Michael Cumberlege's aim was to arrive at a layout which was comfortable and not flashy. His was definitely not a "tarting up" exercise. He observed that a yacht's accommodation is rather like that of a railway carriage, which in those days was either first class or third, there being no middle way. You either lived afloat in sumptuous opulence, beneath chandeliers reflected in mirrors, or you made do with sleeping on a sail-bag and using a bucket. *Jolie Brise* was never *totally* spartan, but she was rough in terms of accommodation, even though a cook/steward presided below decks. But if her accommodation tended in any direction, it was towards the third class rather than the first. It was Michael Cumberlege's intention to steer a middle course – to provide something good-looking and liveable but not opulent and impractical.

The brief interregnum of Warren Ferrier and Brownlow Smith had resulted in the contrivance of an owner's cabin. This was now given improved head-room. It was enlarged too, with the companionway moved for the third time in the boat's life further forward. The result was an elegant compartment with white painted panelling, a double bunk to one side and a single bunk to the other. There was also added a dressing-table beneath a pleasantly moulded mirror, redolent of an Edwardian steam-yacht. We always refer to it as the Captain's vanity table. Beneath the companionway steps, double doors open to reveal double mirrors, so that this owner's cabin is better supplied with looking-glasses than most houses I know and, indeed, only in an Eton High Street tailor's have I come across anything to compare.

Tucked in where E. G. Martin had his chart table, another panelled door gave, and gives to this day, onto the owner's washroom and lavatory. For the installation of this latter – the ubiquitous Baby Blake – they had to sail to Marseilles, because the import duty from England to Majorca on this vital piece of equipment would have doubled its cost. The midships lavatory, which was the cause of dispute between Bobby Somerset and Fred Crossley, was removed altogether and a crew's lavatory was now provided far up in the forecastle.

Installed in Marseilles, too, was the Gardner diesel which was to serve her more or less faithfully until 1979.

This replaced the paraffin motor with which Bobby Somerset had had such a love-hate relationship. But the patent feathering propeller remained, complete with its brass control wheel, which I myself more than once have twiddled in a frenzy when reverse, rather than ahead, has suddenly been required.

Forward of this owner's cabin, the companionway, in its new position, now led into a smaller saloon than *Jolie Brise* had had hitherto, with just one settee bunk on either side, rather than the two bunks end-to-end which had survived so long from her pilot days.

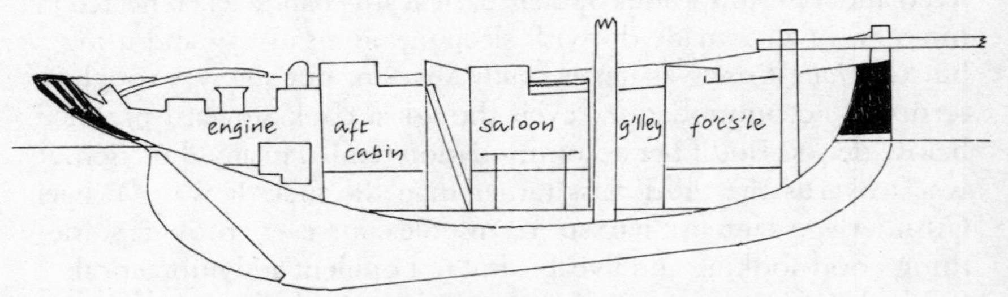

Compare with drawings on pages 51 and 127)

The zinc tank under the table had to go, but with careful adaption was split in two and incorporated in the new water-system, both under the floor and in the header-tank concealed within the coachroof. A natty little locker for signal flags was contrived, as were glass-fronted drinks cabinets and bookcases, these with leaded glass in the English cottage style for, much as the great yachts were contrived to be salt-water palaces, this was to be a salt-water cottage. Indeed, these leaded lights put one in mind of the earliest of motorcar-drawn caravans, which had little bay windows and lattice work.

Certainly Mr Mortimer and his friends, as they descended from the glaring Mediterranean sun or the all-too-teasing mistral, would find themselves in a fanciful but solid evocation of an English rural interior.

Forward again, much remained as before, except that in place of the original lavatory, opening to starboard of the galley, a shower-bath had been contrived as an essential of the American way of life. It operated from a cistern, again in the new coach-roof.

Mr Mortimer must have been well pleased when the next spring, that of 1935, he came across from the States to meet his skipper and his transformed boat. It had been a busy winter, complete with linguistic problems – Cumberlege speaking Spanish, the shipwrights Mallorquín and the deck-hands Breton. The work, too, lasted one month longer than expected. But all the materials had been put to good account; everything that had been stripped out of her was somehow used again, so that when complete there was not enough left over "to make a rabbit hutch". So, with floors of well-seasoned pitch-pine and fittings of African teak, she lay there ready to greet her owner. And as he stepped aboard he probably came upon another of Michael Cumberlege's contrivances. The helmsman's bench had been adapted so that it could be removed, inverted and used as a gang-plank, so essential in Mediterranean harbours where yachts moor stern-on to the quay.

And where did they sail to? Well, in that first summer they covered 7,000 miles. A gentleman's cruising yacht she might be, but such mileage is equivalent to crossing the Atlantic and coming half-way back again. No mere pottering this, although confined within the Mediterranean Sea, to Algiers, Ibiza, Sardinia, Monte

Carlo, Taormina, Crete, Rhodes, the Dalmatian coast, the Greek Islands and Venice.

Perhaps all those places were not visited within the first year. Some would be visited again and again over the four years that Mr Mortimer had her.

I like to think of her, discreet among the steam-yachts in Monte Carlo, gliding across the lagoon at Venice, sailing into Rhodes, where Bobby Somerset was later to lose his life, or along the Cretan coast, where Michael Cumberlege was himself so shortly to die. Untroubled those passages must have been with her artist owner aboard. I like to think of him, perhaps beneath an awning on the after deck, painting pictures of the little harbours they visited, the rugged, olive-clad hill-sides, the sudden storms. He would sail with two friends – always the same two, male and female – as well as a Breton sailor and a Breton cook, and sometimes his skipper Michael's own charming, very beautiful, Canadian wife.

She must have had a moderating effect on the two extremes of Michael's character. On the one hand, he was a poet; on the other, a good man with his fists. Once a crew on one of his commands – *Jolie Brise* perhaps – had made as if to go ashore, contrary to the owner's instructions. Michael laid them all out cold in a neat line on the deck where they awaited his master's return, for all the world like a bag of grouse set out for the record after a shoot on the glorious twelth.

These were the years of the Prince of Wales and Mrs Simpson, cruising those same waters in the steam-yacht *Nahlin*. These were the last of the days when children rushed to see, as they entered some Bulgarian harbour, whether or not their daddy's was the largest steam-yacht there. But Mr Mortimer, as he sat at *Jolie Brise*'s ten-foot tiller, must surely have conceded that sail was best, and the plyers of those wine-dark seas that *he* would acknowledge would be Michael Cumberlege's own father in his schooner, or that other legendary naval yachtsman, Admiral Goldsmith, exploring the Greek Islands in a gaff cutter of similar dimensions to *Jolie Brise*, but crewed only by his wife and daughters.

But lest she grow soft on such sailing, *Jolie Brise* returned each winter to Southampton and had more than one rough passage across "the Bay". Mr Mortimer's family came originally from England, to which they had come with William the Conqueror from Normandy, so that to have a boat built in Normandy, maintained in England, and sailed in the civilized waters of the Mediterranean must indeed have been a happy combination. Sadly, it was one that could not last forever.

Yes, war was on its way again. Mr Mortimer's journeys across the Atlantic, like those of the civilized travellers in the novels of Henry James, had now to come to an end, while it fell to Michael Cumberlege to find his vocation and lose his life under arms beside that same Mediterranean sea. *Jolie Brise* went north again across the Bay to Southampton for the last time – for the time being at least – and was put up for sale once more.

PART SEVEN

1938–1946

CHAPTER THIRTY-THREE

For the Duration . . .

War. Would *Jolie Brise* survive? She had survived the war before but then as a young ship, just built, serving a working purpose. Would people still want sailing yachts of such size after it was all over? Would they still be able to afford the crews and the materials to keep such a boat in commission? So must many have asked as yachtsmen laid up their boats in 1939. The hope for *Jolie Brise*'s survival was the more remote because she had no English owner. No one who was putting her away in mothballs, to return one day. She was on the market for sale, but who would want her?

Luckily, whether in war or peace, slump or boom, there is always a man with an eye to the future, a dash of imagination and a nose for a bargain. He is such a man as we have yet to see on the decks of *Jolie Brise*. Those who have been concerned with her until now have been pilots and fishermen, yes, but among the "gentry" no one, be they English or American, who has been involved in big business, dealing and negotiation. All her yachting owners have had more or less private resources. None have been, in the popular term, "captains of industry", but luckily such a man now comes into *Jolie Brise*'s life. Some fifty-five tons of twenty-six-year-old oak boat would hardly seem something which a business man would focus his eyes on at the beginning of a major war. But William Stannard did just that. His firm at Biddulph in Staffordshire had been established in 1845, but his interests did not rest just there. He was a man very much of the north-west, a member of the Hoylake Sailing Club and with friends in and around Liverpool and the Mersey. But business had taken him south to London and an address in Baker

Street. I knew that he was concerned with a famous firm that makes disinfectant for babies' bottles. Indeed, my pursuit of this strand in *Jolie Brise*'s life began by noting the address of Richardson-Vicks Ltd. from a bottle of theirs which I found on a chemist's shelf.

As with William Stannard's business aspirations, so too, it seemed, with his sailing ambitions. His business interests had moved to London and his sailing interests to the Solent. He was a man of forty, we were on the verge of war, he would probably have to drop his business concerns in the service of his country, but he could foresee a day when things would be back to normal again.

And so it was that he bought *Jolie Brise*, not to sail, but to lay down, as it were, like a good bottle of claret, ready for sunnier days. In his mind, too, was the idea of using her as a mother-ship for another vessel which he bought about the same time, the lovely twelve-metre yacht *Vanity*. It was a wonderful idea, one to warm the heart at depressing times in the war-years to come. An old friend of his, Frank Gibson of Hoylake, remembers indeed a letter from Stannard including a photograph of "*JB*", saying what fun they would all have when the war was over.

And what fun it would have been too, a re-creation of those days when Bobby Somerset had sailed *Jolie Brise* to Cowes and used her as a floating hotel during Cowes Week while he raced his friends' twelve-metres.

But it was not to be. Instead the Royal Navy requisitioned *Jolie Brise*, so that she has the strange distinction of having served in the French Navy during the latter part of the First World War, and in the British Navy in the Second. Were this a work of fiction, I would tell you that she was present at Dunkirk. But she did not join that famous little fleet. Indeed, had she done so, her draught of over ten feet would probably have left her stranded there, her bones shot up upon the shore of her native land with no more tale to tell. No, *Jolie Brise*'s war was far more prosaic. She was laid up at Shoreham, and indeed was of little or no use to the Admiralty. One suspects they just saw such a massive, well-built vessel and felt that she *might* serve some purpose sometime, some conversion perhaps to an MFV or makeshift minesweeper. Some forgotten unit might get posted to her as their own private accommodation, WRNS perhaps, or observers, watching for aircraft from some east-coast estuary.

But no, her fate was to lie in her mud berth in Shoreham, probably no different from any of the other yachts that lay around our coasts in mud berths through those long war years.

She had, I know from later correspondence, at least one visitor during that time. He was Bobby Somerset, now in the Navy himself. Imagine him in his navy blue raincoat and peaked cap, standing huddled on a winter's afternoon, looking at the hull of his old boat, a sad sight, but secure and with her timbers kept wet on every rising tide. She lay facing north-west, he records, so that her port quarter caught the midday sun. That was the same quarter which had suffered in the *Adriana* encounter. Hot and dry during those wartime summers, it was to give trouble again – and yet again, as Richard Sowman and Johnny Nance, Shipwrights, were all too well aware in this last winter of 1980–81.

However, my image of Somerset on that war-time afternoon may be quite wrong. Not wrapped at all against the elements, his stiff collar may instead have been chafing his neck in the summer sunshine. *Jolie Brise*'s timbers could have been enticingly warm to the touch. Only the whine of a Spitfire overhead would have reminded him that there were sterner things in the air than day-dreaming about sailing summer seas again. He must have thought wistfully then of past years, and wondered if he and the old boat would survive the war, and if either of them would ever sail again.

Peace came, but, when the Navy tried to gentle *Jolie Brise* away from her mud berth again, she refused to move. They had to dredge a channel for her, so silted up had her mooring become, before they could return her to her owner.

William Stannard did his sums and wondered if his dream could now be effected. A successful business man he may have been, but in those immediate post-war years there was a critical absence of supplies for things in general and yachts in particular. He might just commission *Vanity*, the twelve-metre, or *Jolie Brise*, one or the other, but not both. It was the dilemma Somerset had had when he had owned both *Jolie Brise* and *Penboch* fifteen years before.

In any event, Stannard was thinking of buying a house at Warsash, well placed for the Hamble and Cowes, so that the idea of a floating mother-ship now had less attraction than when it had first come to his mind. Sadly, *Jolie Brise*, having hardly moved an inch under his ownership, indeed having almost taken root over six years of enforced idleness, was now put up for sale again. And who now would think of buying her, with the market if anything more desperate than it had been in that last year of peace? Before we follow this new thread, let us see how others concerned with the *Jolie Brise* had fared in the war.

Alexandre Paris, her designer, was still alive in France, E. G. Martin, back in the Navy, had been serving in the Rescue Tug Service in Campbeltown but had had to retire, complete with barometer and silver cigarette-case, due to ill health in 1944. Back in London, in yet another bachelor establishment, he had died on April 7th 1945 at the age of sixty-four. He had been complaining of a chesty feeling, but his housekeeper had left him for a visit to friends and he had been dead in his chair when she came back. He had sailed in the 1938 Fastnet in a new boat, *Griffin*, which he shared with H. E. West. Traditionally built at Pinmill, she had a gaff mainsail and a stem-head rig – it was strange except amongst Thames barges, and she was after all built among them, to have a gaff rig without a bowsprit. So, happily, Martin had sailed again in his last possible Fastnet, enjoying the race which he and *Jolie Brise* had inaugurated. On his death, West promptly gave *Griffin* to the Royal Ocean Racing Club for members without boats to sail, and as a memorial to Martin, their founder. But while it was thus guaranteed that Martin's name would not be forgotten, that of *Jolie Brise* had certainly been swept from most people's minds.

A third figure in our tale, Michael Cumberlege, had served on secret missions in the Mediterranean and had been involved with the blocking of the Corinth Canal before he lost either his life, or his freedom, in the hills of Crete. In any event, that cheerful young adventurer who had done so much for *Jolie Brise* was never seen again. As he looked down from those arid Cretan hills in those last days did he, I wonder, fancy he saw the outline of a trim gaff cutter on the shiny waters so far below? War and peace for him must have made a headier contrast than even Tolstoy could contrive.

For the rest, the two figures in the dinghy we saw sailing up Portsmouth Harbour were now husband and wife. They had travelled the world together in the service of their country. They had left Singapore shortly before its fall and had hoped that their own boat *Frisk* would have been used by someone to escape, perhaps to Australia. In those wanderings they had drawn up plans for their ideal yacht for the waters back at home and, incidentally, given birth to me. Returned to England at last, my father had experienced the sort of restrictions which confronted those who wanted to sail again. He bought a half-finished boat and called her *Frisk* as well, as indeed all our family boats are called. As an example of the restrictions, he was unable to get a licence for wood to build her mast and had to make do for a season with something quite unsuitable. With him, and in her, I acquired my love of sailing.

And in all those years that I and my family cruised in European waters, my mother would talk of *Jolie Brise* and whenever she saw a gaff cutter upon the horizon she would say, "That is something like her but not as beautiful," and so I, representative of a new generation, grew to think of the old boat as something of a talisman. But neither my mother nor I, nor anyone, ever expected to see her under sail in post-war waters. To many she was just a legend now. Some assumed she was broken up; others said she was "somewhere in the Med", or "last seen in Nassau" or again "didn't she go to New York?" However, no one was inquisitive enough to follow up the threads. But all the time there she was, in relatively good heart, albeit in no order to excite the eye, in her mud berth in Shoreham.

As it was, the people who found *Jolie Brise* knew nothing of the legend, nothing of the boat, nothing of her previous owners, nothing of sailing. They came upon her and fell in love with her and, to their innocent eye, she represented a dream-ship. A part of that dream would be to sail in her, away from war-weary England, to a new life in New Zealand on the other side of the world.

They represent one of that host of people who now sail the world in boats big and small. They are people who have never sailed before, people not brought up to yachting with a capital "Y", either as gentry or crew, or indeed to working under sail as pilots or fishermen, people who simply want to sail away from it all. Another phase in *Jolie Brise*'s life, another function, had begun. Let us eavesdrop on board her, back over these thirty-five post-war years.

CHAPTER THIRTY-FOUR

Antipodes?

It is a late evening in early May. *Jolie Brise*, out of her mud berth at last, lies alongside a jetty. Her mast is up but her rigging is in a certain amount of disarray and her familiar black hull is in the process of being painted white for tropical waters, of which the warm water from Shoreham power station and the worms which thrive in it are just a foretaste.

Her skipper is Sandy*, a local man, who kept an unofficial eye on *Jolie Brise* for William Stannard throughout the war. He is ashore now, but down below we find four people. In the after cabin are Lilian and Jim. Jim is Jim Worsdell, an engineer from London, just thirty-two, the same age as Bobby Somerset when he took on *Jolie Brise*.

War has widened Jim's horizons. He had risen to Captain serving in India attached to a New Zealand division. He made good friends then, one of them Bob Smith*, also a Captain and an Indian Army man, refreshingly irrepressible, who was sleeping that very night in the saloon, a partner in this project.

Jim turned over and looked at his dark-haired wife, Lilian. She had all the looks and the perky 1940's way of doing her hair that a Battle of Britain fighter-pilot would hope to find waiting for him on the ground after an afternoon's sortie over Sussex. Jim had found her in Baghdad. No, she had not been a resourceful WAAF, pushing round symbols on an underground operation table while the war in

* These names have been changed.

the air raged overhead but, just as exciting, entailing early responsibility, she had been a nurse. The two had married in Alexandria and come home to a world which neither of them knew any more, which was a long way from the officers' mess and, for a girl, the liberated bustle of working life. Still worse, it was a long way off from the sun, of which they were both growing fond. Worse still, Lilian was not well. But, even as he turned in his sleep, Jim wondered whether he was not ill too. When they came home they had gone back to Lilian's home-town of Chesterfield and had bought a house at 25 Rhodes Avenue, Highfields. They had only lived in it a few months in that year of 1946 and now the house was sold for about a sixth of the price of the £3,000 invested in this old wooden boat. Perhaps he was ill to throw away security like that but, if he was, there were others just as mad. Bob Smith perhaps, a bachelor, had little to lose, as perhaps had Nash, his engineer friend from Sheffield, who was also sleeping aboard that night; but there were also three other good solid Chesterfield people with much at stake who had faith in Jim's project. Syd and Barbara Brown had been working together in the grocery business in Chesterfield for eighteen years, and Miss Tinley, not in the first flush of youth, was the daughter of a respected boot- and shoe-shop owner there. £700 apiece they were all stumping up. No, Jim was certainly not alone in his madness. If you had wanted a passage to New Zealand on a liner you would have to have waited eighteen months but if, like the Worsdells, you wanted to emigrate or, like Miss Tinley, hoped to see relations on the other side of the world, the idea of buying your own boat, cocking a snook at the shipping lines and sailing there must surely have made sense.

We leave Jim to fall asleep at last and as eventually the sun creeps through the skylight in that after cabin, let us imagine now his wife Lilian waking up. Perhaps in her mind she too has doubts, particularly in the early morning. But she looks across the cabin at Jim with his neat military moustache and his bushy dark hair and a face which, even to people not blinded by love, would convey a degree of quiet confidence.

She slips out of her bunk, opens the double mirrored doors and brushes her hair, looking first to one mirror, then the other. Yes, this cabin really is as comfortable as her old bedroom and the house they will never see again.

She walks through into the saloon, so reassuringly like the parlour of some English country cottage, and into the galley – and there was her real comfort, her real link with the land. Jim had arranged the fitting of a coal-fired Esse cooker. There it stood, cream and warm, and all it needed was a black cat sitting beside it to make her believe that this *was* a country cottage.

She walks back into the saloon again, a slight shiver running up her back on this early summer morning. That too will soon be gone when they are in the warm Mediterranean waters, or out in the Indian Ocean – remember that heat on the troop-ship coming home!

What it would all be like heeled at forty-five degrees with plates sliding from the table-tops or seas crashing onto the skylights, all that is mercifully beyond her imagination. There is enough here that is reassuringly like life ashore to raise her spirits, as they prepare for a voyage of equally incomprehensible distance.

By day-time all is bustle, some is frustration, as they puzzle over the rigging and sort out the sails. Jim is on good terms with the Gardner diesel, for he after all is an engineer and hopes to set up a motor business in New Zealand. But as for the sails, will they ever get them up and set, as in that amazing photograph of her under sail which William Stannard's agent had shown them? Certainly when there is a following wind and not too much of it, but otherwise the old Gardner will do the work.

And what about steering the boat, and all the rope-work? Well, Sandy is coming with them. He will be skipper and he knows a thing or two, or at least he should do. He has lived in Shoreham all his life. And as for navigation? John is coming, and he is a Merchant Navy officer. He will be their navigator, and there is nothing to fear.

No, their real problem is shortage of stores. Sandy had made enquiries about registering *Jolie Brise*, so that as a registered ship she could take on board seaman's rations. But he had come back with the news that there was already a *Jolie Brise* on the books and, since the authorities would not allow two boats of the same name to be registered, *Jolie Brise* would have to change her name. Amazingly, no one tumbled to the fact that their *Jolie Brise* was in fact the selfsame ship, and that she was already registered, so in good faith they commit that heinous crime of giving a ship a new name, and the black *Jolie Brise* becomes the white *Pleasant Breeze*.

Time is money, and they are anxious to be away. They only bought her in early May. They hope to sail in July, and someone has calculated that the passage will take them three months. One by one on the quayside arrive their acquaintances, who have decided to join in on the venture. Just how well do they know them already? How much do they like them? How well will they like each other after a few nights at sea, let alone after several thousand miles?

The only other married couple are Syd and Barbara Brown. They are not just giving up a house but their grocery business as well. They have not just arrived back from abroad like the Worsdells. They are giving up a whole life in Chesterfield. Syd is the President of the Chesterfield District Cage Bird Society and a successful breeder of canaries, and he is the son of Harry Brown, the well known Derbyshire postman. It has been a long war and he is coming for the good of his health; and if he fancies New Zealand he and Barbara will be staying there.

And so they look down on the relatively diminutive deck of *Jolie Brise* and wonder what they have let themselves in for. As does poor Miss Tinley, a Chesterfield spinster, comfortably placed in provincial life, in a town far inland from the sea, but she seeks a little adventure and a visit to her relations overseas. What can she have thought as she looked down upon the *Pleasant Breeze*, our own *Jolie Brise*?

There must have been many who chanced by that group of people working on their boat, who sat and watched and tossed out the occasional sentence of gratuitous advice. One such, who has no name and, if this were a film, would appear in the credits as "an old yachtsman", cast doubt upon the soundness of her spars.

"I know just the place, the chap will fix you up at cost price, perfect spars, suit her a treat."

From a quayside onlooker, he rapidly promoted himself to a commanding position on *Jolie Brise*'s deck and had shortly organized them all.

It was all a little puzzling, but he seemed to know what he was doing and he spoke with such calm authority. But why did he put himself to such trouble on their behalf?

"No trouble at all," and indeed it was not, for all the old boy was looking for was a sail in a famous old boat.

And it was a grand sail too, as the old cutter, under way at last for the first time in seven years, reached past the chalk cliffs of Sussex on a late evening in May. The spirits of all on board were uplifted as that solid deck came to life. Even the mainsail had been coaxed up the mainmast, hoop by hoop, and the thirty-eight-foot boom was not as daunting as they had feared. Someone had ventured out on the seventeen-foot bowsprit, Bob Smith perhaps, and put the jib up too.

And up through the kitchen chimney came the marvellous smell of roast beef as Lilian prepared a meal of a lifetime, complete with Yorkshire pudding; a feast for people all too used to strictly rationed food and a foretaste of the years ahead, living in New Zealand.

The old boat ticked off the miles in calm, sheltered water. If it was to be like this all the way, surely their dreams would be coming true? But the cruel irony was that that first heart-lifting sail was in the wrong direction. They were sailing not westwards towards the Bay of Biscay and the Mediterranean, the Suez Canal and the Indian Ocean, but eastwards, further and further up the English Channel to the Thames Estuary and Strood, near Rochester. That was the place where the "old yachtsman" knew just the chap who could fix them up with the spars he said they needed. And this sail up-Channel was a cruel lifting of the spirits because, with our prevailing winds from the west, such a sail is always easier to come by than is a "downhill" passage out of the Channel into the Atlantic. So their trip to Strood was taking them backwards, not forwards, and they would have to be fighting back every mile so comfortably slipped by on this their first passage.

However, they were that much more confident when they had nosed up the estuary to Rochester and come to berth at the yacht-yard at Strood. But here the "old yachtsman", after briefly introducing them to a Mr Puttifer, spirited himself away. He had had his sail and he was for home. Mr Puttifer had gone as a young man to America. Now he had returned to his old country and was interested in making a living out of anything that floated. He must have viewed with some amusement these young people setting out, as he had done, to find fortune abroad. But as for spars, he had nothing particularly suitable, nor indeed was there much that needed to be replaced. It had all been a waste of time and when *Jolie Brise* did eventually sail she did not take new spars with her. Indeed, she left one behind, her spinnaker boom, sitting on the rack in Mr Puttifer's shed.

So they had been taken for a ride, or rather, taken for a sail, but spirits were still high and, certainly, back at home the crew of *Pleasant Breeze* had acquired a certain fame. The north-country newspapers hungered for romantic stories in austere peace-time Britain, after those war-time years of tragedy and drama. Each member of the consortium was duly featured and they must have read those articles with a mixture of pride and amusement. Lilian in an unguarded moment had told a reporter, "My husband intends to paint each sail with a number, so that if the skipper wants one lowered in a hurry we shall know at once which it is. You see, we don't even know their names." Lilian was clearly the star of the show and armchair sailors back at home were told that, "She would wear slacks and a seaman's jersey on board. She would sunbathe in the tropics, have a dip over the side when the sun gets too hot, lend a hand with the tiller and prepare meals in the neat little galley." The old boat too, of course, featured as a heroine. She is variously described as "a Norwegian seventy-three tonner, sixty feet long", and "formerly a wealthy Frenchman's pleasure yacht, cruising to the West Indies and racing from Cowes".

"She can," readers were told, "make more than seventeen knots under sail and, when they are becalmed, five and a half knots under engine." The matter of navigation clearly worries the reporter but he can reassure his readers by saying that, "they have chosen the Mediterranean route, instead of the shorter one across the Atlantic through the Panama Canal, because they can keep well inshore almost all the way to Colombo". And finally, all these matters resolved, everything he can promise his readers is neatly tied up to assure this adventurous little group a romantic passage in all the best traditions of a B-movie. Indeed, before you have finished reading the article, you can almost imagine them already there, starting a new life in New Zealand.

"When winds from the west begin to stir the Mediterranean and early June sunshine warms the sea", we see them setting out upon this ideal adventure. We are told that, "Hazards of storm and reef do not worry them. In their minds' eye they can see already a misty landfall – New Zealand rising out of the sea." All heart-stirring stuff, which the people back home at Chesterfield must have enjoyed reading, but which in the minds of poor Jim and Lilian on board *Pleasant Breeze*, far up a creek in the Thames Estuary, must already have been setting seeds of doubt as, slowly, they were beginning to learn of the great gulf between fiction and reality, and of the 16,000 miles between England and New Zealand.

Had they read *The Yachting World* of about the same date they might indeed have abandoned the project altogether. There the "Walrus", otherwise known as Group Captain Teddy Haylock, was offering out titbits of news on yachting matters in his usual personal and somewhat critical style. In this July number it was a godsend to be able to print a photograph of the *Queen Elizabeth*, in recognition that her starboard side had now been repainted in peace-time colours, as well as a classic photograph of that other queen, *Jolie Brise*. And his comment?

> "There are many indications that a number of long-distance cruises are contemplated. Frequently both the people and the craft are unsuited to the hazards of such a voyage and, every now and then, I open my daily paper and see that yet another such party has come to grief. The latest venture is a project by a crew of four men and three women, to sail the late E. G. Martin's *Jolie Brise* to New Zealand . . . Such a fine ship will be welcomed in New Zealand waters, though her departure will raise pangs of sentiment and regret in the hearts of many of the old hands at ocean racing in this country."

A brief, dismissive paragraph, redolent of the implication that here was a bunch of land-lubber duffers, not thoroughgoing yachtsmen, daring to take a famous old boat to New Zealand. Perhaps they were, but none of those "old hands" had had enough "sentiment and regret" to step forward and put her to more appropriate use.

But if the column is a little snooty in its tone, there went with it a friendly warning which they would have done well to have heeded.

July 17th. They are all on board at last, the boat is crammed with stores and at 1.00 pm they leave Strood and the Medway. At 2.30 pm, out past Rochester, they have lunch. Their troubles seem to have been shaken off at last, but there is a speck rapidly approaching across the water astern of them and at 3.45 pm they are boarded by the river police. Syd and Barbara Brown have omitted to pay £250 tax on the sale of their property. It is apparently a last grasp at them by the old country. Sandy, the skipper, and Jim also go aboard the launch. Eventually the police wave amiably enough and they are left chugging eastwards into the evening.

They drop anchor for the night off Sheerness. Awake at 5.00 am they find the old cutter drifting out into the Thames Estuary. They set sail and soon find themselves pitching into heavy seas with a strong head wind.

Five hours later, incredibly, they drop anchor in exposed waters off Margate. Sandy, their trusted skipper, seems more to be trusted with a boat in a mud berth than one at sea, but they have yet to realize this. He seems loath to do other than motor into a head wind, and has a touching faith in his anchor off an exposed shore. Needless to say the motion is bad, all feel sick, one anchor is lost and the lavatory bowl is broken.

Three of the men go ashore for spares, but there is little to be found, not even cigarettes, and they cruise round off Margate for that day and the next, anchoring and dragging in the strong easterly winds, until the weather moderates on the Friday afternoon. They run alongside a French trawler and borrow an anchor in exchange for cigarettes. The French also throw across some fish, which they enjoy for their tea, and they have a quiet night without an anchor watch.

At ten o'clock next morning the French come alongside again and ask for their anchor back. They hand it over with a loaf of bread and hope to motor across the Channel while the sea is calm, and at least find themselves in a foreign country. But it is a faint hope. The calm simply precedes a switch in the wind to the west, heading them as they come round into the English Channel, bucketing into adverse tides.

There are three sea-sick women and six hungry men. They keep going through two nights, at least having learned their lesson about not anchoring off exposed shores, but they have a frantic determination to keep moving in the right direction at whatever the cost and the cost is total chaos down below. The after cabin is flooded with water: doubtless the hull, long resting in mud, has not yet fully "taken up".

The galley, with its new shelves and Esse cooker, so trim and tidy in harbour, and the forecastle are ankle-deep in spilt anthracite, more like a stoke-hole on a tramp steamer than a floating home. There is no sleep for anybody and eventually, late on Monday afternoon, they abandon the idea of heading for Le Havre and put into Littlehampton. They reseal their bonded stores and the ship seems very quiet and still as they spend the night alongside, just ten miles west of Shoreham, from where they had started – ten miles down and sixteen thousand to go.

Next day, new work and repair work is put in hand and Anne Tinley announces that she is going home. The adventure of a lifetime for the spinster of Chesterfield is not to be. How sensible! There is a wave of relief amongst the rest of them, and something of affection and respect as they see her go.

One day at Littlehampton turns into two, and then three, and then four, five and six. They are licking their wounds and reassuring themselves. Bob Smith shaves at last and all the men are clean-shaven again. On the Friday, Lilian has a shampoo and set at 10.30 am. She and Jim spend the night together at the Dophin Hotel on the Monday, thankful to be away from the general bustle on the boat. The following Wednesday Jim buys her a night-light. It is silver, in the shape of a Roman lamp, and is a homely addition to the cabin. Lilian sends one of her family a birthday card – yet another reminder of the family she is leaving. The links are hard to break.

But at last on August 4th at 5.00 pm it is high tide and they motor out into a very calm and hazy sea; but the haze rapidly turns into thick fog and Sandy drops anchor off Sandown on the Isle of Wight. Barbara Brown and Lilian try to cook bread in the Esse, but even the stove is temperamental and provides a very erratic heat. They are under way again at eleven o'clock the next morning (who would wish to lie anchored off Sandown for that length of time it is hard to imagine). They make fair speed but, as they round St Catherine's, hit a choppy sea and adverse tides, surprise surprise, off the Needles.

Skipper Sandy, as he tries to motor against the elements, westward down the Channel, bucketing from one exposed anchorage to another, must by now have felt his authority dwindling. How much kinder it would have been had they set sail from a western port, with a fair wind, and been able to teach themselves how to sail the boat in the open sea! But no, fate has not been so kind. A gesture is needed to bring light relief. Sandy solemly unscrews the new name-board bearing that atrocious name *Pleasant Breeze* and, with due ceremony, casts it adrift.

The women turn in for the night and the men, quite unaccustomed to the routine of watches and night passages, sail on, not westwards, but southwards, indeed not much more than sixty miles from Sandown, so that Lilian awakes to find the boat in Cherbourg.

August 6th now, and she goes ashore at midday. It is a depressing looking town and only fruit and vegetables are plentiful, but not cheap. They are still there the next day. The cooker is not working at all. All the meals are late. It is raining and eight mackerel cost thirty francs each. The day after they are still there. They have made friends with a half-English woman in a shop where they can cash bread-coupons, acquire a piece of veal under the counter and buy four films for their cameras.

On Saturday, four days in harbour, John, the Merchant Navy navigator, and Beck, Sandy's mate, come back rather too happy at 1.00 am. Jim, neither owner nor skipper, but none the less leader of the expedition, has two rows with John. The girls, Lilian and Barbara, are fed up with the men and the next day, Sunday, the three "crew", Sandy, John and Beck come back aboard merry again. Somehow democracy and the old cutter do not seem to go together. The shareholders in the enterprise form an uneasy partnership, while the crew have little respect for them and, in any event, hardly seem to know their job. It is all getting Lilian down and she takes to her bunk, her nerves shot to pieces, overcome by weariness. There is a slight diversion as she takes some photographs of the boat. Jim, worried stiff about what they have taken on, and the mounting bad feeling between the eight people aboard and his own wife's illness, trudges a solitary five miles out to an American base. He manages to get some sodium salicytate for Lilian.

Bob Smith embarks on some plain talking and the air is momentarily cleared. By August 13th, the ship's company are on better terms. Jim is still low and worried and Lilian still confined to her bunk. On Wednesday 14th she manages to sit up for an hour.

On the fifteenth it is VJ Day and a national holiday, and Cherbourg is alive with carnival, all that mocking pleasure and activity surrounding the troubled ship. It is a beautiful sunny day and Lilian is feeling much better; she gets up for several hours. At 5.00 pm they motor out to the outer harbour and anchor, ready to set sail on the next day.

But the next day dawns, it starts dull and then it rains and then the wind rises to gale force; the anchor drags and they drift towards the shore. Sandy starts the engine, but they go aground. John the navigator goes ashore to get help; a French naval tug comes by, breaking five tow-ropes as fifty-five tons of boat blowing onto the shore present a formidable task to tow clear. On the fifth attempt the whole of the starboard bulwark is torn away.

John appears with a fishing boat and eventually they manage to haul in the anchor and get free. A sorry sight, they return to the inner harbour, having paid their salvagers seven English pounds and two bottles of Scotch whisky. Everyone is desperately depressed, except for Bob Smith, and the crew go off to drown their sorrows. A gale roars through the rigging, even in the inner harbour, and they have a sleepless night.

August 17th and the gale has abated, but there is no setting sail now. They go into dry-dock to make hasty repairs. August 18th, Sunday, out of dry-dock again and back to their old all-too-accustomed mooring. Yet another ship's conference with Bob making the running and all, bar the weather, seems to be calm again. But there is a week of rain and gales, until at last on August 24th, although there is fog in the early morning, the weather clears and they finally set off. Proposed destination, Lisbon. Lilian, by now confined to her bunk, is past caring.

On August 25th they were past Ushant and could be said to have just about embarked on their world trip, having cleared the Channel at last. They had been talking about a passage to New Zealand lasting a mere three months, but they had taken six weeks just to get so far. As they rounded into the Bay of Biscay so the wind headed them; but instead of tacking out into the Atlantic, Sandy the skipper returns to his old form of motoring straight into wind, aided and abetted perhaps by John, the Merchant Navy navigator, used to ships which point where they are going. At four o'clock the engine packs up and Sandy decides to pack it in. He turns for home. Even though they get the engine running again within the hour, they continue to head for home. Falmouth is reached on Monday, August 26th. That first step on a world cruise had been so soon retracted.

I wonder who recognized that white cutter *Pleasant Breeze* as the former rakish black *Jolie Brise*? How differently she must have sailed *into* Falmouth that day than on the spring morning in 1926 when she had set out from there so purposefully on her first transatlantic voyage. The two married couples, Jim and Lilian and Barbara and Syd, quickly decide that their dream is at an end. Jim soon has his wife in hospital and, as he sits by her bed-side, they have to recast their dreams. New Zealand, perhaps, later, if they can get a passage by steamer, but, as Lilian Worsdell says in her sad little diary of those days, "For the time being, finis".

But for us and *Jolie Brise*, not finis at all. Better times and better hands lay ahead, or promised to. In the meantime she was to fare still worse. No one remembers quite how, but the Royal Bermuda Yacht Club, remembering her visit there in 1926 and her heroic rescue of the crew of the *Adriana* in 1932, offered to buy her if she could be sailed there. By now Bob Smith had assumed the crown. Sandy had gone home, but he and John the navigator and two hands, one from Falmouth, proposed to take on the voyage. Bob, as agent for the partners, was to take his share of the eventual sale and send the rest of the money back home. How many days she spent in Falmouth while this change of plan was effected is not recorded, but there are two chairs still in the saloon of *Jolie Brise* which they pinched from a Falmouth church; which church is not recorded either, but one day we would like to return them, even though by now they have acquired a character which is almost part of the fabric of the ship. They certainly lend her an ecclesiastical air, however ill-gained.

And so the cutter sets out again southward on her first leg towards Spain, on what must have been her fourteenth or fifteenth crossing of the Bay of Biscay, and it was certainly to be her last for over thirty years. It was hardly to be in the style to which she was accustomed, and the robust old girl must have been thankful for her white disguise and change of name. As before, the sails were only used when there was a fair wind. Inevitably in the late summer they encountered bad weather, and they limped into Vigo with the engine being greased with margarine, the only lubrication they had. There Bob Smith and John sent the two hands back home; more than likely the hands had had enough. The two men pushed on round the coast to Lisbon at last.

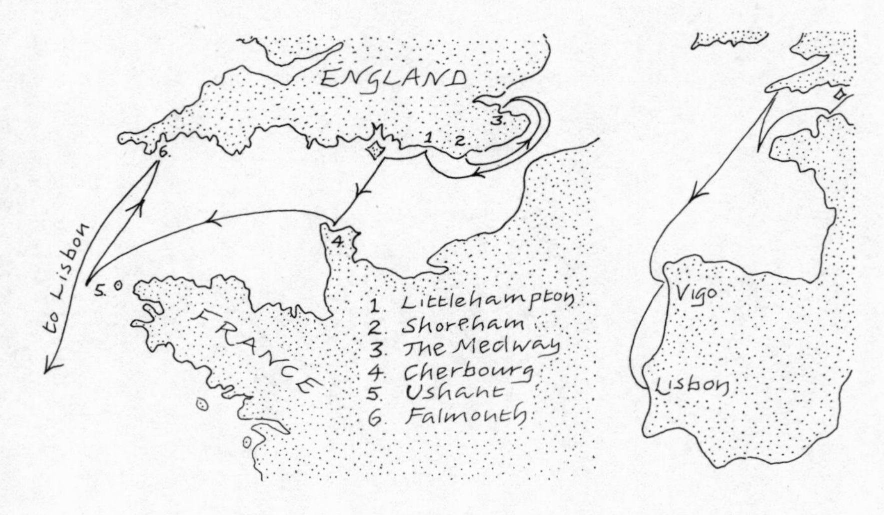

PART EIGHT

1946–1975

CHAPTER THIRTY-FIVE

Lobato to the Rescue

Luis de Guimarães Lobato hurried through the archway into the great Praça do Comẽrcio, most beautiful of Lisbon's baroque squares. The mellow autumn light flooded across the pavements and though the arcades to where the great equestrian statue at its centre pointed the way towards the quays on the River Tagus; and it was there that Luis Lobato was heading, a small vital man in his early thirties, dark, with a twinkle in his eyes. He had heard that there was a battered old English cutter recently arrived. Indeed, the ship's chandler had told him she was so battered she was going for scrap.

Soon he was on the quay, glancing up and down looking for her, shading his eyes looking across the swift-flowing Tagus waters to the distant shore; and presently he came to her. But this was not just an old English cutter, this was *Jolie Brise*! He could tell despite the white paint and the curiously ill-set rigging. He knew just who she was, despite her battered bulwarks. He looked down from the quay at the two men on the deck below.

"*Jolie Brise?*"

"Yes, that's right."

Lobato knew because Lobato was an Anglophile; he had a passion for things English, and a passion for boats. Indeed, as an engineer he had just spent some time in London as part of Sir Patrick Abercrombie's team, replanning the metropolis, and now he was turning his hand to similar plans for Lisbon. He knew about boats, because he had his own little twenty-foot sloop in which he ventured up and down the coast. When in London he had haunted that mecca of yachtsmen, Captain O. M. Watts, yacht chandler, in Albemarle Street; and he consumed avidly every book on sailing that came his way, including E. G. Martin's *Deep Water Cruising*; and he had feasted his eyes on picture after picture of *Jolie Brise*. It was not surprising, then, that this agile, vital man recognized the boat he had never seen, but knew so much about, despite her sorry state and her disguise. His English was good; Bob Smith's Portuguese non-existent. He climbed aboard, looked around, briefly discussed her future, heard of her terrible passage, shook his head when Bob said she was going for scrap.

"What price are you being offered?" he asked.

The figure was equivalent to some £3,000. Scrap she might be, but these were years when materials were in short supply and the two hundred pounds' worth of lead alone which Bobby Somerset had installed in her bilges was now worth a fortune.

Lobato was quickly ashore again and told Smith to do nothing until his return.

Soon he was canvassing his friends around the yacht club, just across the quay from the Monastery of St Jeronimos. Soon he was looking for his friends up and down the corridors of the University, and, even quicker than Jim Worsdell had found backers for his ill-fated purchase of the ship, Lobato had persuaded seven of them to join in a more felicitous venture – saving *Jolie Brise*.

Their names, like his own, ring out with fine Portuguese sonority, enough to put even Bobby Somerset's many names in the shade. Here is that splendid roll-call of subscribers. Chief among them was Adriano Vaz Pinto. Then, with Lobato, there were Antonio Francisco de Aguiar, Antonio Manuel de Vasconcelos, Joao Cardoso de Lemos, Jose Rebelo Vaz Pinto, Manuel Alegria da Cunha, and, finally, Augusto Cavaco. And from these people the money was found. But yet, her arrival in Lisbon and her conditon and the tale which Bob Smith told seemed all so improbable that the purchase was not effected until Lobato had been several times to the English Consul, and reference had been made back to England to discover whether or not Bob Smith was indeed authorized to sell the boat. But at last, on December 8th 1946, her ownership passed to this splendid consortium. As Luis Lobato and Bob Smith had a drink in the cabin to seal the deal, Bob wrote an entry in sixteenth century Nepalese script, scrawling several lines across a page of the ship's log. What he wrote has yet, even to this day, to be translated. Perhaps it is as well that we should not know, because having written it he took the money and boarded a steamer bound for Mombasa and was never heard of again. It seems that the co-owners of *Jolie Brise* have never had a penny back from him in recompense.

There was still much to be done, but there was time in which to do it, and the resources too. All those men with splendidly mellifluous names, though they sound like knights in armour and, indeed, had acted fast to save a damsel in distress, were in fact, like Luis Lobato, engineers. They were practical men, living in Lisbon, looking for a boat, not to voyage the world in, but to lie in the basin by Lisbon's yacht club, the second oldest in the world, to sail up and down the Tagus and to sally forth from time to time in one or another of Portugal's handful of off-shore races.

Indeed, it is hard to imagine a more suitable harbour or a more suitable country in which *Jolie Brise* could have sought a golden retirement. There was no yacht-building tradition there, but the colourful Tagus barges and fishing-boats all came from small yards along the water-front, where traditional boat-building skills were still alive. Blacksmiths too could be found who could be persuaded to copy or improvise iron-work for a ship. Certainly fine sails and complex chandlery were another matter. But Lobato, from his time in England, knew immediately the right thing to do, and he opened an account with Captain O. M. Watts.

It would be some time before these young men with their giant cutter could sail proudly up and down the Tagus, along the water-front of Europe's most western and perhaps most elegant of capitals. Indeed, it was not until 1950 that *Jolie Brise* appeared again in Lloyds Register of Yachts as under the ownership of the senior partner, Vaz Pinto. Her own name was listed again as *Jolie Brise*, ex *Pleasant Breeze*, ex *Jolie Brise*. In those intervening years her port quarter had been completely rebuilt, as had been the bulwarks ripped out of her in the Cherbourg fiasco. She had been completely re-rigged too and painted a glistening black again, set off by a discreet white line.

Lobato entered into a lengthy correspondence, both with Bobby Somerset and with William Stannard. Somerset, now living in Hampshire, wrote often. He had acquired a typewriter and seemed to delight in the gadget. Pages of advice tumbled into Luis Lobato's post-box. "Shorten the boom" was the most repeated exhortation; and then long thoughts aloud about which sail was made just when and where, and the provenance of her present sails.

Bobby confessed he had not sailed himself for fifteen years, but was going to skipper *Griffin* in the first post-war Santander Race. Lobato was urged to bring *Jolie Brise* back to England and join in the race. Bobby had little hope of success in *Griffin*, but he would dearly like to see his old boat at the starting line. "Failing that," said Bobby, "why not sail up to Santander and meet us?" but he had not realized, I suspect, just how convalescent his old boat was and, in any event, the yachtsmen of Lisbon are loath to sail north. (Who can blame them?) So, as *Jolie Brise* did not come to Bobby, Bobby came to her, just a year or so after she had found her new home. He sailed up the Tagus in his great *Iolare*, the fine ship that marked his return to serious sailing.

On board was his son David, today heir presumptive to the Duke of Beaufort in his late father's place. Today he sells pictures in Mayfair, not far from where John Gage's son runs a pub in Knightsbridge. (How pre-war eyebrows would have risen at such commercial involvement!) A young man then, David must have looked with curiosity at the boat which his father had had when he was just a babe in arms.

However, someone else aboard *Iolare* remembered the old boat vividly. This was Maclean Buckley, "a proper Ocean Racing Club sort", Lobato recalls today, who had raced in *Jolie Brise* so often and had been friends with Bobby Somerset so long. He was a man dedicated to sailing and also to such intriguing ventures as running the Eton College shop and (with Somerset himself) an "International" airline between England and Scotland.

By now *Jolie Brise* was lying in the basin beside the yacht club and she and *Iolare* must have made a pretty sight together there. Bobby Somerset's brains were picked and his memories ransacked on just how her rigging should be put to rights. And there is a splendid photograph of Somerset and Lobato at some yacht club function, her former owner and the present – Somerset languid, older, but handsome as ever, Lobato the younger man, eager to learn. Soon *Iolare* was to sail southward again and, as she sailed down the Algarve coast, Maclean Buckley sat at her cabin table and wrote to Luis Lobato, saying how splendid it was to see the old boat "saved from death three times but risen like a phoenix yet again".

William Stannard wrote equally enthusiastically. He by now had sailed the twelve-metre *Vanity* to Denmark and was steadily working his way through a succession of boats – hardly ever the same boat two years running – with all the rapidity of a born business man and an enthusiast. He never came out to Lisbon; indeed, he wrote of the problems back at home and the near-impossibility of travel – "the only way we can come and see *Jolie Brise* would be for you to sail over here to fetch us!" But he does retrieve the spinnaker boom from Mr Puttifer's yard in Strood and pays thirty-three pounds for it on Lobato's behalf. Endless correspondence ensues with problems of currency and export, second only to the problems which surrounded the despatch of a new Baby Blake lavatory bowl from Captain O. M. Watts – broken, you will remember, off Margate.

One item from England had to be brought by a friend as hand-luggage, arriving battered and broken. This was Bobby Somerset's own model of his old boat, not as excellent as that which stands in pride of place in the Royal Ocean Racing Club's club-rooms in Park Place, nor as the brilliant models recently made by van den Heuvel in Holland, or Dole Robbe in France. No, this is very much an amateur affair, but the more precious for that, as it was made lovingly by the boat's owner. It came as a tribute to Lobato for his work in saving *Jolie Brise* – but not before the Bank of England had solemly written enquiring where he had acquired the money to purchase it.

Somerset made one further visit to Lisbon but, in true form, he had a row with the Customs and cleared out in a huff before he could make contact again with his old boat and his new friend. It foreshadowed a little bureaucratic problem Luis Lobato was himself to have many years hence. The two men did not meet again, and it comes as a shock to Lobato, as to so many, when he buys a copy of the *Telegraph* in Italy one day in 1965 and reads the tragic tale of Bobby Somerset's death by drowning. He had fought his way below in an attempt to save the lives of two girls and his dog as his yacht sank in the entrance to Rhodes harbour. Near death in the trenches of the First World War, near death in the calm waters of Lulworth Cove, in peril when saving *Adriana*'s crew, the luck of that courageous and engaging man had at last eluded him.

In those years of the early 'fifties *Jolie Brise*, now in top form again, had a professional crew of two, drawn from the Fishermen's School, and her seven owners, the engineers, were famous in racing circles. Other competitors were amused and impressed by that all-engineer crew, bringing with them an echo of the races in British waters when *Jolie Brise* raced against the Royal Engineers in *Ilex*.

There was no *Ilex* to race against on the Tagus, but there was *Foxhound*, that fine Nicholson-designed cutter, sister-ship to *Bloodhound*, later to be owned by our Duke of Edinburgh. *Foxhound* and *Jolie Brise* make good sparring partners because *Foxhound* had been one of the first ocean racers to be built specifically for the Fastnet Race which *Jolie Brise* had helped to inaugurate; and though the two boats look so different, their underwater lines aft of amidships are in fact remarkably similar. And there were other great old yachts to race against too, because Lisbon in the post-war years was as much a refuge for fine boats as it was for kings in exile – such kings, indeed, as would from time to time sail upon *Jolie Brise*, on whose decks, as it happens, the present King of Spain got an early taste of the sea. The races she entered were southward down the coast to the Algarve, out to sea to the Farres, and north-west to the Berlengas Islands. Despite suggestions from Somerset, the Portuguese never took handicapping rules too seriously and seldom ventured further than their own coastal waters – and perhaps it was just as well, as it was just that sort of circumstance which could give *Jolie Brise*'s keen young owners exciting competitive sailing in steady weather, and often with the fast reaching winds which suit her so much. Indeed, perhaps one of the finest photographs of *Jolie Brise* at speed comes from those years, while the saloon is still decorated with the medallions of wins and placings in those friendly races.

There were only two excitements from that time: one was the breaking of the bowsprit in grand style just off the Torre de Belem, so all yachting Lisbon had a grand-stand view. Its fine replacement survived until 1979 when it snapped, pitching into short seas, revealing a knot the size of a fist previously hidden from view. The second matter of note was a whirlwind off Cape St Vincent. Luis Lobato mercifully saw it coming and sailed the boat under a full press of canvas round with it, the water lashing up to the companionway. One neighbour with less foresight was dismasted. These apart, those were fair winds and steady seas in which *Jolie Brise* raced in the 1950s.

CHAPTER THIRTY-SIX

Family Boat

Yet again was to come another of *Jolie Brise*'s retirements from racing, and with it perhaps the most placid and enjoyable period of her life. In 1955 Vaz Pinto ceases to appear as her principal owner in Lloyds Register of Yachts. The bright band of racing engineers is disbanded and Luis Lobato becomes her sole owner. And with this change she becomes, for the first and only time in her life, a true family boat.

That sonorous list of the seven engineers who together had saved *Jolie Brise* gives way to a list of seven other equally splendid names. It is headed by Luis Lobato himself, husband and father, then comes Maria Teresa, Luis's beautiful and amusing wife, on whom Bobby Somerset had complimented him – "I wish my wife was as sea-worthy", and then their children. First to confuse with the reversal of her mother's own names, Teresa Maria, then Antonio, followed by Leonor, Pedro, and Maria Yoao. A family boat indeed! And over the next twenty years that family were to be in and out of *Jolie Brise*, year in year out, regarding her as a floating extension of their own home. There she would lie off the yacht club with always a friendly paid hand to help a young child, or they would moor off Cascais, then just a little fishing village out of the mouth of the Tagus, where the children could swim from the beach and father could come down from the office in the long summer evenings. Or again, they would have a regular mooring at Sesimbra, a few miles down the coast to the south of the Tagus, beneath its high Roman fortress.

And to Luis Lobato's own children would be added innumerable children of fellow members of the club, of which he was to become in time both President and Commodore. Indeed, there seemed no end to the numbers of children that the venerable old boat could accommodate. There would be photograph after photograph in the album of Emilio, the cheerful paid hand, totally surrounded by them. Almost by coincidence, *Jolie Brise* became a school afloat and many a child learned the first rudiments of sail on her decks and up her mast, a foretaste of her life today.

As the children grew older and their tastes and interests grew more sophisticated, they would actually have dances on board. The table in the saloon would be unscrewed and put aside; and what more splendid place for a young party could there be than in the old boat's cabin, down on the water-front, so close to the centre of the great humming city? Or again, there might be barbecues ashore on the beach with fish cooked over an open fire. Back on board, Maria Teresa cooked indomitably at the Esse stove. Not here were there the cooks and staff which families, even in post-war Portugal, then still enjoyed. On board she herself had to turn to, and she enjoyed it to the full. However, she was not always a galley slave, particularly when another paid hand, Manuel Pedro, made one of his famous fish soups.

As the children grew older, too, there came the summer cruises, southward down to the Algarve and to Gibraltar; and from these came those nostalgic, jerky family films, in which friends from school, children of different ages, and capers with dinghies in harbour all feature. Well remembered was a run through the Straits of Gibraltar at a steady seven knots with just a staysail set.

Sometimes they would penetrate further, perhaps to Majorca, where Michael Cumberlege had refitted her, or to one of the new yachting harbours on the French Mediterranean coast. But there was nothing ambitious in these cruises, other than to have fun, and for the family to spend its time together, to be away from home for a week or two and to sleep aboard.

An exciting role which *Jolie Brise* would sometimes adopt on these family adventures would be that of sword-fish hunter. She would be motored into wind and into the path of the sun, so neither sound nor shadow would warn of her approach. The harpoonist would perch bold and precarious on the end of the bowsprit, while his assistant would be ready with fathoms of light line and a huge cork float on the foredeck. If the harpoon met its mark, the line would race out and the float would be jettisoned to be pursued for the capture and the kill.

We have no relic of *Jolie Brise*'s tunny fishing days, but these sword-fishing sorties have left one souvenir – the huge cork float. It is this which the skipper to this day uses as his seat at the head of the breakfast-table in *Jolie Brise*'s saloon.

It was in these years, too, that *Jolie Brise* was something of an object of pilgrimage. Just who came to see her and just who they were was never too clear to the ever hospitable Lobatos. In ports all over Europe, we find people today who say that they have sailed in her out of the Tagus.

But two in particular feature in our story. One was Colin Mudie, who in his tiny boat *Sopranino* put into Lisbon in that famous transatlantic crossing of the 1950s. I was to find his name in her visitors' book, and he remembered her well when I visited him in his drawing-office just three years ago, for it was his advice as a naval architect that I sought over the installation of a new engine – advice which he kindly gave free for the pleasure of being associated with this fine old ship again.

And another visitor was dear Lilian Worsdell in 1964. She looked round the boat and was pleased to see the Esse cooker still in place, and the shelves in the galley which she had contrived with such care all those years before, when with great optimism they had first planned their New Zealand trip in the harbour at Shoreham. Ever since that sad day when she and her husband Jim had stepped ashore at Falmouth they had hoped in some way, someday, to buy *Jolie Brise* back again. The brief note from Bob Smith (with no cheque enclosed) to the effect that he had disposed of her for scrap had given her no hope that she would ever set eyes on the old cutter again. But there she was, trim and beautiful on the waters of the Tagus. Lilian herself was heading south to Australia, by ship, and Jim was flying there. They had lived in many countries since that first set-back to their globe-trotting plans back in 1946. Now at last that old wound was healed and they could look back with pleasure, rather than regret, at their time with the old boat – pleasure which I am glad to say continues as we happily correspond with them, we who sail her now, letters passing regularly between us and them in their retirement in Australia.

CHAPTER THIRTY-SEVEN

Solent Ghost

There would seem to be little reason why *Jolie Brise*, in this her Indian summer, need ever move again to new waters. Her owner, now a man of some eminence, had been variously Deputy Mayor, a Professor of Planning at the University, Co-founder of the new Roman Catholic University, a man of international repute as a Trustee of the Gulbenkian Foundation, and an honorary member of our own Royal Institute of British Architects. Luis Lobato's position, and his ability to maintain and keep, *Jolie Brise* in the way that she should be looked after, seemed impregnable. Indeed, she herself had become almost as much a feature of the Lisbon water-front as the Torre de Belem, or the giant monument to the navigators, in the shadow of which she lay moored. She had played her part too in the construction of another landmark, the great Tagus Bridge, for it was from her decks that engineer Lobato and the engineers from England had done the necessary survey work and supervised the construction.

However, all was to change, and that change is best symbolized by that bridge itself, for it now bears the name of *Ponte 25 de Abril*, that so-recent date in 1975 when old-world Portugal was overtaken by a revolution, which shook all that symbolized capitalism and wealth, however justly gained. Ironically, *Jolie Brise*, built as a work-boat, first a pilot, then a fishing-boat, was now a symbol of wealth. Old Monsieur Paumelle would have laughed at the idea, but it was no laughing matter. As such a symbol she was all too vulnerable. That huge weight of Normandy oak, those highly inflammable sails, were only too easy a target for a spectacular, politically inspired conflagration in a key location on Lisbon's water-front. It would have been an ignominious end to have burnt to the waterline, as did *Adriana* all those years before. But fortunately loyalties die hard and, although two attempts were made to set *Jolie Brise* alight, her paid crew, sleeping aboard, frustrated them both.

Less happy was the fate of many former crowned heads and aristocracy, who no longer found Portugal a peaceful haven. Many fled, leaving their little palaces rapidly to be plundered to bare shells. The Lobatos' position was of course less precarious, but Luis Lobato was the product of a more conservative régime and now he found himself, almost overnight, faced with the uncertainties of a Communist revolution, and uncertain too of what his family could in future call their own.

Not to be over-dramatic, the old order had changed and there was no place for *Jolie Brise* in the new. Movement in and out of the country was heavily restricted, but there was one rendezvous which the old boat must surely attend.

The Royal Ocean Racing Club had invited Senhor Lobato to take *Jolie Brise* to the fiftieth anniversary celebrations of the Fastnet Race at Cowes. There was much shaking of heads among new officials, much argument, speculation, filling in of forms but at last, after two days' negotiation, Luis Lobato had permission to sail his boat out of the Tagus, almost thirty years after she had limped in with Bob Smith at the helm. Permission to leave came early in the morning; by six o'clock the Lobato family were on board. Their loyal skipper rowed out to the boat and helped them prepare sail and then went back to the quay to wave and wave again as they slipped out of the yacht basin. And so *Jolie Brise* pointed her bowsprit to the Atlantic and her counter to the sun rising above the Tagus Bridge – *Ponte 25 de Abril*. Behind that waving man a police van had arrived to watch the depature.

There is a feeling of relief on board after the tensions of the months before, almost of holiday as for once they sailed north, not south, that family party. They had on board a Portuguese Air Marshal, equally at variance with the new régime, and heaven-sent as a navigator. They had too his son and two English undergraduates from Cambridge.

By sunset of the same day they had the Berlengas Islands abeam, those islands which in her Portuguese racing days had marked the turning point of so many races.

Their first port of call was Bilbao in Spain and there were meetings there with old friends. Then came a happy sail across the Bay of Biscay to Quiberon Bay. Arriving one sunny morning among a host of sailing dinghies, they dropped anchor to be greeted by Antonio, who had come out to join them from his college in England, to complete the family party. Thence they sailed north again, met with fog and calm in mid-Channel and finally, out of the haze, raised the Needles Light.

And so, fifty years after that first Fastnet Race, *Jolie Brise* came again to Cowes. You might think it was a triumphant return but it was one such as Rip Van Winkle might have made. The racing machines of 1975 were so very different from this pilot cutter of 1913, and far too few gave her a look, other than as just "an old gaffer". She should by rights have picked up her skirts and entered the race, but Senhor Lobato had only a family crew, a light one at that. Indeed, strange to relate, this was the first time in her long life that she had ever been sailed without professional help.

I would like to report that she was moored in pride of place in Cowes, but this was not the case. She was secured on piles up the Medina River, emerging to sail, well laden in hospitable Lobato tradition, like a ghost at the banquet, through the small racing yachts in those days of Cowes Week which precede the Fastnet.

However, there were three memorable highlights: a shipwright sailed with her who had worked with her in the 1920s and J. van den Heuvel came over from Holland and saw at last, face to face, the boat of which for several years he had been building a model. But, best of all, Owen Aisher gave a small party at the Royal Yacht Squadron, where the Duke of Edinburgh left no doubt about his admiration for the Lobatos' efforts, and the significance that he placed on the continuing welfare of a fine old boat. The crowning moment was to come the next day when, sailing past *Britannia*, Luis Lobato made to dip his ensign in salute, but the Prince gestured to him from the bridge, implying that he should delay. So it was that the Royal Yacht first dipped her ensign to *Jolie Brise* and *Jolie Brise* then replied, rather than vice versa. This generous and almost unprecedented gesture of respect from Her Majesty's yacht to the older vessel was deeply appreciated. *Jolie Brise* was a ghost of Cowes no more; she had indeed returned.

Once again that inimitable marine photographer, Mr Beken, came fussing round in his launch to add more pictures of her to his files, and once again yachting editors could slip a picture of *Jolie Brise* into their columns whenever they had space to spare for a beautiful boat. It was as if the intervening decades had never been.

PART NINE

1975–1981

CHAPTER THIRTY-EIGHT

London pied-à-terre

As the Fastnet fleet of 1975 sailed westward, so the only yacht ever to win that classic race three times set her bowsprit eastward up the English Channel and into the Thames Estuary, that *via dolorosa* which had so early and cruelly dashed the Worsdells' hope of sailing to New Zealand. However, now she was flying her green and red Portuguese ensign where once had flown the *tricolore* of France, the red, the blue and the white ensigns of Britain, and the Stars and Stripes of America.

On this occasion she sailed past Rochester right up-stream and past the palace of Greenwich and the National Maritime Museum, in whose Yachting Gallery she already held a special place. Finally she came to Tower Bridge in the Pool of London, to turn into St Katherine's Dock. From the water-front of one capital she had come to rest in another. She was to perform a last service to the family which she had served for thirty years, that of a London *pied-à-terre* – or *pied-en-eau* – for Senhora Lobato and her two sons, both now at college in England. And it was there that *Jolie Brise* really came back into the headlines again, with Londoners viewing her with amazement, as if she had floated out of the pages of the history books. *Country Life*, not without exaggeration, celebrated her return with an article headed "The Most Famous Ocean Racer in the World".

Naturally Senhor Lobato returned to Portugal and naturally too, for a man with such gifts, the new régime came to terms with him rather than vice versa, so that he continued to serve his country. But the question remained. Pleasant as it was to have a floating London home, what should become of *Jolie Brise*? Too many boats had put down roots that way and never sailed again. This could not be allowed to happen to *Jolie Brise*.

Marvellous though it would be, too, to have *Jolie Brise* back on the water-front in the yacht basin at Lisbon, the revolution, bloodless though it was, and politics, quick though they were to flow into more moderate channels again, meant that Portugal was no longer a place where a yacht like *Jolie Brise* could flourish in private hands. I know that for myself because last February I flew out to Lisbon and found that charming city and lovely country basking in benign sunshine, but no yachts slid gracefully past the Torre de Belem, ivory-white in the water of the Tagus. There is no longer a glistening array of varnish, paint-work and brass in the yacht basin by the world's second oldest yacht club. No, like us in England, yachtsmen of Portugal have now taken to the small plastic boat and the tin mast; and they have done so for the same reasons. For better or worse, labour has become prohibitively expensive. Indeed, a dedicated, undemanding shipwright or deck-hand, skipper or sailmaker, is now not so much too expensive to employ, as just no longer in existence at all.

Senhor Lobato could see all this and knew that, even if he were to bring *Jolie Brise* back to the port where she had spent almost half of the sixty-four years of her life, there just would not be the skills available to keep her to the standard at which, over the years, it had been his pride that she should be maintained. And so, sadly, he resolved to sell her. There were obviously many, crackpotted and serious, rich and poor, who were interested in buying her, because, so different from 1946, the late 1970s was the era of conservation when famous boats were no longer just "old gaffers" and wooden boats were indeed items of rarity.

In the summer of '76 he and his family sailed *Jolie Brise* to her first home in Le Havre, a place so sadly changed after two wars from the days when *Jolie Brise* first slid down the ways in 1913. They had hoped for instant recognition. Certainly, as they lay alongside, there were one or two quayside personalities who, primed with a glass or two, would remember anything that they were prompted to remember about the old boat. But, rightly or wrongly, her native country did not seem to be the home in which he would like her to end her days – I think perhaps wrongly, as I know now, through my researches for this book, quite how much the *cognoscenti* of France value the heritage of their Le Havre pilots in general, and the boats of Paumelle in particular. But be that as it may, *Jolie Brise* sailed back again to London and there a friend I have recently made was one of many who longed to own her. This was Frank Essen who, as I write, splendid man that he is, is sailing the only gaff rigged boat, indeed the only boat with a wooden mast, in the 1981 Transatlantic Race. Frank surveyed *Jolie Brise* from stem to stern and sadly decided that, for an individual such as he, she was no boat to be taken on single-handed. He had an American friend, keen to buy her if he decided not to do so, and to this friend in the United States he sent the following report – "If you are a man you will buy this boat, if you are a mouse you will not." Across the telegraph came the distinct reply, "I am a mouse," yet another catch-phrase in the old boat's history.

CHAPTER THIRTY-NINE

Dauntsey's School

Onto the centre of the stage, and I do apologize, steps your author. It is rather like a producer taking a part in his own play. No, I am not about to produce my cheque-book and purchase *Jolie Brise* to present her to the nation. Indeed, I am not talking about the 1970s now but the 1950s, for it was then that I was sent to a small, ancient and little-known public school in the Wiltshire countryside. Dauntsey's was and is a happy place. It ploughs a quiet furrow in what is grandiosely known as the Education of British Youth. Its unspectacular Victorian buildings lie in the palm of the downs on the edge of Salisbury Plain in the village of West Lavington from where, in the sixteenth century, one William Dauntsey went to London in search of fame and fortune. He became Lord Mayor and, mindful of his roots, founded a school in his home-village. That school grew in the last century from a small ancient building in the village to a substantial institution whose new buildings were worthy of the attention on opening day of Joseph Chamberlain, no less.

In the 1920s Dauntsey's cast off its sixteenth- and nineteenth-century mantles and adopted something of the *avant-garde* with H. G. Wells as one of its Governors. It became the first school of its type to adopt shorts – not just for the boys but for the masters too. In so doing, it led the way for Bryanston and Gordonstoun. But by the time that I was to arrive there, this new approach to education had mellowed to a quiet, unassuming, civilized community where one lived and let live. There were the tough rugger chaps and the boys who collected newts. I was neither the one nor the other, but I grew fond of the place, as generations have done, and in many respects that corner of Wiltshire became home for me.

But at no time did I ever connect Dauntsey's with sailing; indeed, when I was there I was never further from the sea. Sailing for me was my family tradition; it was something for the holidays in our faithful old boat *Frisk*. There was certainly no sailing club, though there was a Combined Cadet Force in which I, with my Air Force background, rose to the dizzy rank of Flight Sergeant. There were others who, under our Scottish classics master, served in a Naval section, but they seldom got nearer to the sea than a whaler on the nearby Erlestoke Lake.

I left Dauntsey's for Durham University with the sage advice from my housemaster that old boys who returned too precipitately, with sports cars and girlfriends, were not as welcome as those who had found their feet and come back to the school in the fullness of time. I took his advice and it was some twenty years later that, driving south from Argyllshire, I found myself passing through West Lavington. I stopped for a drink in a pub called The Bridge, where my history master had sent me on many an occasion to retrieve the exercise books which he had left there by mistake the night before. In that pub I left my wallet and had to backtrack forty miles the next day to pick it up. That day happened to be Speech Day and so I returned to the fold, finding myself, at last, an old boy visiting my old school.

I was amazed to find my old housemaster looking no older, but my classics master, looking equally ageless, was no longer in charge of the Naval section of the CCF. Indeed, there was no CCF in existence at all. However, a master with the mien of an amiable heron, new to me, though in fact our paths had nearly crossed, explained that now the CCF had been disbanded and in its place the boys and girls had the choice of social services and a variety of other extra-mural activities. Did I say girls? Yes, now, as in so many other schools, there were girls too. And who was he? He was Bill Parish, the Commodore, grand title, of none other than the Dauntsey's School Sailing Club. He explained that after the CCF had been disbanded a group of boys had pestered him, knowing of his interest in sailing, to start a sailing club. With no boat, they had advertised in the press for some kind owner of some embarrassingly large yacht to go into partnership with a bunch of schoolchildren, whose eagerness to work on the boat in the winter, and to sail her in summer, would be in direct contrast to their total lack of financial resources.

There had been little response to that advertisement, until had come a brief letter from one Commander Newcombe Hoare, simply instructing them to report to Weymouth and his yacht *Griffin*. And so had begun a happy partnership. This *Griffin* was not the *Griffin* that E. G. Martin had co-owned, not the *Griffin* which had been given to the Royal Ocean Racing Club in his memory, but her successor, in a way no less famous, which, when she herself had been superseded as the RORC club boat, had been acquired by Hoare and some other ocean-racing friends. The tale amazed and delighted me. It also made me a little sad that when I had been at the school there was no sailing club which I could have joined. Perhaps it was as well because had there been a school boat such as *Griffin* in my time, how would I have divided my loyalties between the family boat and her?

Bill Parish sold me a raffle ticket in aid of the sailing club and for the first time in my life I won a prize. But Bill Parish gave me something else – an invitation to sail in *Griffin* three weeks hence. Sadly, that invitation could never be fulfilled, because on the evening before I was due to join the boat a severe gale forced her from her moorings in Portland Harbour and (through no fault of the sailing club) she foundered, a total loss, on Portland breakwater.

It was a particularly cruel blow because, in the winter before, she had been ferried to the school, for a long and total overhaul. My letter of condolence to Bill seemed very inadequate and I am touched, now that I know him so much better, to find that letter still on his files.

But he and the club were quick to pick themselves up again. With their kind and equally bereaved Newcombe Hoare, they sought for a replacement boat. One such was *Marabu*, the German fifty-square-metre sister-ship to *Overlord*, one of the "windfalls" which it so happened my father had been in charge of capturing from Germany, for use in our own waters by our own services. In a circular letter, Bill Parish let me know that the purchase of *Marabu* was in the wind. I wrote back and said that a German sausage (for fifty square metres are very long and narrow and sail on their ears) was no boat for a school sailing club. Much more suitable would be a gaff cutter, perhaps such as *Dyarchy*. *Dyarchy*, I knew, would never be available because I know her owner well, but I never expected the response that I got some weeks later when Bill Parish, perhaps, I think, a little diverted by my letter about *Marabu*, fine boat though she be, wrote me an astounding letter. He wrote to say that *Jolie Brise* has been acquired for the use of the club. I must confess I had not even known of her return to English waters, but almost from the cradle it had been a name which my mother had so often repeated to me. I was over the moon.

CHAPTER FORTY

Parish and Goddard

This was how it had come about. Senhor Lobato had finally decided that his old boat would be best preserved if she were to belong to a museum, but at the same time continue an active life of sail training. Commander Newcombe Hoare and Mr Dennis Harewood put their heads together – Hoare as the former partner in *Griffin* (sadly so shortly to die) with Dauntsey's School Sailing Club, and Harewood as Chairman of the Exeter Maritime Museum with its parent body, the International Sailing Craft Association. The idea rapidly took seed in fertile soil and onto the scene, centre stage, now comes Bill Parish himself and David Goddard, the Exeter Maritime Museum's Director and indeed creator. Parish and Goddard are very similar men, both single-minded and unflappable.

Bill Parish had hoped to go into the Navy, but was thwarted by ill health, though not before he had had a sound training in seamanship. He had then taken a degree in mathematics, bought his own Morecambe Bay prawner, run a charter boat business in the Mediterranean and then found his real vocation teaching mathematics at Dauntsey's, where he now heads his department, as well as a family of a wife and four sons.

David Goddard, a retired Major home from India, had developed a passion for native sailing craft. By monumental disregard of problems, he had taken over the fine old warehouses on the quay at Exeter and filled them with improbable craft from all corners of the world. Jostling for space in the canal basin there he had gathered round him Arab dhows, Chinese junks and highly painted boats from the Tagus.

Both men are English to the roots; neither motivated by money, nor perturbed by lack of it. Somehow they looked right standing on *Jolie Brise*'s deck, Bill with his pipe and studied lack of nautical dress in the "yachty" sense of the word, and David Goddard in his cavalry twill trousers, large brown leather shoes and a voice which would be useful in a fog. These were the two men who together contrived a partnership perhaps still more remarkable than any that *Jolie Brise* had seen before. David Goddard would have her in his museum to undertake major reconstruction work during winter months; he would provide, too, a dormitory in a warehouse where boys and girls from Dauntsey's could come down in term-time, and during the winter holidays, to carry out the running maintenance on the boat. Bill Parish, in his turn, would organize all of this and see that the boat was properly sailed throughout European waters in the summer months, so that *Jolie Brise*'s silhouette would, little by little, become a familiar sight again.

The personalities fitted, the interests of the two men and the organizations which they represented were complementary. There was now just a matter of money, something which – history repeating itself – neither had. *Jolie Brise* had cost perhaps £500 to build and had cost E. G. Martin maybe some £300 to buy. She had changed hands in the 'twenties and early 'thirties for perhaps £1,000 or £2,000. She had cost the Worsdells £3,000 just after the war, and the "scrap price" for which she had been sold to Senhor Lobato and his friends had been much the same. Now in 1977 that figure had risen to some £27,000, surprising for a sixty-four-year-old boat, but one which is entirely justifiable when you reflect that to build such a boat today, even if there were sufficient amounts of oak available, would cost some £300,000 Many noughts had been added to the cost of sailing as well as the cost of living since Monsieur Paumelle first laid *Jolie Brise*'s keel, but if the cause is right the money can be found.

Dauntsey's School Sailing Club is an independent organization, just like any other club within the school. It was not for the Governors just to write out a cheque and buy the boat to give to the club, even if they could. No, she was not to be just a floating extension to the school; they would help, of course, and had kept a watchful eye on that handful of pupils who had asked Mr Parish to take them sailing some years before. However, that small school club had, amazingly, acquired some assets for itself over the years. There was the share in *Griffin* and the money from her insurance.

Commander Hoare, their old partner, was happy too to be associated in this new venture, and placed some of his money in the project. Further money was to come from many quarters, most significant of all the Science Museum, and, most appropriately, the Royal Ocean Racing Club, of which *Jolie Brise* was a founder member, as well as the Mercers Company, which had included William Dauntsey among their number so many centuries before. And so in 1977, as a result of a complicated transaction, Dauntsey's School Sailing Club gathered together the finance which they then lent, interest free, to the Exeter Maritime Museum, which in its turn bought the boat. Where there is a will there is a way, and the way had been found.

But that, of course, was just the beginning because in the four years in which the Museum has owned her, many many more thousands of pounds have been spent on her. Money has had to be raised for a new engine and major reconstruction works, and this the Museum has boldly undertaken. Money too has been needed for new rigging, a new suit of sails and new spars. Here the boys and girls of the Sailing Club and the club's many friends and patrons have raised the money, in ways great and small, in the club's book-shop, fêtes in the village at West Lavington, sponsored paddles in canoes, auctions, or proceeds from lectures from helpful people like Chay Blyth – endless efforts, so familiar to all fund-raisers. No, neither the Museum nor the Sailing Club have had their fine boat handed to them on a plate. And that is how it should be.

I am going to mention no names of those to whom the club and the Museum are so indebted. To pick and choose would be impossible, but they and we who sail in her are grateful to everyone who has helped to make the dream come true. Those of them who read these lines can in a sense take this whole tale as our "thank-you".

CHAPTER FORTY-ONE

Sailing Today

But enough of financial problems; they seldom perturbed E. G. Martin or Bobby Somerset, so why should they perturb *Jolie Brise*'s new owners? More important, what is it like to sail this amazing boat? How is she, now that she comes so vividly across the horizon sailing towards us, not just a legend or a photograph, but a boat ready to weigh anchor and be outward bound on fresh adventures?

It was in the spring of 1979 that she finally left St Katherine's Dock, and a crew of boys and girls worked her westwards into the English Channel. I was invited to join her at Gosport. There I went and waited; she was a day late, and with me were various parents and their children, waiting to join the boat too. I did not resent the delay. After all, I had waited years enough for a chance of setting foot on *Jolie Brise* and another day did no more than heighten the anticipation. I sat in a pub in old Portsmouth, which commands the entrance to the harbour, but no gaff cutter came.

It was late on the second evening that, finally, up the harbour slipped that dark gaff silhouette. She was coming back to Camper & Nicholson's, where from time to time she had lain in the 1920s. They had had a hard beat from Honfleur and we exchanged pleasantries in the dark as kit-bags and bodies came ashore, and her new crew went aboard.

The next day we had hoped to sail but there were various troubles, particularly with the engine fitted by Mr Mortimer in 1934. But I was not sorry that we were not sailing straight away. Just to walk from the stern up that fifty-six feet of deck until high in the bows; just to shin out on the seventeen feet of bowsprit; just to climb the ratlines to the hounds and look down upon that mackerel-tailed stern; just to sit in that calm, dark, deep saloon and wait for bacon and eggs to be handed round from the Esse in the galley and, when thus satiated, to polish the brass binnacle and see her deck and mast and rigging reflected in it, or the brass cap of her rudder head, which reads "*Jolie Brise Havre 1913 Paumelle Constr.*"; just to feel, in Martin's words, the "massive compactness" of that exquisite piece of floating furniture, was quite enough to comprehend in one day, without actually setting sail.

However, we *did* set sail on the next. Up went the gaff as we pulled on throat and peak halyards and then on throat and peak stretchers. (Even now I have yet to be totally familiar with all that cordage.) You strain your eyes up the mast to work out what runs where. It is like looking up the tracery of some fan vault in a cathedral, to trace some rib high in the ceiling from its source on the pillar by your side. The situation is helped by the number of willing hands – she sails with up to fourteen, twice the number that Martin would have favoured – but it is equally hindered by the sheer number of people gazing aloft.

On that first day, all of us more or less unfamiliar with the boat, and myself most of all, we set off down the Solent with geography master John Rushworth in command. After the fluster and fuss of getting everything hoisted, we all sat back on the capping rail and suddenly the whole majesty of the boat seeped through our senses. Effortlessly she reached down the Solent, solid as a rock, lofty as a mountain, with hardly any fuss astern, and it seemed, in no time at all, that the last of the downs of the Isle of Wight and of the wooded shores of the New Forest had finally slipped by, as if *they* and not the ship were moving.

Greatest delight of all was to take that famous ten-foot tiller, to sit just wherever her weather helm dictated at the most comfortable point along that eight foot of helmsman's bench, or to stand with the helmhead at your hip and your feet braced on the duck-board beneath you, and see how her bowsprit end slowly but so surely responded as you brought her into wind. All this was magical.

Later in that first sail of mine, we sailed through the race off St Albans Head. The fierce little waves clapped at her hull. We had stowed everything below and waited with some consternation for the troubled water. She went through it with no more concern than a police horse walking through a clamorous crowd.

That evening we picked up *Jolie Brise*'s new mooring in Portland

Harbour, which was briefly to be her home-port, courtesy of Her Majesty's Harbour Master. It was just fifty-six years after E. G. Martin had made his first landfall there when he brought her from her native France to England, and her new life. Yet another new life awaited her as we looked back from the launch leaving her that evening. How small the perfection of her lines made her look in the midst of that immense harbour!

It was August before I set foot on board *Jolie Brise* again, this time at that new miraculous marina at Brighton – how Lilian Worsdell would have loved to have put in there when they buffeted their way westward down the Channel in 1946. But we were eastward bound and lazed our way over to Boulogne. *Moules marinière* the next day and, by evening, we were reaching down to Cap Gris-Nez, our long boom end skimming the waves as *Jolie Brise* made her powerful way.

Bill Parish was the "daddy" of the ship, and his flute-playing niece our cook. At Wolverston on the Orwell it was her family who entertained all fifteen of us and joined us to sail coastwise to Great Yarmouth. Jo Stokes, an old friend of mine, came too, clasping his favourite book – E. G. Martin's *Deep Water Cruising*. We were running that day, 6th August, and I would lie in the bowsprit net, watching her spread wings and powerful straight forefoot between my toes. We had torrential thunderstorms as we made Yarmouth and the brigantine *Marquese* appeared and reappeared in the squalls with all the drama of a Cotman seascape. Yarmouth was almost as full of sail training vessels as it once was of the herring fleet.

August 9th showed *Jolie Brise* in one of her less admirable but understandable aspects. It was the morning of the start of the Tall Ships Race to Oslo but we could not even leave harbour because we could not turn her under motor, let alone make up against the flood tide. The old Gardner engine was not only lacking in puff but the propeller mounted on her port quarter meant that a turn to port was well nigh impossible. A tow was attempted but this too failed and in these early days of our sailing her, when everything on deck was just a little ripe, cleats would pop overboard with all the ease of waistcoat buttons shooting off the chest of a fat man. So we stayed alongside; we scrubbed the decks, watched others go and waited for the ebb. Never a racing man, I found crossing the line three hours late was far more pleasant than the general fuss, jostle, bad temper and ill feeling that usually accompanies the racing scene – or does these days, but surely not when *Jolie Brise* held sway as ocean-racing queen.

At midnight we slipped through some of the fleet off Smiths Knowle and sailed into a grey day of head winds and gas rigs in the ill-named Placid Field. We sailed close to one rig, happily christened *Captain Salt*, towering above us and the Dutch schooner *Sleidericht*, one of only two other sails we saw that day.

The next day was greyer still; I had to cook my own breakfast. But the day after was a blessed reach along the Jutland shore in pursuit of the ketch *Rona*.

Ian Procter – energetic rugger master during my days at school – calmly sat at his sewing machine on the foredeck mending the ravages of our two days' windward beat. The sight of him was somewhat reminiscent of Sidney Briggs sewing a counterpane on *Jolie Brise*'s spinnaker in the course of the 1926 Bermuda Race. How happily such scenes repeat themselves on those broad decks as season follows season! If Bill Parish is the driving force behind the sailing club, Ian Procter is his trusty henchman, dedicating most of his spare time to looking after the ship. He had viewed with equanimity "his" Esse cooker being extinguished when we had stowed the topsail on the chimney the night before. It just goes to show that sailing makes us all more philosophical and forgiving – he was certainly more so than as I remember him when I was a trembling youth in the upper fourth.

The joy of *Jolie Brise* on long days at sea like these is that 117 feet of broad capped bulwark gives everyone somewhere to sit and chat or shelter and snooze, or you can walk around her deck, breasting the slope to her bow, to run down the other side to the sweep of her counter behind. If somebody wants to listen to pop up forward on Radio 1, they can happily do so without reducing the enjoyment of someone else listening to a Beethoven symphony on Radio 3 at the other end of the ship. For meals too, it is almost like being on a liner. Two or three of us have a quiet drink forward of the mast followed by our supper, while an equally civilized group will have a favourite spot on the after deck.

That night we sailed anti-clockwise round the Skagerrak with the light broad reaching wind which the old girl really loves. This was Bill Parish's trump card. He decided on the longer route to benefit from the northward current. The direct route to Oslo fjord would risk a foul current, disastrous if the night fell calm.

And so it was that the next day, Sunday 13th August, we crossed the finishing line with the bulk of the fleet bearing down on us from the west. It was a perfect sail at sunset up the fjord, and at the end of the day we learnt that we had come second. *Jolie Brise* was now tasting a new form of racing in that happy, eccentric band of tall ships, and she had found that, yet again, she was not after all outclassed.

My next encounter with *Jolie Brise* was a special one. I was not just to sail in her but to skipper her as well and, with a group of fourteen, I arrived on the quayside at Santander. Bill Parish, deceptively casual, had decided that he trusted me and with no sign of nerves or second thoughts put his bags ashore and took his own crew home on the steamer. She was mine to command. It was a daunting but exciting prospect, particularly as he had slotted her with great ingenuity into an almost inaccessible berth in an inner basin. There was going to be no chance for me simply to slip her moorings and work things out as we went along.

As always, getting to sea is the headache with this great little ship. But once out there with sails set, with routine shipboard life ahead, all falls in to a happy pattern. With growing pleasure and increasing confidence, I sailed her in and out of those fine, deep, eucalyptus-clad *rías* of Northern Spain. More often than not, even though now she had a new engine, I found it easier to manoeuvre under sail than under power. For instance, how easy it was in a bay in the Ría del Ferrol to weigh anchor with mainsail set and sail quietly towards the beach, and then to back the staysail to bring her head round, knowing that she would always come, however inexpert the finger on the helm – and then with freed sheets to sail out to the open sea. More and more, I was finding that she was as much a joy in confined waters to sail as she was out in the broad ocean, and that her characteristics were such that she would suffer fools gladly, but, with the right hand on the helm and the right eye on the sails, she could instantly be transformed from a comfortable slow old thing to a boat with a magical turn of speed.

However, that particular cruise will always be in my mind, not just because it was my first taste of skippering her. No, there was another reason too, which I have already touched on. We were sailing home to the English Channel when, fifty-four years after her first triumph in the Fastnet Race, *Jolie Brise* found herself by chance on the fringe of the storm which made the 1979 Fastnet the most infamous in that race's otherwise distinguished history. We were south-west of Ushant. Force 5 rose to Force 9 in half an hour. We lowered the mainsail down-wind as the seas were already too steep to face – no small problem with that thirty-eight feet of boom. That done, I sent all hands below. One boy watched in the companionway while either myself or my mate, fellow old boy Colin Berry, helmed her through the night.

At 0400 when I was on watch we were knocked down by a rogue wave. *Jolie Brise* recovered, shook herself like an old Labrador and took us on our way again. I sat shivering, wedged between the helmsman's bench and the boom lashed to the deck. As we had tipped over, I had actually been standing on the inside of the port bulwarks. The water had come almost to her companionway and her port cross-trees, normally fifty-five feet about the deck, dipped into the sea. It had been a cataclysmic moment and when I looked round to find that all was still in place I could hardly believe it – though I should have known *Jolie Brise* better. What I feared, when Colin relieved me, was that I would go below to find the cabin in total disarray and the crew frightened and demoralized. I need not have worried, for it was more like entering the library of a London club. From the roar of the following seas and the relentless howl of the wind in the rigging, I found below total calm and my cook, the only girl on board, casually asking if anyone had seen her handbag.

Just before dawn the lights of Ushant appeared comfortably on the starboard bow and we entered the English Channel. Fortunately it was only now that the gale had veered to the west. We could still run before it in the right shipping lane along the French shore. That night, in more moderate seas, we found ourselves south of the shipping lane and clear of the coast. Lights occluded by waves hindered visual identification of our position, but a DF fix confirmed that it would be prudent to heave to. With one boy on watch at a time, we had a comfortable night and in the course of it learned that, just with one headsail set, *Jolie Brise* could still lie as peacefully hove to as when she was a pilot cutter. After eggs and bacon the next day we hoisted the main, sailed north across the shipping lanes at right angles and then set course for Poole. The BBC was making us all too aware of the disasters to the north of us, all the more distressing because the father of one boy was skippering a Fastnet boat. Only later was his safety confirmed. And so it was, with another gale coming up behind us, that we scudded up the coast past the Isle of Purbeck. As we sailed up to Poole quay another yacht called out,

"Where have you come from, Alderney?"

"No, Coruña." Silence, then,

"You were never out in that?" We had been, and the boat had come through unscathed, as had her crew and her towering rigging, which had sagged and sung like a violin, but had more than amply demonstrated that old-fashioned lanyards and rope, designed to give rather than resist, have always been more seamanlike than tensioned masts and bottle screws.

No, our only mishap was a cracked whisky glass. Would that *Jolie Brise*'s modern counterparts, in the still more furious waters round the Fastnet in those stormy days, had suffered so slightly too.

Last year proved that *Jolie Brise* was not too old to make new landfalls. Already we had introduced her to Norway, but now she joined in the Tall Ships Races in the Baltic, and I took her on the final cruise of the year from the river Orwell on the east coast. First stop was Peterhead and on that 400 mile passage I remember thick fog off Yarmouth, Flamborough Head in the setting sun, a squall off the hills above Whitby as the fishing-boats put out before daybreak, and a brilliant day reaching in calm water with an off-shore wind, up past the castles of Northumberland and the Farnes. Colin Berry, again my mate, said,

"This is Grace Darling country, isn't it?"

"The Farnes are famous for their birds but I don't know about grey starlings," was my long-remembered reply. Of such silly memories are cruises made.

We dragged anchor fiendishly in Peterhead's outer harbour with a Force 10 blowing *off shore* – and put to sea again four days later to find too little wind. Too long we spent ambling through the Caledonian Canal. One dare not complain about the pace on a canal which might so easily be closed, but it really did seem, with the delay, that it would have been quicker to have gone round the top, as indeed most fishermen now do. But had we done so, we would not have climbed a hill in Scotland's very centre and seen the scar of the Great Rift stretching from horizon to horizon, Ben Nevis to Loch Ness. Lock work was good training too, because the real art is not so much in getting *Jolie Brise* to go, but in getting her to stop.

And it was pleasant to see her, rugged as a highland castle, moored so quietly beneath those highland hills.

Schedule pressing, it was our misfortune to have to motor down Loch Linnhe in the dark. We found ourselves at dawn entering the Sound of Islay, tribute to navigator John Clay. We sat on the bulwarks, eating porridge and counting the distilleries as the tide rushed us through. In a sense we were lucky to have had no wind on this long narrow south-west leg, for otherwise it would have been bound to have been opposing us from the prevailing south-west. But now we had good sailing, bar a few hours stemming a foul tide off the Mull of Kintyre, and we picked up a ship's buoy in Arran's Lamlash that evening. Our cook, Nicky Flemming, had parents on the island and they entertained us liberally before half our crew left for the south. Depleted from thirteen to seven, ours was a civilized voyage home, for now *Jolie Brise* was back to the numbers for which she had been built. Ailsa Craig at supper-time in the evening sun was a memorable sight. Ten knots through the North Channel made my night watch a joy.

It fell calm in the Irish Sea and the next night we were slipping past Arklow and Wicklow. At noon off the Tuskar, to avoid a foul tide, we slipped into Rosslare – and straight out again. Never pretty, it is now all ferry terminal and brash hotels, and even for a pint of Guinness we felt disinclined to lower anchor, sails and dinghy. We now had a slow beat to Land's End in Fastnet water where the thrice Fastnet winner really should have made better time.

One night the Smalls was twenty miles to the south, the next twenty miles to the north, but better wind there came and we reached down the North Cornish coast to the Longships in fine style. It was calm as we motored into Plymouth the next day and in our four hour stay the crew of seven became five, including Colin Berry's sister Sue, who had joined us. And that was a fine sail off the breakwater at 5.00 pm and creaming past the Needles at 7.00 am to discover that whereas the Solent had been *Jolie Brise*'s stamping ground in racing days, she is in fact too deep to enter most Solent harbours. We lay at the end of Lymington River waiting our tide to cross the bar into Beaulieu, dozing quietly and listening to the radio antics of the Royal Cruising Club's fleet making eastward before we too, now depleted to three, sailed quietly down to join them for the Club's centenary – the club of which E. G. Martin had once been such a prominent member, to which Bobby Somerset had belonged, and under whose burgee Bill Parish and I sometimes sail *Jolie Brise* today.

Two thoughts, looking back upon that cruise: one was that our brief sail round Rosslare Harbour and our failure to drop anchor there got *Jolie Brise* as close to visiting Ireland as she has ever been. It is strange that a boat who has spent such a major proportion of her life sailing round Ireland's most famous lighthouse should never have moored in an Irish harbour! The other thought was that that depressing flog to windward from Ireland to Land's End made evident all too clearly that *Jolie Brise*, however brilliant reaching or running in light airs or strong winds, however comfortable hoved to, is an absolute pig in a head wind with anything of a sea. I thought perhaps it was us, but having talked to Jack Crossley and Alfred Broom, both deck-hands aboard her in the 'twenties, they too have confirmed that "whatever the books say" nothing could persuade her to move in such conditions. It is her failing, and if one is to love a boat as we do, it is as well that she should have failings, for it is a pleasure to forgive those that we love.

My most recent experience of *Jolie Brise* was skippering her for just a week this very month (June 1981). Eterna Watches of Switzerland had asked to charter her for the week leading up to the Transatlantic Race. It was a hectic time taking their guests sailing, short tacking up the Tamar close to her old home at Ince Castle and sailing out into Plymouth Sound. There her two transatlantic voyages had finished; from there she had set out on the Santander Races. There too had ended her six Fastnets, three times as victor.

It was a pleasurable week because some of her guests had never sailed before while others, on the contrary, were preparing for the Transatlantic Race or had circumnavigated the globe. To have Clare Francis at the helm, or Frank Essen, entering the only gaff rigged boat in the race, or the two Hammick sisters, was a pleasure, as it was to watch how they reacted to this boat, so solid beneath them, and which by rights should have vanished into the clouds of history years ago. Better still was to sail out of Plymouth Sound, having seen Mr Mashford who had rebuilt her bulwarks in the 1920s, Mr Broad who had scrubbed her bottom for Bobby Somerset and others who had been part of her crew racing round the buoys, but best of all we took with us Jack Crossley and had him sitting at the helm as we creamed up the Solent the next day, where he had not been since he sailed in her there in 1931, We had on board too Richard Sowman who, with Johnny Nance and David Chase, had put so much work and craftsmanship, shipwrights that they are, into *Jolie Brise* at the Exeter Maritime Museum. Colin Berry was with me then, my mate on all the three occasions that I have skippered her. For two whole seasons he had been on board, sailing some 8,000 miles with her, and had, I believe, become as adept in his knowledge of the boat as Sidney Briggs or Fred Crossley – no small achievement for a "bloody amateur!".

We left her on the piles at Bucklers Hard, quietly waiting to take her youthful crews on a crammed calendar of summer voyages. A fortnight later she took up Solent racing again, in the form of the Round-the-Island Race. Of a thousand entries, she had the second stiffest handicap, second only to the ship Colin Berry is to race in Round the World, because it seems that past form is taken into account. Three Fastnet wins have not been forgotten.

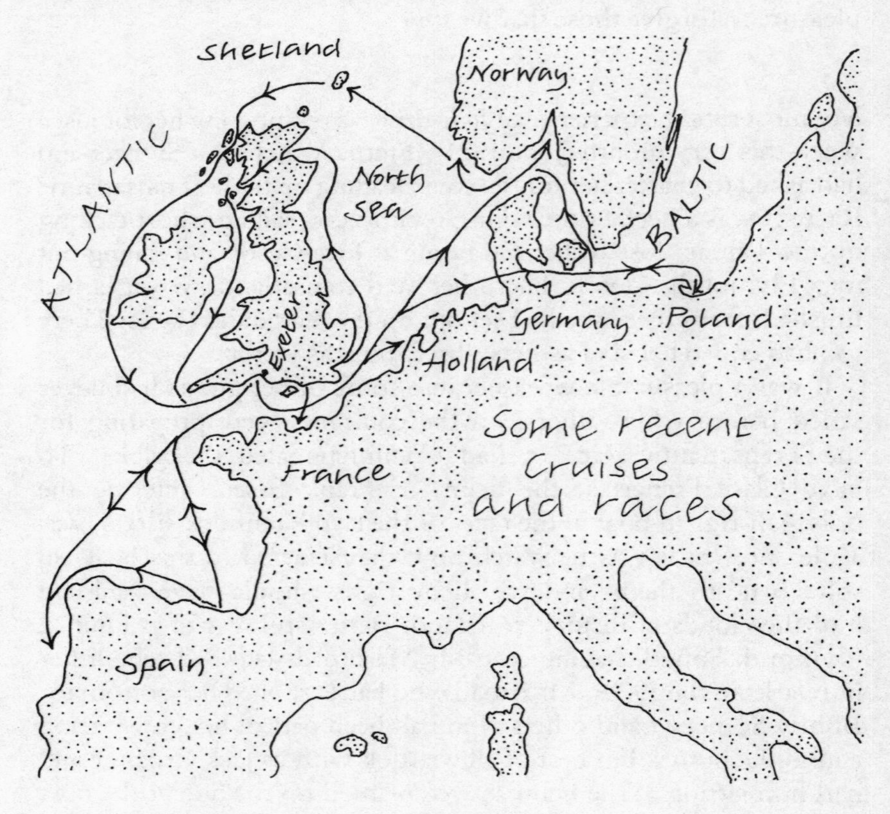

Now, as I write, she is in Poland. When I have finally corrected this script, I shall be off to fetch her from the north of Scotland.

Next year she races to Lisbon with the tall ships of the Sail Training Association – and who is going to organize the events there for those great ships and youth drawn from the world over? Luis Lobato, of course.

CHAPTER FORTY TWO

Where We Came In

So there it is, David, you in your back-room in Poland Street. That is the tale, so far at least. As gripping as a tale about Hornblower or Bolitho? Not as neat perhaps, but with just as much scope for a sequel.

But it is not *just* the tale of a tall ship. It is the tale of so much that has slid beneath her bows in this century, of which she has seen so much more than either you or I. It is a tale of so much social and international change, and changes in the way in which we enjoy ourselves when we go sailing. I have done my best to tell it for her but, sphinx-like, she could tell *so* much more, this phoenix of the seas.

If you chance upon *Jolie Brise* alongside some quay at home or abroad, give her a hail. Climb down the ratlines and drop onto her deck, as I had Monet do upon another pilot cutter, earlier in the story. I hope you will be made as welcome as you would have been in the days of Dagier or Hervette, Martin or Somerset, Brownlow Smith, Warren Ferrier, Gage or Mortimer, Worsdell or Lobato. Spare a thought, too, for the spirit of Paumelle and Paris, Sydney Briggs and Fred Crossley, Bill from the Shambles Light and Michael Cumberlege. Remember poor Clarence Kozlay, who failed to gain the safety of her decks, and *Adriana* who slid beneath the waves. Send up a prayer of thanksgiving for her deliverance from one or two whom we shall not name. And if you are really fanciful, conjure up a picture of Napoleon hovering over her, like something on a Courvoisier bottle, the author of the decree under which she was built.

You may see her mastless and ripped apart by energetic shipwrights in the basin at Exeter, or you may see her, a cloud of white canvas on a summer's day, sailing toward some new horizon. But when I think of her, I always think of the day when I first trod her decks, just four years ago.

"Do you see that girl with the camera?" one of the boys asked another.

"The one with the navy blue jersey?"

"Yes – I could have sworn she has been past several times."

"Must fancy you."

"Nonsense – the boat more like."

I looked up to see who they were talking about.

There on the upper deck of the Gosport Ferry was the trim figure of a dark-haired girl.

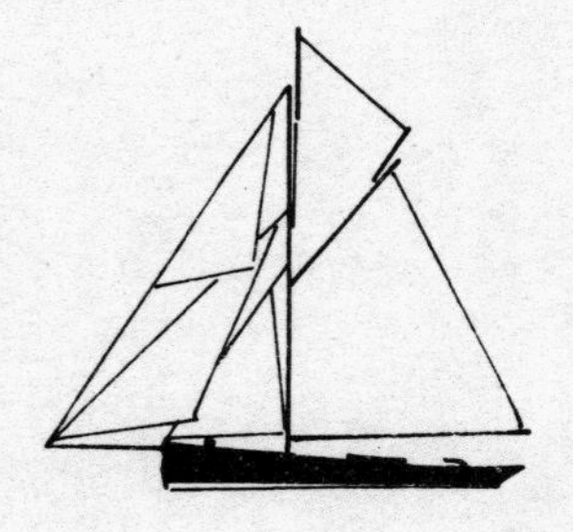